CHINESE

the essence of Asian cooking

CHINESE

the essence of Asian cooking

LINDA DOESER

HERMES HOUSE

This edition published by Hermes House

Hermes House is an imprint of
Anness Publishing Limited
Hermes House
88–89 Blackfriars Road
London SE1 8HA

A CIP catalogue record for this book is available from the British Library.

Publisher: Joanna Lorenz
Project Editor: Linda Doeser
Copy Editor: Harriette Lanzer
Designer: Ian Sandom

Photography: Karl Adamson, Edward Allwright, David Armstrong, Steve Baxter, James Duncan, Michelle Garrett, Amanda Heywood, Patrick McLeavey, Michael Michaels and Thomas Odulate
Styling: Madeleine Brehaut, Michelle Garrett, Maria Kelly, Blake Minton and Kirsty Rawlings
Food for Photography: Carla Capalbo, Kit Chan, Elizabeth Wolf-Cohen, Joanne Craig, Nicola Fowler, Carole Handslip, Jane Hartshorn, Shehzad Husain, Wendy Lee, Lucy McKelvie, Annie Nichols, Jane Stevenson and Steven Wheeler
Illustrations: Madeleine David

Front cover shows Singapore Noodles. For recipe see page 193.

Previously published as *Best-Ever Chinese & Asian*

1 3 5 7 9 10 8 6 4 2

NOTES

For all recipes, quantities are given in both metric and imperial measures and, where appropriate, measures are also given in standard cups and spoons. Follow one set, but not a mixture, because they are not interchangeable.
Standard spoon and cup measures are level.
1 tsp = 5ml, 1 tbsp = 15ml, 1 cup = 250ml/8fl oz
Australian standard tablespoons are 20ml. Australian readers should use 3 tsp in place of 1 tbsp for measuring small quantities of gelatine, cornflour, salt, etc.
Medium eggs are used unless otherwise stated.

Contents

Introduction

Chinese and Asian food is increasingly popular in the West, and our hunger for greater experience of oriental cuisines continues unabated. This book, with its extensive and wide-ranging collection of recipes, goes a long way towards appeasing the appetite for new gastronomic discoveries.

From the simple and familiar, such as Spring Rolls with Sweet Chilli Dipping Sauce, to the more elaborate and unusual, like Lion's Head Casserole, there is something here to attract every cook. Stunning starters, including Cheat's Shark's Fin Soup and Lacy Duck Egg Nets, fabulous fish and seafood dishes, like Doedoeh of Fish, and mouth-watering meat and poultry, such as Paper-thin Lamb with Spring Onions and Chicken Teriyaki, are all here. The vibrant vegetable dishes include Chinese Potatoes with Chilli Beans and Spiced Tofu Stir-fry, and there are sensational salads such as Sweet-and-sour Fruit and Vegetable Salad. Noodle and rice recipes each have a section to themselves, and desserts are represented by such delights as Mango with Sticky Rice and Thai Coconut Cream.

Every recipe is temptingly illustrated with a full-colour photograph of the finished dish, and clear step-by-step instructions and photographs show you how to achieve this end result. Additional guidance is provided by the sections on ingredients, techniques and equipment.

With its heavy reliance on wok cooking and fresh ingredients, Chinese and Asian food is fast and nutritious as well as gastronomically and visually stimulating. A feast of exotic flavours is waiting to burst from the pages of this book into a kitchen near you.

INGREDIENTS

Bamboo shoots Mild-flavoured, tender shoots of the young bamboo, widely available fresh, or sliced or halved in cans.

Basil Several different types of basil are used in Asian cooking. Thai cooks use two varieties, holy and sweet basil, but ordinary basil works well.

Bean curd See under Tofu.

Beansprouts Shoots of the mung bean, usually available from supermarkets. They add a crisp texture to stir-fries.

Black bean sauce Made of salted black beans crushed and mixed with flour and spices (such as ginger, garlic or chilli) to form a thickish paste. It is sold in jars or cans and, once opened, should be kept in the refrigerator.

Cardamom pods Available both as small green pods and larger black pods containing seeds, they have a strong aromatic quality.

Cashew nuts Whole cashew nuts feature prominently in Chinese stir-fries, especially those with chicken.

Cassia bark A form of cinnamon, but with a more robust flavour.

Chilli bean sauce Made from fermented bean paste mixed with hot chilli and other seasonings. Sold in jars, some chilli bean sauces are quite mild, but some are very hot. You will have to try out the various brands yourself to see which one is to your taste.

Chilli oil Made from dried red chillies, garlic, onions, salt and vegetable oil, this is used more as a dip than as a cooking ingredient.

Chilli sauce A very hot sauce made from chillies, vinegar, sugar and salt. Usually sold in bottles, it should be used sparingly in cooking or as a dip. Tabasco sauce can be a substitute.

Chillies There is a wide range of fresh and dried chillies from which to choose. Generally the larger the chilli, the milder the flavour, but there are some exceptions, and the only way to gauge potency is by taste. Remove the seeds for a milder flavour. Whether using dried or fresh chillies, take care when preparing them as their seeds and flesh can "burn": wash your hands immediately afterwards or, better still, wear rubber gloves – and never rub your eyes.

Chinese cabbage Also known as Chinese leaves, two sorts are widely available. The most commonly seen variety has a pale green colour and tightly wrapped elongated head, and about two-thirds of the cabbage is stem which has a crunchy texture. The other type has a shorter and fatter head with curlier, pale yellow or green leaves, and white stems.

Chinese chives Better known as garlic chives, these are sometimes sold with their flowers.

Chinese five-spice powder This flavouring contains star anise, pepper, fennel, cloves and cinnamon.

Chinese pancakes Thin flour and water pancakes with no added seasonings or spices. They are available fresh or frozen.

Chinese rice wine Made from glutinous rice, this is also known as yellow wine – *huang jin* or *chiew* – because of its colour. The best variety is called Shao Hsing or Shaoxing and comes from the south-east of China. Dry sherry may be used as a substitute.

Coconut milk and cream Coconut milk should not be confused with the "milk" or juice found inside a fresh coconut (though the latter makes a refreshing drink). The coconut milk used for cooking is produced from the white flesh of the nut. If left to stand, the thick part of the milk will rise to the surface like cream.

To make your own, break open a fresh coconut and remove the brown inner skin from the flesh. Grate sufficient flesh to measure 400ml/14 fl oz/1⅔ cups. Place the grated flesh, together with 300ml/½ pint/1¼ cups water, in a blender or food processor fitted with a metal blade and process for 1 minute. Strain the mixture through a sieve lined with muslin into a bowl. Gather up the corners of the muslin and squeeze out the liquid. The coconut milk is then ready to use, but you should stir it before use.

Coconut milk is also available in cans, as a soluble powder and as creamed coconut which is sold in block form. Powder and creamed coconut make a poor milk, but are useful for sauces and dressings.

Coriander Fresh coriander has a strong, pungent smell that combines well with other rich flavours. The white coriander root is used when the green colouring is not required. The seeds are also used, whole and ground.

Cornflour paste To make cornflour paste, mix 4 parts cornflour with about 5 parts cold water until smooth.

Cumin Available as whole seeds and as a powder, cumin has a strong, slightly bitter flavour and is used mainly in Indian recipes, and also in many Asian dishes.

Curry paste Curry paste is traditionally made by pounding fresh herbs and spices in a mortar with a pestle. The two types of Thai curry paste, red and green, are made with red and green chillies respectively. Other ingredients vary with individual cooks, but red curry paste typically contains ginger, shallots, garlic, coriander and cumin seeds and lime juice, as well as chillies. Herbs and flavourings in green curry paste usually include spring onions, fresh coriander, kaffir lime leaves, ginger, garlic and lemon grass. Making curry paste is time-consuming, but it tastes excellent and keeps well. Ready-made pastes, available in packets and tubs, are satisfactory substitutes.

Top shelf, left to right: *garlic, ginger, lemon grass, dried shrimps, Thai fish sauce, Szechuan peppercorns, sweet chilli sauce, ground coriander, galangal, Chinese five-spice powder, fresh green chillies*
Middle shelf: *dried red chillies, peanuts (skins on), cardamom pods, cashew nuts (in jar), peanuts (skins off), kaffir lime leaves, tamarind, hoisin sauce, salted black beans, chilli oil*
Bottom shelf, back row: *sake, rice vinegar, Chinese rice wine*
Bottom shelf, middle row: *sesame oil, mirin, peanut oil, fresh coriander, cumin seeds*
Bottom shelf, front row: *basil, dried shrimp paste, red and green chillies, flaked coconut and creamed coconut, light soy sauce, oyster sauce, pieces of coconut, whole coconut*

Dashi Light Japanese stock, available in powder form. The flavour derives from kelp seaweed. Diluted vegetable stock made from a cube may be substituted.

Dried shrimps and shrimp paste Dried shrimps are tiny shrimps that are salted and dried. They are used as a seasoning for stir-fried dishes. Soak them first in warm water until soft, then either process them in a blender or food processor or pound them in a mortar with a pestle. Shrimp paste, also known as *terasi*, is a dark, odorous paste made from fermented shrimps. Use sparingly.

Fish sauce The most commonly used flavouring in Thai food. Fish sauce (*nam pla*) is used in Thai cooking in the same way as soy sauce is used in Chinese dishes. It is made from salted anchovies and has a strong, salty flavour.

Galangal Fresh galangal, also known as *lengkuas*, tastes and looks a little like ginger with a pinkish tinge to its skin. Prepare it in the same way. It is also available dried and ground.

Garlic Garlic, together with ginger, is an indispensable ingredient in Chinese and Asian cooking.

Ginger Fresh ginger root has a sharp, distinctive flavour. Choose firm, plump pieces of fresh root with unwrinkled, shiny skins.

Gram flour Made from ground chick-peas, this flour has a unique flavour and is worth seeking out in Indian food stores.

Hoisin sauce A thick, dark brownish-red sauce which is sweet and spicy.

Kaffir lime leaves These are used rather like bay leaves, but to give an aromatic lime flavour to dishes. The fresh leaves are available from oriental food stores and can be frozen for future use.

Lemon grass Also known as citronella, lemon grass has a long, pale green stalk and a bulbous end similar to that of a spring onion. Only the bottom 13cm/5in are used. It has a woody texture and an aromatic, lemony scent. Unless finely chopped, it is always removed before serving because it is so fibrous.

Lengkuas See under Galangal.

Mirin A mild, sweet, Japanese rice wine used in cooking.

Miso A fermented bean paste that adds richness and flavour to Japanese soups.

Mooli A member of the radish family with a fresh, slightly peppery taste and white skin and flesh. Unlike other radishes, it is good when cooked, but should be salted and allowed to drain first, as it has a high water content. It is widely used in Chinese cooking and may be carved into an elaborate garnish.

Mushrooms Chinese shiitake mushrooms are used both fresh and dried to add texture and flavour to a dish. Wood ears are used in their dried form. All dried mushrooms need to be soaked in warm water for 20–30 minutes before use. Dried mushrooms are expensive, but a small quantity goes a long way.

Noodles: Cellophane noodles, also known as bean thread, transparent or glass noodles, are made from ground mung beans. Dried noodles must be soaked in hot water before cooking.

Egg noodles are made from wheat flour, egg and water. The dough is flattened and then shredded or extruded through a pasta machine to the required shape and thickness.

Rice noodles are made from ground rice and water. They range in thickness from very thin to wide ribbons and sheets. Dried ribbon rice noodles are usually sold tied together in bundles. Fresh rice noodles are also available. Rinse rice noodles in warm water and drain before use.

Rice vermicelli are thin, brittle noodles that look like white hair and are sold in large bundles. They cook almost instantly in hot liquid, provided the noodles are first soaked in warm water. They can also be deep-fried.

Somen noodles are delicate, thin, white Japanese noodles made from wheat flour in dried form, usually tied in bundles held together with a paper band.

Udon noodles, also Japanese, are made of wheat flour and water. They are usually round, but can also be flat and are available fresh, precooked or dried.

Nori Paper-thin sheets of Japanese seaweed.

Oyster sauce Made from oyster extract, this is used in many Asian fish dishes, soups and sauces.

Pak choi Also known as bok choi, this is a leaf vegetable with long, smooth, milky white stems and dark green foliage.

Palm sugar Strongly flavoured, hard brown sugar made from the sap of the coconut palm tree. It is available in oriental stores. If you have trouble finding it, use soft dark brown sugar instead.

Peanut oil This oil can be heated to a high temperature, making it perfect for stir-frying and deep-frying.

Peanuts Used in wok cookery to add flavour and a crunchy texture. The thin red skins must be removed before cooking, by immersing the peanuts in boiling water for a few minutes and then rubbing off the skins.

Red bean paste A reddish-brown paste made from puréed red beans and crystallized sugar. It is sold in cans.

Rice Long-grain rice is generally used for savoury dishes. There are many high-quality varieties, coming from a range of countries. Basmati, which means fragrant in Hindi, is generally acknowledged as the king of rices. Thai jasmine rice is also fragrant and slightly sticky.

Rice vinegar There are two basic types of rice vinegar: red vinegar is made from fermented rice and has a distinctive dark colour and depth of flavour; white vinegar is stronger in flavour as it is distilled from rice. If rice vinegar is unavailable, cider vinegar may be substituted.

Sake A strong, powerful, fortified rice wine from Japan.

Dried noodles

1 ribbon noodles, 2 somen noodles, 3 udon noodles, 4 soba noodles, 5 egg ribbon noodles, 6 medium egg noodles, 7 cellophane noodles, 8 rice sheets, 9 rice vermicelli, 10 egg noodles, 11 rice ribbon noodles

Sesame oil This is used more for flavouring than for cooking. It is very intensely flavoured, so only a little is required.

Soy sauce A major seasoning ingredient in Asian cooking, this is made from fermented soy beans combined with yeast, salt and sugar. Chinese soy sauce falls into two main categories: light and dark. Light soy sauce has more flavour than the sweeter dark soy sauce, which gives food a rich, reddish colour.

Spring roll wrappers Paper-thin wrappers made from wheat or rice flour and water. Wheat wrappers are usually sold frozen and should be thawed and separated before use. Rice flour wrappers are dry and must be soaked before use.

Sweet potato The sweet richness of this red tuber marries well with the hot-and-sour flavours of South-east Asia. In Japan the sweet potato is used to make delicious candies and sweetmeats.

Szechuan peppercorns Also known as *farchiew*, these aromatic red peppercorns are best used roasted and ground. They are not so hot as either white or black peppercorns, but do add a unique taste.

Tamarind The brown, sticky pulp of the bean-like seed pod of the tamarind tree. It is used in Thai and Indonesian cooking to add tartness to recipes, rather as western cooks use vinegar or lemon juice. It is usually sold dried or pulped. The pulp is diluted with water and strained before use. Soak 25g/1oz tamarind pulp in 150ml/¼ pint/⅔ cup warm water for about 10 minutes. Squeeze out as much tamarind juice as possible by pressing all the liquid through a sieve.

Terasi See under Dried Shrimps and Shrimp Paste.

Tofu This custard-like preparation of puréed and pressed soya beans, also known as bean curd, is high in protein. Plain tofu is bland in flavour but readily absorbs the flavours of the food with which it is cooked. Tofu is also available smoked and marinated. Firm blocks of tofu are best suited to stir-frying.

Turmeric A member of the ginger family, turmeric is a rich, golden-coloured root. If you are using the fresh root, wear rubber gloves when peeling it to avoid staining your skin. Turmeric is also available in powder form.

Wasabi This is an edible root, which is used in Japanese cooking to make a condiment with a sharp, pungent and fiery flavour. It is very similar to horseradish and is available fresh, and in powder and paste form.

Water chestnuts Walnut-sized bulbs from an Asian water plant that look like sweet chestnuts. They are sold fresh by some oriental food stores, but are more readily available canned.

Wonton wrappers Small, paper-thin squares of wheat flour and egg dough.

Top shelf, left to right: *fresh egg noodles, wonton wrappers, water chestnuts, cellophane noodles, gram flour, spring roll wrappers*
Middle shelf: *dried Chinese mushrooms, pak choi, tofu, dried egg noodles, Chinese pancakes*
Bottom shelf, at back: *rice; (in basket) mangetouts, baby sweetcorn, shallots, shiitake mushrooms; Chinese cabbage, rice vermicelli*
Bottom shelf, at front: *bamboo shoots, beansprouts, wood ears (mushrooms), spring onions, yard-long beans*

Yard-long beans Long, thin beans similar to French beans but three or four times longer. Cut into smaller lengths and use just like ordinary green beans.

Yellow bean sauce A thick paste made from salted, fermented yellow soya beans, crushed with flour and sugar.

EQUIPMENT

You don't need specialist equipment to produce a Chinese or Asian meal – you can even use a heavy-based frying pan instead of a wok in many instances. However, the items listed below will make your oriental dishes easier and more pleasant to prepare.

Wok There are many different varieties of wok available. All are bowl-shaped with gently sloping sides that allow the heat to spread rapidly and evenly over the surface. One that is about 35cm/14in in diameter is a useful size for most families, allowing adequate room for deep-frying, steaming and braising, as well as stir-frying.

Originally always made from cast iron, woks are now manufactured in a number of different metals. Cast iron remains very popular as it is an excellent conductor of heat and develops a patina over a period of time that makes it virtually non-stick. Carbon steel is also a good choice, but stainless steel tends to scorch. Non-stick woks are available but are not really very efficient because they cannot withstand the high heat required for wok cooking. They are also expensive.

Woks may have an ear-shaped handle or two made from metal or wood, a single long handle or both. Wooden handles are safer.

Seasoning the wok New woks, apart from those with a non-stick lining, must be seasoned. Many need to be scrubbed first with a cream cleanser to remove the manufacturer's protective coating of oil. Once the oil has been removed, place the wok over a low heat and add about 30ml/2 tbsp vegetable oil. Rub the oil over the entire inside surface of the wok with a pad of kitchen paper. Heat the wok slowly for 10–15 minutes, then wipe off the oil with more kitchen paper. The paper will become black. Repeat this process of coating, heating and wiping several times until the paper is clean. Once the wok has been seasoned, it should not be scrubbed again. After use, just wash it in hot water without using any detergent, then wipe it completely dry before storage.

Wok accessories There is a range of accessories available to go with woks, but they are by no means essential.

Lid This is a useful addition, particularly if you want to use the wok for steaming and braising, as well as frying. Usually made of aluminium, it is a close-fitting, dome-shaped cover. Some woks are sold already supplied with matching lids. However, any snug-fitting, dome-shaped saucepan lid is an adequate substitute.

Stand This provides a secure base for the wok when it is used for steaming, braising or deep-frying and is a particularly useful accessory. Stands are always made of metal but vary in form, usually either a simple open-sided frame or a solid metal ring with holes punched around the sides.

Trivet This is essential for steaming to support the plate above the water level. Trivets are made of wood or metal.

Scoop This is a long, often wooden-handled, metal spatula with a wooden end used to toss ingredients during stir-frying. Any good, long-handled spoon can be used instead, although it does not have quite the same action.

Bamboo steamer This fits inside the wok where it should rest safely perched on the sloping sides. Bamboo steamers range in size from small for dumplings and dim sum to those large enough to hold a whole fish.

Bamboo strainer This wide, flat, metal strainer with a long bamboo handle makes lifting foods from steam or hot oil easier. A slotted metal spoon can also be used.

Other equipment Most equipment required for cooking the recipes in this book will be found in any kitchen. However, specialist tools are generally simple and inexpensive, especially if you seek out authentic implements from oriental stores.

A selection of cooking utensils, clockwise from top: bamboo steamer, pestle and mortar, chopping board with cleaver, chef's knife and small paring knife, wok with lid and draining wire, wok scoop

Cleaver No Chinese cook would be without one. This is an all-purpose cutting tool, available in various weights and sizes. It is easy to use and serves many purposes from chopping up bones to precision cutting, such as deveining prawns. It is a superb instrument for slicing vegetables thinly. It must be kept very sharp.

Pestle and mortar Usually made of earthenware or stone, this is extremely useful for grinding small amounts of spices and for pounding ingredients together to make pastes.

Food processor This is a quick and easy alternative to the pestle and mortar for grinding spices and making pastes. It can also be used for chopping and slicing vegetables.

COOKING TECHNIQUES

STIR-FRYING

This quick technique retains the fresh flavour, colour and texture of ingredients, and its success depends upon having all that you require ready prepared before starting to cook.

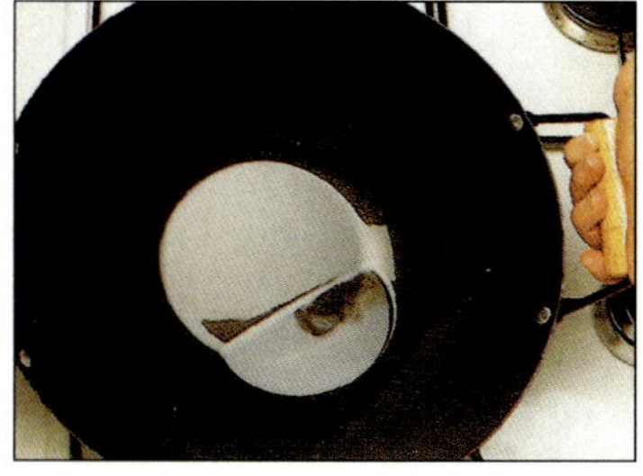

1 Heat an empty wok over a high heat. This prevents food sticking and will ensure an even heat. Add the oil and swirl it around so that it coats the base and halfway up the sides of the wok. It is important that the oil is hot when the food is added, so that it will start to cook immediately.

2 Add the ingredients in the order specified in the recipe. Aromatics (garlic, ginger, spring onions) are usually added first: do not wait for the oil to get so hot that it is almost smoking or they will burn and become bitter. Toss them in the oil for a few seconds. Next add the main ingredients that require longer cooking, such as dense vegetables or meat. Follow with the faster-cooking items. Toss the ingredients from the centre of the wok to the sides using a wok scoop, long-handled spoon or wooden spatula.

DEEP-FRYING

A wok is ideal for deep-frying as it uses far less oil than a deep-fat fryer. Make sure that it is fully secure on its stand before adding the oil and never leave the wok unattended.

1 Put the wok on a stand and half-fill with oil. Heat until the required temperature registers on a thermometer. Alternatively, test it by dropping in a small piece of food: if bubbles form all over the surface of the food, the oil is ready.

2 Carefully add the food to the oil, using long wooden chopsticks or tongs, and move it around to prevent it sticking. Use a bamboo strainer or slotted spoon to remove the food. Drain on kitchen paper before serving.

STEAMING

Steamed foods are cooked by a gentle moist heat, which must circulate freely in order for the food to cook. Steaming is increasingly popular with health-conscious cooks as it preserves flavour and nutrients. It is perfect for vegetables, meat, poultry and especially fish. The easiest way to steam food in a wok is using a bamboo steamer.

USING A BAMBOO STEAMER

1 Put the wok on a stand. Pour in sufficient boiling water to come about 5cm/2in up the sides and bring back to simmering point. Carefully put the bamboo steamer into the wok so that it rests securely against the sloping sides without touching the surface of the water.

2 Cover the steamer with its matching lid and cook for the time recommended in the recipe. Check the water level from time to time and top up with boiling water if necessary.

USING A WOK AS A STEAMER

Put a trivet in the wok, then place the wok securely on its stand. Pour in sufficient boiling water to come just below the trivet. Carefully place a plate containing the food to be steamed on the trivet. Cover the wok with its lid, bring the water back to the boil, then lower the heat so that it is simmering gently. Steam for the time recommended in the recipe. Check the water level from time to time and top up with boiling water if necessary.

Soups and Starters

The delicious soups in this chapter can be served as a first course or as part of a selection of main course dishes, as they do in China. The recipes even include an unusual and satisfying Japanese breakfast soup. Many of the mouth-watering starters – a variety of spring rolls with spicy dipping sauces, dim sum, wontons and tempura – need no introduction, as they are long-established favourites in the West. Others are lesser known, but just as tasty. Try Lacy Duck Egg Nets from Thailand or Spicy Meat Patties with Coconut from Indonesia, for example.

Basic Stock

This stock is used not only as the basis for soup making, but also for general cooking whenever liquid is required instead of plain water.

Ingredients

Makes 2.25 litres/4 pints/10½ cups

- 675g/1½lb chicken pieces, skinned
- 675g/1½lb pork spareribs
- 3.25 litres/6 pints/15 cups cold water
- 3–4 pieces fresh root ginger, unpeeled and crushed
- 3–4 spring onions, each tied into a knot
- 45–60ml/3–4 tbsp Chinese rice wine or dry sherry

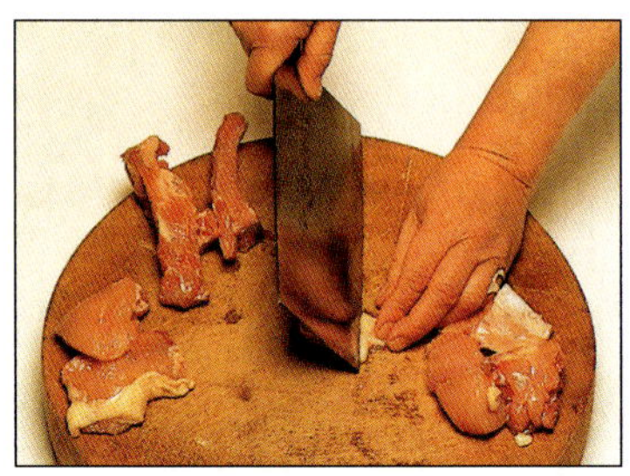

1 Trim off any excess fat from the chicken and spareribs and chop them into large pieces.

2 Place the chicken, spareribs and water in a large saucepan. Add the ginger and spring onion knots.

3 Bring to the boil and, using a sieve, skim off the froth. Reduce the heat and simmer, uncovered, for 2–3 hours.

4 Strain the stock, discarding the chicken, pork, ginger and spring onions, and return it to the pan. Add the rice wine or dry sherry and bring to the boil. Simmer for 2–3 minutes. Refrigerate the stock when cool. It will keep for up to 4–5 days. Alternatively, it can be frozen in small containers and defrosted when required.

Chicken Wonton Soup with Prawns

This soup is a more luxurious version of the familiar, basic Wonton Soup and is almost a meal in itself.

Ingredients

Serves 4

275g/10oz boneless chicken breast, skinned
200g/7oz prawn tails, raw or cooked
5ml/1 tsp finely chopped fresh root ginger
2 spring onions, finely chopped
1 egg
10ml/2 tsp oyster sauce (optional)
1 packet wonton wrappers
15ml/1 tbsp cornflour paste
900ml/1½ pints/3¾ cups chicken stock
¼ cucumber, peeled and diced
salt and ground black pepper
1 spring onion, roughly shredded, 4 sprigs fresh coriander and 1 tomato, skinned, seeded and diced, to garnish

1 Place the chicken breast, 150g/5oz of the prawn tails, the ginger and spring onions in a food processor and process for 2–3 minutes. Add the egg, oyster sauce and seasoning and process briefly. Set aside.

2 Place 8 wonton wrappers at a time on a surface, moisten the edges with cornflour paste and place 2.5ml/½ tsp of the chicken and prawn mixture in the centre of each. Fold them in half and pinch to seal. Simmer in salted water for 4 minutes.

3 Bring the chicken stock to the boil, add the remaining prawn tails and the cucumber and simmer for 3–4 minutes. Add the filled wontons and simmer for 3–4 minutes to warm through. Garnish with the spring onion, coriander and diced tomato and serve hot.

Thai Chicken Soup

The subtle combination of herbs, spices and creamed coconut makes this satisfying soup a special treat.

INGREDIENTS

Serves 4
15ml/1 tbsp vegetable oil
1 garlic clove, finely chopped
2 x 6oz boneless chicken breasts, skinned and chopped
2.5ml/½ tsp ground turmeric
1.5ml/¼ tsp hot chilli powder
75g/3oz creamed coconut
900ml/1½ pints/3¾ cups hot chicken stock
30ml/2 tbsp lemon or lime juice
30ml/2 tbsp crunchy peanut butter
350g/12oz thread egg noodles, broken into small pieces
15ml/1 tbsp finely chopped spring onion
15ml/1 tbsp chopped fresh coriander
salt and ground black pepper
30ml/2 tbsp desiccated coconut and ½ fresh red chilli, seeded and finely chopped, to garnish

1 Heat the oil in a large pan and fry the garlic for 1 minute until lightly golden. Add the chicken, turmeric and chilli powder and stir-fry for a further 3–4 minutes.

2 Crumble the creamed coconut into the hot chicken stock and stir until dissolved. Pour on to the chicken and add the lemon or lime juice, peanut butter and egg noodles.

3 Cover and simmer for about 15 minutes. Add the spring onion and coriander, then season well and cook for a further 5 minutes.

4 Meanwhile, place the desiccated coconut and chopped chilli in a small frying pan and heat for 2–3 minutes, stirring frequently, until the coconut is lightly browned.

5 Serve the soup in bowls sprinkled with the fried coconut and chilli.

Chinese Tofu and Lettuce Soup

This light, clear soup is brimful of nourishing, tasty vegetables.

INGREDIENTS

Serves 4

- 30ml/2 tbsp groundnut or sunflower oil
- 200g/7oz smoked or marinated tofu, cubed
- 3 spring onions, sliced diagonally
- 2 garlic cloves, cut in thin strips
- 1 carrot, thinly sliced in rounds
- 1 litre/1¾ pints/4 cups vegetable stock
- 30ml/2 tbsp soy sauce
- 15ml/1 tbsp dry sherry or vermouth
- 5ml/1 tsp sugar
- 115g/4oz Cos lettuce, shredded
- salt and ground black pepper

1 Heat the oil in a preheated wok, then stir-fry the tofu cubes until browned. Drain and set aside on kitchen paper.

2 Add the onions, garlic and carrot to the wok and stir-fry for 2 minutes. Pour in the stock, soy sauce, dry sherry or vermouth, sugar and lettuce. Heat through gently for 1 minute, season to taste and serve hot.

Crab and Egg Noodle Broth

This delicious broth is the ideal solution when you are hungry, time is short and you need a fast, nutritious and filling meal.

Ingredients

Serves 4

75g/3oz thin egg noodles
25g/1oz/2 tbsp unsalted butter
1 small bunch spring onions, chopped
1 celery stick, sliced
1 medium carrot, cut into batons
1.2 litres/2 pints/5 cups chicken stock
60ml/4 tbsp dry sherry
115g/4oz white crab meat, fresh or frozen
pinch of celery salt
pinch of cayenne pepper
10ml/2 tsp lemon juice
1 small bunch coriander or flat-leaf parsley, roughly chopped, to garnish

1 Bring a large saucepan of salted water to the boil. Toss in the egg noodles and cook according to the instructions on the packet. Cool under cold running water and leave immersed in water until required.

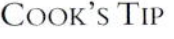

Cook's Tip

Fresh and frozen crab meat have a better flavour than canned crab, which tends to taste rather bland.

2 Heat the butter in another large pan, add the spring onions, celery and carrot, cover and cook the vegetables over a gentle heat for 3-4 minutes until soft.

3 Add the chicken stock and dry sherry, bring to the boil and simmer for a further 5 minutes.

4 Flake the crab meat between your fingers on to a plate and remove any stray pieces of shell.

5 Drain the noodles and add to the broth together with the crab meat. Season to taste with celery salt and cayenne pepper and stir in the lemon juice. Return to a simmer.

6 Ladle the broth into shallow soup plates, scatter with roughly chopped coriander or parsley and serve immediately.

Cheat's Shark's Fin Soup

Shark's fin soup is a renowned delicacy. In this poor man's vegetarian version cellophane noodles, cut into short lengths, mimic shark's fin needles.

INGREDIENTS

Serves 4–6

4 dried Chinese mushrooms
25ml/1½ tbsp dried wood ears
115g/4oz cellophane noodles
30ml/2 tbsp vegetable oil
2 carrots, cut into fine strips
115g/4oz canned bamboo shoots, rinsed, drained and cut into fine strips
1 litre/1¾ pints/4 cups vegetable stock
15ml/1 tbsp soy sauce
15ml/1 tbsp arrowroot or potato flour
30ml/2 tbsp water
1 egg white, beaten (optional)
5ml/1 tsp sesame oil
salt and freshly ground black pepper
2 spring onions, finely chopped, to garnish
Chinese red vinegar, to serve (optional)

1 Soak the mushrooms and wood ears separately in warm water for 20 minutes. Drain well. Remove and discard the stems from the mushrooms and slice the caps thinly. Cut the wood ears into fine strips, discarding any hard bits. Soak the noodles in hot water until soft. Drain and cut into short lengths. Leave until required.

2 Heat the oil in a large saucepan. Add the mushrooms and stir-fry for 2 minutes. Add the wood ears, stir-fry for 2 minutes, then stir in the carrots, bamboo shoots and noodles.

3 Add the stock to the pan. Bring to the boil, reduce the heat and simmer gently for 15–20 minutes. Season with salt, pepper and soy sauce.

4 Blend the arrowroot or potato flour with a little water. Pour into the soup, stirring all the time to prevent lumps from forming as the soup continues to simmer.

5 Remove the pan from the heat. Stir in the egg white if using, so that it sets to form small threads in the hot soup. Stir in the sesame oil, then pour the soup into individual bowls. Sprinkle each portion with chopped spring onions and offer the Chinese red vinegar separately, if using.

Miso Breakfast Soup

Miso is a fermented bean paste that adds richness and flavour to many of Japan's favourite soups. It is available in health food stores. This unusual soup provides a nourishing start to the day.

INGREDIENTS

Serves 4

3 shiitake mushrooms, fresh or dried
1.2 litres/2 pints/5 cups vegetable stock
60ml/4 tbsp miso paste
115g/4oz tofu, cut into large dice
1 spring onion, green part only, sliced, to garnish

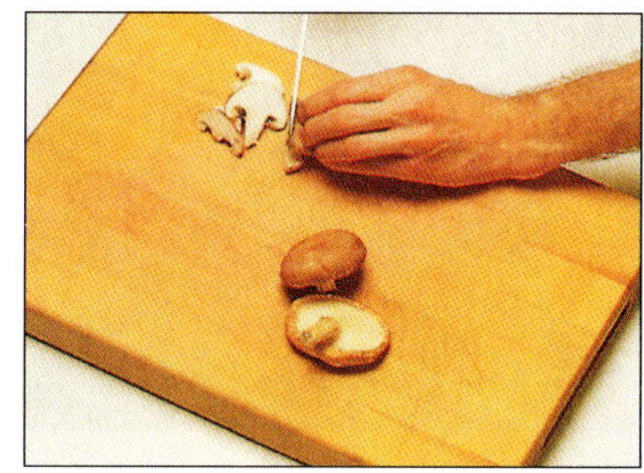

1 If using dried mushrooms, soak them in hot water for 3–4 minutes, then drain. Slice the mushrooms thinly and set aside.

2 Bring the stock to the boil in a large saucepan. Stir in the miso paste and mushrooms, lower the heat and simmer for 5 minutes.

3 Ladle the broth into 4 soup bowls and divide the tofu between them. Sprinkle over the spring onion and serve immediately.

Noodle Soup with Pork and Szechuan Pickle

Ingredients

Serves 4

1 litre/1¾ pints/4 cups chicken stock
350g/12oz egg noodles
15ml/1 tbsp dried shrimps, soaked in water
30ml/2 tbsp vegetable oil
225g/8oz lean pork, finely shredded
15ml/1 tbsp yellow bean paste
15ml/1 tbsp soy sauce
115g/4oz Szechuan hot pickle, rinsed, drained and shredded
pinch of sugar
salt and freshly ground black pepper
2 spring onions, finely sliced, to garnish

1 Bring the stock to the boil in a large saucepan. Add the noodles and cook until almost tender. Drain the dried shrimps, rinse them under cold water, drain again and add to the stock. Lower the heat and simmer for a further 2 minutes. Keep hot. Heat the oil in a frying pan or wok. Add the pork and stir-fry over a high heat for about 3 minutes.

2 Add the bean paste and soy sauce to the pork; stir-fry for 1 minute more. Add the hot pickle with a pinch of sugar. Stir-fry for 1 minute more.

3 Divide the noodles and soup among individual serving bowls. Spoon the pork mixture on top, then sprinkle with the spring onions and serve at once.

Snapper, Tomato and Tamarind Noodle Soup

Tamarind gives this light, fragrant noodle soup a slightly sour taste.

Ingredients

Serves 4

2 litres/3½ pints/8 cups water
1kg/2¼lb red snapper (or other red fish such as mullet)
1 onion, sliced
50g/2oz tamarind pods
15ml/1 tbsp fish sauce
15ml/1 tbsp sugar
30ml/2 tbsp vegetable oil
2 garlic cloves, finely chopped
2 lemon grass stalks, very finely chopped
4 ripe tomatoes, roughly chopped
30ml/2 tbsp yellow bean paste
225g/8oz rice vermicelli, soaked in warm water until soft
115g/4oz beansprouts
8–10 basil or mint sprigs
25g/1oz roasted peanuts, ground
salt and freshly ground black pepper

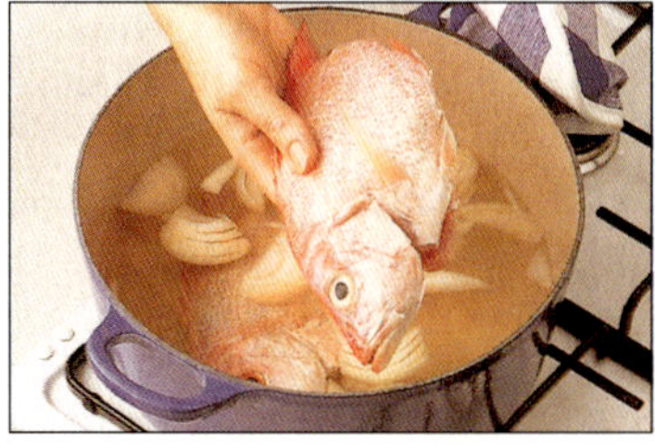

1 Bring the water to the boil in a saucepan. Lower the heat and add the fish and onion, with 2.5ml/½ tsp salt. Simmer gently until the fish is cooked through.

2 Remove the fish from the stock; set aside. Add the tamarind, fish sauce and sugar to the stock. Cook for 5 minutes, then strain the stock into a large jug or bowl. Carefully remove all of the bones from the fish, keeping the flesh in big pieces.

3 Heat the oil in a large frying pan. Add the garlic and lemon grass and fry for a few seconds. Stir in the tomatoes and bean paste. Cook gently for 5–7 minutes, until the tomatoes are soft. Add the stock, bring back to a simmer and adjust the seasoning.

4 Drain the vermicelli. Plunge it into a saucepan of boiling water for a few minutes, drain and divide among individual serving bowls. Add the beansprouts, fish and basil or mint, and sprinkle the ground peanuts on top. Top up each bowl with the hot soup.

Beef Noodle Soup

A steaming bowl, packed with delicious flavours and a taste of the Orient, will be welcome on cold winter days.

Ingredients

Serves 4

10g/¼oz dried porcini mushrooms
150 ml/¼ pint/⅔ cup boiling water
6 spring onions
115g/4oz carrots
350g/12oz rump steak
about 30 ml/2 tbsp sunflower oil
1 garlic clove, crushed
2.5 cm/1in piece fresh root ginger, peeled and finely chopped
1.2 litres/2 pints /5 cups beef stock
45 ml/3 tbsp light soy sauce
60 ml/4 tbsp Chinese rice wine or dry sherry
75g/3oz thin egg noodles
75g/3oz spinach, shredded
salt and ground black pepper

1 Break the mushrooms into small pieces, place in a bowl and pour over the boiling water. Set aside to soak for 15 minutes.

2 Shred the spring onions and carrots into 5cm/2in-long fine strips. Trim any fat off the rump steak and slice into thin strips.

3 Heat the oil in a large saucepan and cook the beef in batches until browned, adding a little more oil if necessary. Remove the beef with a slotted spoon and set aside to drain on kitchen paper.

4 Add the garlic, ginger, spring onions and carrots to the pan and stir-fry for 3 minutes.

5 Add the beef stock, the mushrooms and their soaking liquid, the soy sauce, rice wine or dry sherry and plenty of seasoning. Bring to the boil and simmer, covered, for 10 minutes.

6 Break up the noodles slightly and add to the pan, with the spinach. Simmer gently for 5 minutes, or until the beef is tender. Adjust the seasoning before serving.

Pork and Noodle Broth with Prawns

This delicately flavoured Vietnamese soup is very quick and easy to make, but tastes really special.

Ingredients

Serves 4–6

350g/12oz pork chops or fillet
225g/8oz raw prawn tails or cooked prawns
150g/5oz thin egg noodles
15ml/1 tbsp vegetable oil
10ml/2 tsp sesame oil
4 shallots or 1 medium onion, sliced
15ml/1 tbsp finely sliced fresh root ginger
1 garlic clove, crushed
5ml/1 tsp sugar
1.5 litres/2½ pints/6¼ cups chicken stock
2 kaffir lime leaves
45ml/3 tbsp fish sauce
juice of ½ lime
4 sprigs fresh coriander and 2 spring onions, green parts only, chopped, to garnish

1 If you are using pork chops, trim away any fat and the bones. Place the meat in the freezer for 30 minutes to firm, but not freeze, it. Slice the pork thinly and set aside. Peel and devein the prawns, if using raw prawn tails.

2 Bring a large saucepan of salted water to the boil and simmer the noodles according to the instructions on the packet. Drain and refresh under cold running water. Set aside.

3 Heat the vegetable and sesame oils in a preheated wok, add the shallots or onion and stir-fry for 3–4 minutes, until evenly browned. Remove from the wok and set aside.

4 Add the ginger, garlic, sugar and chicken stock to the wok and bring to a simmer. Add the lime leaves, fish sauce and lime juice. Add the pork, then simmer for 15 minutes. Add the prawns and noodles and simmer for 3–4 minutes to heat through. Serve in shallow bowls, garnished with coriander sprigs, the green parts of the spring onion and the browned shallots or onion.

Hanoi Beef and Noodle Soup

Millions of North Vietnamese eat this fragrant soup for breakfast.

Ingredients

Serves 4–6

1 onion
1.5kg/3–3½lb beef shank with bones
2.5cm/1in fresh root ginger
1 star anise
1 bay leaf
2 whole cloves
2.5ml/½ tsp fennel seeds
1 piece of cassia bark or cinnamon stick
3 litres/5 pints/12½ cups water
fish sauce, to taste
juice of 1 lime
150g/5oz fillet steak
450g/1lb fresh flat rice noodles
salt and freshly ground black pepper

For the accompaniments

1 small red onion, sliced into rings
115g/4oz beansprouts
2 red chillies, seeded and sliced
2 spring onions, finely sliced
handful of coriander leaves
lime wedges

1 Cut the onion in half. Grill under a high heat, cut side up, until the exposed sides are caramelized, and deep brown. Set aside.

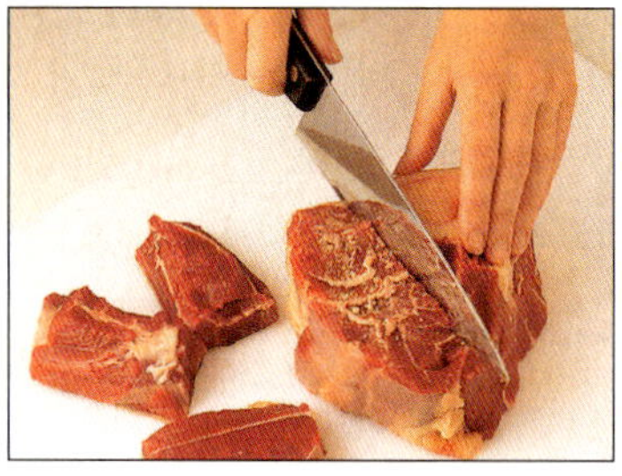

2 Cut the meat into large chunks and then place with the bones in a large saucepan or stock pot. Add the caramelized onion with the ginger, star anise, bay leaf, cloves, fennel seeds and cassia bark or cinnamon stick.

3 Add the water, bring to the boil, reduce the heat and simmer gently for 2–3 hours, skimming off the fat and scum from time to time.

4 Using a slotted spoon, remove the meat from the stock; when cool enough to handle, cut into small pieces, discarding the bones. Strain the stock and return to the pan or stock pot together with the meat. Bring back to the boil and season with the fish sauce and lime juice.

5 Slice the fillet steak very thinly and then chill until required. Place the accompaniments in separate bowls.

6 Cook the noodles in a large saucepan of boiling water until just tender. Drain and divide among individual serving bowls. Arrange the thinly sliced steak over the noodles, pour the hot stock on top and serve, offering the accompaniments separately so that each person may garnish their soup as they like.

Tamarind Soup with Peanuts and Vegetables

Sayur Asam is a colourful and refreshing soup from Jakarta with more than a hint of sharpness.

Ingredients

Serves 4 or 8 as part of a buffet

For the spice paste

5 shallots or 1 medium red onion, sliced
3 garlic cloves, crushed
2.5cm/1in *lengkuas*, peeled and sliced
1–2 fresh red chillies, seeded and sliced
25g/1oz raw peanuts
1cm/½in cube *terasi*, prepared
1.2 litres/2 pints/5 cups well-flavoured stock
50–75g/2–3oz salted peanuts, lightly crushed
15–30ml/1–2 tbsp dark brown sugar
5ml/1 tsp tamarind pulp, soaked in 75ml/5 tbsp warm water for 15 minutes
salt

For the vegetables

1 chayote, thinly peeled, seeds removed, flesh finely sliced
115g/4oz French beans, trimmed and finely sliced
50g/2oz sweetcorn kernels (optional)
handful green leaves, such as watercress, rocket or Chinese leaves, finely shredded
1 fresh green chilli, sliced, to garnish

1 Prepare the spice paste by grinding the shallots or onion, garlic, *lengkuas*, chillies, raw peanuts and *terasi* to a paste in a food processor or with a pestle and mortar.

2 Pour in some of the stock to moisten and then pour this mixture into a pan or wok, adding the rest of the stock. Cook for 15 minutes with the lightly crushed peanuts and sugar.

3 Strain the tamarind, discarding the seeds, and reserve the juice.

4 About 5 minutes before serving, add the chayote slices, beans and sweetcorn, if using, to the soup and cook fairly rapidly. At the last minute, add the green leaves and salt to taste.

5 Add the tamarind juice and taste for seasoning. Serve, garnished with slices of green chilli.

Prawn Crackers

These are a popular addition to many Chinese and other Far Eastern dishes and are often served before guests come to the table. Freshly cooked prawn crackers are more delicious than the ready-to-eat variety.

Ingredients

Serves 4–6

300ml/½ pint/1¼ cups vegetable oil
50g/2oz uncooked prawn crackers
fine table salt, to serve

1 Line a tray with kitchen paper. Heat the oil in a large wok until it begins to smoke. Reduce the heat to maintain a steady temperature. Drop 3 or 4 prawn crackers into the oil.

2 After they swell up, remove them from the oil almost immediately before they start to colour. Transfer to the paper-lined tray to drain. Serve sprinkled with salt.

Hot Chilli Prawns

These can be prepared up to 8 hours in advance and are delicious either grilled or barbecued.

Ingredients

Serves 4–6

1 garlic clove, crushed
1cm/½in piece fresh root ginger, finely chopped
1 small fresh red chilli, seeded and chopped
10ml/2 tsp sugar
15ml/1 tbsp light soy sauce
15ml/1 tbsp vegetable oil
5ml/1 tsp sesame oil
juice of 1 lime
675g/1½lb raw prawns
175g/6oz cherry tomatoes
½ cucumber, cut into chunks
salt
1 small bunch coriander, roughly chopped, to garnish
lettuce leaves, to serve

1 Pound the garlic, ginger, chilli and sugar to a paste in a mortar with a pestle. Add the soy sauce, vegetable and sesame oils, lime juice and salt to taste. Place the prawns in a shallow dish and pour over the marinade. Set aside to marinate for up to 8 hours. Soak some bamboo skewers.

2 Thread the prawns, tomatoes and cucumber chunks on to bamboo skewers. Cook under a preheated grill or on a barbecue for 3–4 minutes. Transfer to a serving dish, scatter over the coriander and serve on a bed of lettuce.

Spring Rolls with Sweet Chilli Dipping Sauce

Miniature spring rolls make a delicious starter or unusual finger-food for serving at a party.

INGREDIENTS

Makes 20–24

25g/1oz rice vermicelli noodles
groundnut oil, for deep-frying
5ml/1 tsp grated fresh root ginger
2 spring onions, finely shredded
50g/2oz carrot, finely shredded
50g/2oz mangetouts, shredded
25g/1oz young spinach leaves
50g/2oz fresh beansprouts
15ml/1 tbsp chopped fresh mint
15ml/1 tbsp chopped fresh coriander
30ml/2 tbsp fish sauce
20–24 spring roll wrappers, each 13cm/5in square
1 egg white, lightly beaten

For the dipping sauce

50g/2oz caster sugar
50ml/2fl oz rice vinegar
30ml/2 tbsp water
2 fresh red chillies, seeded and finely chopped

1 First make the dipping sauce. Place the sugar, vinegar and water in a small pan. Heat gently, stirring until the sugar dissolves, then boil rapidly until it forms a light syrup. Stir in the chillies and leave to cool.

2 Soak the noodles according to the packet instructions, then rinse and drain well. Using scissors, snip the noodles into short lengths.

3 Heat 15ml/1 tbsp of the oil in a preheated wok and swirl it around. Add the ginger and spring onions and stir-fry for 15 seconds. Add the carrot and mangetouts and stir-fry for 2–3 minutes. Add the spinach, beansprouts, mint, coriander, fish sauce and noodles and stir-fry for a further minute. Set aside to cool.

4 Soften the spring roll wrappers, following the directions on the packet. Take one spring roll wrapper and arrange it so that it faces you in a diamond shape. Place a spoonful of filling just below the centre, then fold up the bottom point over the filling.

5 Fold in each side, then roll up tightly. Brush the end with beaten egg white to seal. Repeat until all the filling has been used up.

6 Half-fill a wok with oil and heat to 180°C/350°F. Deep-fry the spring rolls in batches for 3–4 minutes until golden and crisp. Drain on kitchen paper. Serve hot with the sweet chilli dipping sauce.

COOK'S TIP

You can cook the spring rolls 2–3 hours in advance, then reheat them on a foil-lined baking sheet at 200°C/400°F/Gas 6 for about 10 minutes.

Crab Spring Rolls and Dipping Sauce

Chilli and grated ginger add a hint of heat to these sensational treats. Serve them as a starter or with other Chinese dishes as part of a main course.

INGREDIENTS

Serves 4–6

15ml/1 tbsp groundnut oil
5ml/1 tsp sesame oil
1 garlic clove, crushed
1 fresh red chilli, seeded and finely sliced
450g/1lb fresh stir-fry vegetables, such as beansprouts and shredded carrots, peppers and mangetouts
30ml/2 tbsp chopped coriander
2.5cm/1in piece of fresh root ginger, grated
15ml/1 tbsp Chinese rice wine or dry sherry
15ml/1 tbsp soy sauce
350g/12oz fresh dressed crab meat (brown and white meat)
12 spring roll wrappers
1 small egg, beaten
oil, for deep-frying
salt and ground black pepper
lime wedges and fresh coriander, to garnish

For the dipping sauce

1 onion, thinly sliced
oil, for deep-frying
1 fresh red chilli, seeded and finely chopped
2 garlic cloves, crushed
60ml/4 tbsp dark soy sauce
20ml/4 tsp lemon juice or 15–25ml/1–1½ tbsp prepared tamarind juice
30ml/2 tbsp hot water

1 First make the sauce. Spread the onion out on kitchen paper and leave to dry for 30 minutes. Then half-fill a wok with oil and heat to 190°C/375°F. Fry the onion in batches until crisp and golden, turning all the time. Drain on kitchen paper.

2 Mix together the chilli, garlic, soy sauce, lemon or tamarind juice and hot water in a bowl.

3 Stir in the onion and leave to stand for 30 minutes.

4 Heat the groundnut and sesame oils in a clean, preheated wok. When hot, stir-fry the crushed garlic and chilli for 1 minute. Add the vegetables, coriander and ginger and stir-fry for 1 minute more. Drizzle over the rice wine or dry sherry and soy sauce. Allow the mixture to bubble up for 1 minute.

5 Using a slotted spoon, transfer the vegetables to a bowl. Set aside until cool, then stir in the crab meat and season with salt and pepper.

6 Soften the spring roll wrappers, following the directions on the packet. Place some of the filling on a wrapper, fold over the front edge and the sides and roll up neatly, sealing the edges with a little beaten egg. Repeat with the remaining wrappers and filling.

7 Heat the oil for deep-frying in the wok and fry the spring rolls in batches, turning several times, until brown and crisp. Remove with a slotted spoon, drain on kitchen paper and keep hot while frying the remainder. Serve at once, garnished with lime wedges and coriander, with the dipping sauce.

Mini Spring Rolls

Eat these irresistibly light and crisp parcels with your fingers. If you like slightly spicier food, sprinkle them with a little cayenne pepper before serving.

INGREDIENTS

Makes 20

1 green chilli
120ml/4fl oz/½ cup vegetable oil
1 small onion, finely chopped
1 garlic clove, crushed
75g/3oz cooked boneless chicken breast, skinned
1 small carrot, cut into fine matchsticks
1 spring onion, finely sliced
1 small red pepper, seeded and cut into fine matchsticks
25g/1oz beansprouts
5ml/1 tsp sesame oil
4 large sheets filo pastry
1 small egg white, lightly beaten
long chives, to garnish (optional)
45ml/3 tbsp light soy sauce, to serve

1 Carefully remove the seeds from the chilli and chop finely, wearing rubber gloves to protect your hands, if necessary.

2 Heat 30ml/2 tbsp of the vegetable oil in a preheated wok. Add the onion, garlic and chilli and stir-fry for 1 minute.

3 Slice the chicken breast very thinly, then add to the wok and fry over a high heat, stirring constantly, until browned.

4 Add the carrot, spring onion and red pepper and stir-fry for 2 minutes. Add the beansprouts, stir in the sesame oil and leave to cool.

5 Cut each sheet of filo pastry into 5 short strips. Place a small amount of filling at one end of each strip, then fold in the long sides and roll up the pastry. Seal and glaze the parcels with the egg white, then chill, uncovered, for 15 minutes before frying.

6 Wipe the wok with kitchen paper, reheat it and add the remaining vegetable oil. When the oil is hot, fry the rolls in batches until crisp and golden brown. Drain on kitchen paper. Serve garnished with long chives with light soy sauce, for dipping.

COOK'S TIP

Be careful to avoid touching your face or eyes when seeding and chopping chillies because they are very potent and may cause burning and irritation to the skin. Try preparing chillies under running water.

Crab, Pork and Mushroom Spring Rolls

If you cannot obtain minced pork, use the meat from the equivalent weight of best-quality pork sausages. Filled spring rolls can be made in advance and kept in the refrigerator until they are ready for frying.

Ingredients

Serves 4–6

25g/1oz rice noodles
50g/2oz shiitake mushrooms, fresh or dried
vegetable oil, for deep-frying
4 spring onions, chopped
1 small carrot, grated
175g/6oz minced pork
115g/4oz white crab meat
5ml/1 tsp fish sauce (optional)
12 frozen spring roll wrappers, defrosted
30ml/2 tbsp cornflour paste
salt and ground black pepper
1 iceberg or Bibb lettuce, separated into leaves
1 bunch fresh mint or basil, coarsely chopped
1 bunch fresh coriander leaves, coarsely chopped
½ cucumber, sliced

1 Bring a large saucepan of salted water to the boil, add the noodles and simmer for 8 minutes. Cut the noodles into finger-length pieces. If the mushrooms are dried, soak them in boiling water for 10 minutes, then drain. Slice the mushrooms thinly.

2 To make the filling, heat 15ml/1 tbsp of the oil in a wok or frying pan, add the spring onions, carrot and pork and cook for 8–10 minutes. Remove from the heat, then add the crab meat, fish sauce, if using, and seasoning. Add the noodles and mushrooms and set aside.

3 To fill the rolls, brush one spring roll wrapper at a time with the cornflour paste, then place 5ml/1 tsp of the filling on to the skin. Fold the edges towards the middle and roll evenly to make a neat cigar shape. The paste will help seal the wrapper.

4 Heat the oil for deep-frying in a wok or deep-fryer until hot. Fry the spring rolls two at a time for 6–8 minutes. Make sure the oil is not too hot or the filling will not heat through properly. Arrange the salad leaves, mint or basil, coriander and cucumber on a serving platter and top with the spring rolls.

Dim Sum

Popular as a snack in China, these tiny dumplings are fast becoming fashionable in many fast-food, as well as specialist, restaurants in the West.

INGREDIENTS

Serves 4

For the dough

150g/5oz/1¼ cups plain flour
50ml/2fl oz/¼ cup boiling water
25ml/1½ tbsp cold water
7.5ml/½ tbsp vegetable oil

For the filling

75g/3oz minced pork
45ml/3 tbsp canned chopped bamboo shoots
7.5ml/½ tbsp light soy sauce
5ml/1 tsp dry sherry
5ml/1 tsp demerara sugar
2.5ml/½ tsp sesame oil
5ml/1 tsp cornflour
lettuce leaves such as iceberg, frisée or Webbs, soy sauce, spring onion curls, sliced fresh red chilli and prawn crackers, to serve

1 To make the dough, sift the flour into a bowl. Stir in the boiling water, then the cold water together with the oil. Mix to form a dough and knead until smooth.

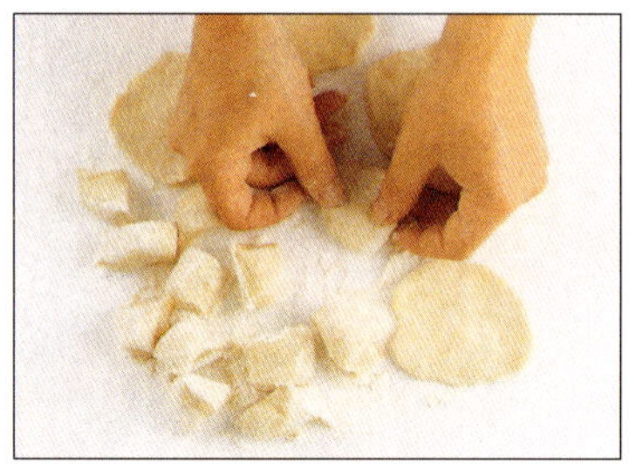

2 Divide the mixture into 16 equal pieces and shape into circles.

3 For the filling, mix together the pork, bamboo shoots, soy sauce, dry sherry, sugar and oil.

4 Add the cornflour and stir well until thoroughly combined.

5 Place a little of the filling in the centre of each dim sum circle. Pinch the edges of the dough together to form little "purses".

6 Line a steamer with a damp tea towel. Place the dim sum in the steamer and steam for 5–10 minutes. Arrange the lettuce leaves on four individual serving plates, top with the dim sum and serve with soy sauce, spring onion curls, sliced red chilli and prawn crackers.

VARIATION

You can replace the pork with cooked, peeled prawns. Sprinkle 15ml/1 tbsp sesame seeds on to the dim sum before cooking, if wished.

Crab and Tofu Dumplings

These little crab and ginger-flavoured dumplings are usually served as a delicious side dish as part of a Japanese meal.

Ingredients

Serves 4–6

115g/4oz frozen white crab meat, thawed
115g/4oz tofu
1 egg yolk
30ml/2 tbsp rice flour or wheat flour
30ml/2 tbsp finely chopped spring onion, green part only
2cm/¾in fresh root ginger, grated
10ml/2 tsp light soy sauce
salt
vegetable oil, for deep-frying
50g/2oz mooli, very finely grated, to serve

For the dipping sauce

120ml/4fl oz vegetable stock
15ml/1 tbsp sugar
45ml/3 tbsp dark soy sauce

1 Squeeze as much moisture out of the crab meat as you can. Press the tofu through a fine strainer with the back of a tablespoon. Combine the tofu and crab meat in a bowl.

2 Add the egg yolk, rice or wheat flour, spring onion, ginger and soy sauce and season to taste with salt. Mix thoroughly to form a light paste.

3 To make the dipping sauce, combine the stock, sugar and soy sauce in a serving bowl.

4 Line a tray with kitchen paper. Heat the vegetable oil in a wok or frying pan to 190°C/375°F. Meanwhile, shape the crab and tofu mixture into thumb-sized pieces. Fry in batches of three at a time for 1–2 minutes. Drain on the kitchen paper and serve with the sauce and mooli.

Steamed Pork and Water Chestnut Wontons

Ginger and Chinese five-spice powder flavour this version of steamed dumplings – a favourite snack in many teahouses.

INGREDIENTS

Makes about 36

2 large Chinese cabbage leaves, plus extra for lining the steamer
2 spring onions, finely chopped
1cm/½in fresh root ginger, chopped
50g/2oz canned water chestnuts, rinsed and finely chopped
225g/8oz minced pork
2.5ml/½ tsp Chinese five-spice powder
15ml/1 tbsp cornflour
15ml/1 tbsp light soy sauce
15ml/1 tbsp Chinese rice wine or dry sherry
10ml/2 tsp sesame oil
generous pinch of caster sugar
about 36 wonton wrappers, each 7.5cm/3in square
light soy sauce and hot chilli oil, for dipping

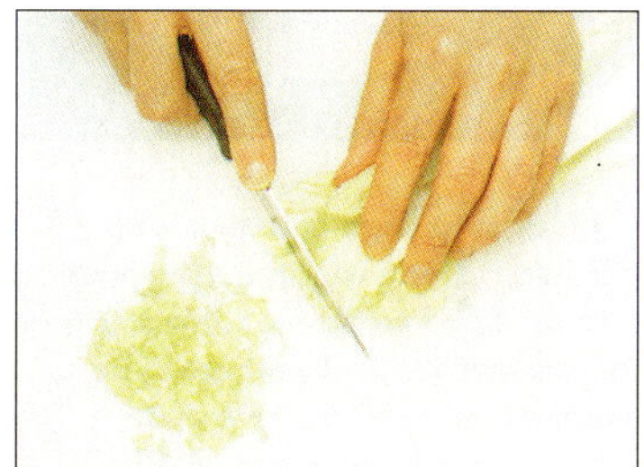

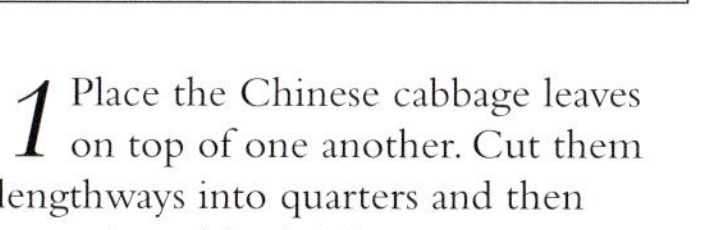

1 Place the Chinese cabbage leaves on top of one another. Cut them lengthways into quarters and then across into thin shreds.

2 Place the shredded Chinese cabbage leaves in a bowl. Add the spring onions, ginger, water chestnuts, pork, five-spice powder, cornflour, soy sauce, rice wine or dry sherry, sesame oil and sugar and mix well.

3 Place a heaped teaspoon of the filling in the centre of the wrapper. Lightly dampen the edges with water.

4 Lift the wrapper up around the filling, gathering it to form a "purse". Squeeze the wrapper firmly around the middle, then tap the bottom to make a flat base. The top should be open. Place the wonton on a tray and cover with a damp tea towel. Repeat.

5 Line a steamer with cabbage leaves and steam the dumplings for 12–15 minutes, until tender. Remove each batch from the steamer as soon as they are cooked, cover with foil and keep warm. Serve hot with soy sauce and chilli oil for dipping.

Seafood Wontons with Coriander Dressing

These tasty wontons resemble tortellini. Water chestnuts add a light crunch to the filling.

INGREDIENTS

Serves 4

225g/8oz raw prawns, peeled and deveined
115g/4oz white crabmeat, picked over
4 canned water chestnuts, finely diced
1 spring onion, finely chopped
1 small green chilli, seeded and finely chopped
2.5ml/½ tsp grated fresh root ginger
1 egg, separated
20–24 wonton wrappers
salt and ground black pepper
coriander leaves, to garnish

For the coriander dressing
30ml/2 tbsp rice vinegar
15ml/1 tbsp chopped pickled ginger
90ml/6 tbsp olive oil
15ml/1 tbsp soy sauce
45ml/3 tbsp chopped coriander
30ml/2 tbsp finely diced red pepper

1 Finely dice the prawns and place them in a bowl. Add the crabmeat, water chestnuts, spring onion, chilli, ginger and egg white. Season with salt and pepper and stir well.

2 Place a wonton wrapper on a board. Put about 5ml/1 tsp of the filling just above the centre of the wrapper. With a pastry brush, moisten the edges of the wrapper with a little of the egg yolk. Bring the bottom of the wrapper up over the filling. Press gently to expel any air, then seal the wrapper neatly in a triangle.

3 For a more elaborate shape, bring the two side points up over the filling, overlap the points and pinch the ends firmly together. Space the filled wontons on a large baking sheet lined with greaseproof paper, so that they do not stick together.

4 Half fill a large saucepan with water. Bring to simmering point. Add the filled wontons, a few at a time, and simmer for 2–3 minutes. The wontons will float to the surface. When ready the wrappers will be translucent and the filling should be cooked. Remove the wontons with a large slotted spoon, drain them briefly, then spread them on trays. Keep warm while cooking the remaining wontons.

5 Make the coriander dressing by whisking all the ingredients together in a bowl. Divide the wontons among serving dishes, drizzle with the dressing and serve garnished with a handful of coriander leaves.

Wonton Flowers with Sweet-and-sour Sauce

These melt-in-the-mouth, crisp dumplings make a delicious first course or snack – and take hardly any time at all to prepare.

Ingredients

Serves 4–6
16–20 wonton wrappers
vegetable oil, for deep-frying

For the sauce
15ml/1 tbsp vegetable oil
30ml/2 tbsp light brown sugar
45ml/3 tbsp rice vinegar
15ml/1 tbsp light soy sauce
15ml/1 tbsp tomato ketchup
45–60ml/3–4 tbsp stock or water
15ml/1 tbsp cornflour paste

1 Pinch the centre of each wonton wrapper and twist it around to form a floral shape.

2 Heat the oil in a wok and deep-fry the floral wontons for 1–2 minutes, until crisp. Remove and drain on kitchen paper.

3 To make the sauce, heat the oil in a wok or frying pan and add the sugar, vinegar, soy sauce, tomato ketchup and stock or water.

4 Stir in the cornflour paste to thicken the sauce. Continue stirring until smooth. Pour a little sauce over the wontons and serve immediately with the remaining sauce.

Seared Scallops with Wonton Crisps

Quick seared scallops with crisp vegetables in a lightly spiced sauce make a delightful starter.

Ingredients

Serves 4

16 medium scallops, halved
oil for deep frying
8 wonton wrappers
45ml/3 tbsp olive oil
1 large carrot, cut into long thin strips
1 large leek, cut into long thin strips
juice of 1 lemon
juice of ½ orange
2 spring onions, finely sliced
30ml/2 tbsp coriander leaves
salt and freshly ground black pepper

For the marinade

5ml/1 tsp Thai red curry paste
5ml/1 tsp grated fresh root ginger
1 garlic clove, finely chopped
15ml/1 tbsp soy sauce
15ml/1 tbsp olive oil

1 Make the marinade by mixing all the ingredients in a bowl. Add the scallops, toss to coat and leave to marinate for about 30 minutes.

2 Heat the oil in a large heavy-based saucepan or deep fryer and deep fry the wonton wrappers in small batches until crisp and golden.

3 When the wrappers are ready, drain them on kitchen paper and set aside until required.

4 Heat half the olive oil in a large frying pan. Add the scallops, with the marinade, and sear over a high heat for about 1 minute or until golden, taking care not to overcook (they should feel firm to the touch but not rubbery). Using a slotted spoon, transfer the scallops to a plate.

5 Add the remaining olive oil to the pan. When hot, add the carrot and leek strips. Toss and turn the vegetables until they start to wilt and soften, but remain crisp. Season to taste with salt and pepper, stir in the lemon and orange juices, and add a little more soy sauce if needed.

6 Return the scallops to the pan, mix lightly with the vegetables and heat for just long enough to warm through. Transfer to a bowl and add the spring onions and coriander. To serve, sandwich a quarter of the mixture between two wonton crisps. Make three more "sandwiches" in the same way and serve at once.

Rice Cakes with Spicy Dipping Sauce

Rice cakes are a classic Thai appetizer. They are easy to make and can be kept in an airtight box almost indefinitely.

INGREDIENTS

Serves 4–6

175g/6oz/1 cup jasmine rice
350ml/12fl oz/1½ cups water
oil for frying and greasing

For the spicy dipping sauce

6–8 dried chillies
2.5ml/½ tsp salt
2 shallots, chopped
2 garlic cloves, chopped
4 coriander roots
10 white peppercorns
250ml/8fl oz/1 cup coconut milk
5ml/1 tsp shrimp paste
115g/4oz minced pork
115g/4oz cherry tomatoes, chopped
15ml/1 tbsp fish sauce
15ml/1 tbsp palm sugar
30ml/2 tbsp tamarind juice
30 ml/2 tbsp coarsely chopped roasted peanuts
2 spring onions, finely chopped

1 Stem the chillies and remove most of the seeds. Soak the chillies in warm water for 20 minutes. Drain and transfer to a mortar.

2 Add the salt and grind with a pestle until the chillies are crushed. Add the shallots, garlic, coriander roots and peppercorns. Pound together until you have a coarse paste.

3 Pour the coconut milk into a saucepan and boil until it begins to separate. Add the pounded chilli paste. Cook for 2–3 minutes until it is fragrant. Stir in the shrimp paste. Cook for another minute.

4 Add the pork, stirring to break up any lumps. Cook for about 5–10 minutes. Add the tomatoes, fish sauce, palm sugar and tamarind juice. Simmer until the sauce thickens.

5 Stir in the chopped peanuts and spring onions. Remove from the heat and leave to cool.

6 Wash the rice in several changes of water. Put in a saucepan, add the water and cover with a tight-fitting lid. Bring to the boil, reduce the heat and simmer gently for about 15 minutes.

7 Remove the lid and fluff up the rice. Turn out on to a lightly greased tray and press down with the back of a large spoon. Leave to dry out overnight in a very low oven until it is completely dry and firm.

8 Remove the rice from the tray and break into bite-size pieces. Heat the oil in a wok or deep-fat fryer.

9 Deep fry the rice cakes in batches for about 1 minute, until they puff up, taking care not to brown them too much. Remove and drain. Serve accompanied with the dipping sauce.

Vegetable Tempura

These deep-fried fritters are based on *Kaki-age*, a Japanese dish that often incorporates fish and prawns as well as vegetables.

Ingredients

Serves 4

2 medium courgettes
½ medium aubergine
1 large carrot
½ small Spanish onion
1 egg
120ml/4fl oz/½ cup iced water
115g/4oz/1 cup plain flour
salt and ground black pepper
vegetable oil, for deep-frying
sea salt flakes, lemon slices and Japanese soy sauce (*shoyu*), to serve

1 Using a potato peeler, pare strips of peel from the courgettes and aubergine to give a striped effect.

2 Cut the courgettes, aubergine and carrot into strips about 7.5–10cm/3–4in long and 3mm/⅛in wide.

3 Put the courgettes, aubergine and carrot into a colander and sprinkle liberally with salt. Leave for about 30 minutes, then rinse thoroughly under cold running water. Drain well.

4 Thinly slice the onion from top to base, discarding the plump pieces in the middle. Separate the layers so that there are lots of fine, long strips. Mix all the vegetables together and season with salt and pepper.

5 Make the batter immediately before frying. Mix the egg and iced water in a bowl, then sift in the flour. Mix briefly with a fork or chopsticks. Do not overmix; the batter should remain lumpy. Add the vegetables to the batter and mix to combine.

6 Half-fill a wok with oil and heat to 180°C/350°F. Scoop up one heaped tablespoon of the mixture at a time and carefully lower it into the oil. Deep-fry in batches for about 3 minutes, until golden brown and crisp. Drain on kitchen paper. Serve each portion with salt, slices of lemon and a tiny bowl of Japanese soy sauce for dipping.

Spicy Spareribs

Fragrant with spices, this authentic Chinese dish makes a great – if slightly messy – starter to an informal meal.

Ingredients

Serves 4

675–900g/1½–2lb meaty pork spareribs
5ml/1 tsp Szechuan peppercorns
30ml/2 tbsp coarse sea salt
2.5ml/½ tsp Chinese five-spice powder
25ml/1½ tbsp cornflour
groundnut oil, for deep-frying
coriander sprigs, to garnish

For the marinade
30ml/2 tbsp light soy sauce
5ml/1 tsp caster sugar
15ml/1 tbsp Chinese rice wine or dry sherry
ground black pepper

1 Using a sharp, heavy cleaver, chop the spareribs into pieces about 5cm/2in long, or ask your butcher to do this for you. Place them in a shallow dish and set aside.

2 Heat a wok to medium heat. Add the Szechuan peppercorns and salt and dry-fry for about 3 minutes, stirring constantly, until the mixture colours slightly. Remove from the heat and stir in the five-spice powder. Set aside to cool.

3 Grind the cooled spice mixture in a mortar with a pestle to a fine powder.

4 Sprinkle 5ml/1 tsp of the spice powder over the spareribs and rub in well with your hands. Add all the marinade ingredients and toss the ribs to coat thoroughly. Cover and leave in the refrigerator to marinate for about 2 hours, turning occasionally.

5 Pour off any excess marinade from the spareribs. Sprinkle the ribs with the cornflour and mix to coat evenly.

6 Half-fill a wok with oil and heat to 180°C/350°F. Deep-fry the spareribs in batches for 3 minutes until golden. Remove and set aside. When all the batches have been cooked, reheat the oil to 180°C/350°F and deep-fry the ribs for a second time for 1–2 minutes, until crisp and thoroughly cooked. Drain on kitchen paper. Transfer the ribs to a warm serving platter and sprinkle over 5–7.5ml/1–1½ tsp of the remaining spice powder. Garnish with coriander sprigs and serve immediately.

Cook's Tip

Any leftover spice powder can be kept in a screw-top jar for several months. Use to rub on the flesh of duck, chicken or pork before cooking.

Barbecue-glazed Chicken Skewers

Known as *yakitori*, this mouth-watering appetizer is often served with pre-dinner drinks in Japan.

INGREDIENTS

Makes 12 skewers and 8 wing pieces

4 chicken thighs, skinned
4 spring onions, blanched and cut into short lengths
8 chicken wings
15ml/1 tbsp grated mooli, to serve (optional)

For the sauce

60ml/4 tbsp sake
75ml/5 tbsp dark soy sauce
30ml/2 tbsp tamari sauce
45ml/3 tbsp sweet sherry
60ml/4 tbsp sugar

1 Bone the chicken thighs and cut the meat into large dice. Thread the spring onions and chicken on to 12 bamboo skewers.

2 To prepare the chicken wings, remove the tip at the first joint. Chop through the second joint, revealing the two narrow bones. Take hold of the bones with a clean cloth and pull, turning the meat around the bones inside out. Remove the smaller bone and set the meat aside.

3 Put all the sauce ingredients into a stainless steel or enamel saucepan and simmer until reduced by two-thirds. Set aside to cool.

4 Cook the skewers of chicken and the wings under a preheated grill without brushing on any oil. When juices begin to emerge from the chicken, baste liberally with the sauce. Cook the chicken on the skewers for a further 3 minutes and cook the wings for a further 5 minutes. Serve with grated mooli, if liked.

Lacy Duck Egg Nets

These parcels are very attractive. Thais have a special dispenser for making the nets. It is cone-shaped with holes at the bottom, to allow the egg mixture to dribble out in threads. You can use a small-hole funnel, a piping bag with a small nozzle or a squeezy bottle.

Ingredients

Makes about 12–15

For the filling

4 coriander roots
2 garlic cloves
10 white peppercorns
pinch of salt
45ml/3 tbsp oil
1 small onion, finely chopped
115g/4oz lean minced pork
75g/3oz shelled prawns, chopped
50g/2oz roasted peanuts, ground
5ml/1 tsp palm sugar
fish sauce, to taste

For the egg nets

6 duck eggs
coriander leaves, to serve, plus extra to garnish
spring onion tassels, to garnish
sliced red chillies, to garnish

1 Using a pestle and mortar, grind the coriander roots, garlic, white peppercorns and salt into a paste.

2 Heat 30ml/2 tbsp of the oil, add the paste and fry until fragrant. Add the onion and cook until softened. Add the pork and prawns and continue to stir-fry until the meat is cooked.

3 Add the peanuts, palm sugar, salt and fish sauce, to taste. Stir the mixture and continue to cook until it becomes a little sticky. Remove from the heat. Transfer the mixture into a bowl and set aside.

4 Beat the duck eggs in a bowl. Grease a non-stick frying pan with the remaining oil and heat. Using a special dispenser or one of the alternatives, trail the eggs across the pan to make a net pattern, about 13cm/5in in diameter.

5 When the net is set, carefully remove it from the pan, and repeat until all the eggs have been used up.

6 To assemble, lay a net on a board, lay a few coriander leaves on it and top with a spoonful of the filling. Turn in the edges to make a neat square shape. Repeat with the rest of the nets. Arrange on a serving dish, garnish with spring onion tassels, coriander leaves and chillies.

Pickled Sweet-and-sour Cucumber

The "pickling" can be done in minutes rather than days – but the more time you have, the better the result.

Ingredients

Serves 6–8
1 slender cucumber, about 30cm/12in long
5ml/1 tsp salt
10ml/2 tsp caster sugar
5ml/1 tsp rice vinegar
2.5ml/½ tsp red chilli oil (optional)
few drops of sesame oil

1 Halve the unpeeled cucumber lengthways. Scrape out the seeds and cut the cucumber into thick chunks.

2 In a bowl, sprinkle the cucumber chunks with the salt and mix well. Leave for at least 20–30 minutes – longer if possible – then pour the juice away.

3 Mix the cucumber with the sugar, vinegar and chilli oil. Sprinkle with the sesame oil just before serving.

Hot-and-sour Cabbage

This popular dish from Szechuan in western China can be served hot or cold.

Ingredients

Serves 6–8
450g/1lb pale green or white cabbage
45–60ml/3–4 tbsp vegetable oil
10–12 red Szechuan peppercorns
few whole dried red chillies
5ml/1 tsp salt
15ml/1 tbsp light brown sugar
15ml/1 tbsp light soy sauce
30ml/2 tbsp rice vinegar
few drops of sesame oil

1 Cut the cabbage leaves into small pieces each roughly 2.5 x 1cm/1 x ½in.

2 Heat the oil in a preheated wok until smoking, then add the peppercorns and chillies.

3 Add the cabbage to the wok and stir-fry for about 1–2 minutes. Add the salt and sugar, continue stirring for 1 minute more, then add the soy sauce, vinegar and sesame oil. Blend well and serve immediately.

Spicy Meat Patties with Coconut

Spicy meat patties, known as *Rempah*, with a hint of coconut, often feature as one of the delicious accompaniments in an Indonesian-style buffet.

INGREDIENTS

Makes 22

115g/4oz freshly grated coconut, or desiccated coconut, soaked in 60–90ml/4–6 tbsp boiling water
350g/12oz finely minced beef
2.5ml/½ tsp each coriander and cumin seeds, dry-fried
1 garlic clove, crushed
a little beaten egg
15–30ml/1–2 tbsp plain flour
groundnut oil for frying
salt
thin lemon or lime wedges, to serve

1 Mix the moistened coconut with the minced beef.

2 Grind the dry-fried coriander and cumin seeds with a pestle and mortar. Add the ground spices to the meat and coconut mixture together with the garlic, salt to taste, and sufficient beaten egg to bind.

3 Divide the meat into evenly sized portions, the size of a walnut, and form into patty shapes.

4 Dust with flour. Heat the oil and then fry the patties for 4–5 minutes until both sides are golden brown and cooked through. Serve with lemon or lime wedges, to squeeze over.

Sweetcorn Fritters

There is no doubt that freshly cooked sweetcorn is best for this recipe, called *Perkedel Jagung*. Do not add salt to the water, because this toughens the outer husk.

INGREDIENTS

Makes 20

2 fresh corn on the cob, or 350g/12oz can sweetcorn kernels
2 macadamia nuts or 4 almonds
1 garlic clove
1 onion, quartered
1cm/½in fresh *lengkuas*, peeled and sliced
5ml/1 tsp ground coriander
30–45ml/2–3 tbsp oil
3 eggs, beaten
30ml/2 tbsp desiccated coconut
2 spring onions, finely shredded
a few celery leaves, finely shredded (optional)
salt

1 Cook the corn on the cob in boiling water for 7–8 minutes. Drain, cool slightly and, using a sharp knife, strip the kernels from the cob. If using canned sweetcorn, drain well.

2 Grind the nuts, garlic, onion, *lengkuas* and coriander to a fine paste in a food processor or pestle and mortar. Heat a little oil and fry the paste until it gives off a spicy aroma.

3 Add the fried spices to the beaten eggs with the coconut, spring onions and celery leaves, if using. Add salt to taste with the corn kernels.

4 Heat the remaining oil in a shallow frying pan. Drop large spoonfuls of batter into the pan and cook for 2–3 minutes until golden. Flip the fritters over with a fish slice and cook until golden brown and crispy. Only cook three or four fritters at a time.

Fish and Seafood

The many islands in the Pacific and the long coastline of mainland China ensure an abundance of wonderful fish and seafood recipes in the cuisines of Asia. Whole fish and fillets are combined with fragrant herbs and marinades and then steamed, baked or fried quickly. The different ways of preparing prawns, mussels, scallops, squid and other seafood are almost endless, from the subtly aromatic Pan-steamed Mussels with Thai Herbs to the robust and spicy Prawns with Chayote in Turmeric Sauce. All are quick to prepare, highly nutritious and utterly delicious.

Steamed Fish with Ginger and Spring Onions

Firm and delicate fish steaks, such as salmon or turbot, can be cooked by this same method.

INGREDIENTS

Serves 4–6

1 sea bass, trout or grey mullet, weighing about 675g/1½lb, gutted
2.5ml/½ tsp salt
15ml/1 tbsp sesame oil
2–3 spring onions, cut in half lengthways
30ml/2 tbsp light soy sauce
30ml/2 tbsp Chinese rice wine or dry sherry
15ml/1 tbsp finely shredded fresh ginger
30ml/2 tbsp vegetable oil
finely shredded spring onions, to garnish

1 Using a sharp knife, score both sides of the fish as far down as the bone with diagonal cuts about 2.5cm/1in apart. Rub the fish all over, inside and out, with salt and sesame oil.

2 Sprinkle the spring onions over a heatproof platter and place the fish on top. Blend together the soy sauce and rice wine or dry sherry with the ginger shreds and pour evenly all over the fish.

3 Place the platter in a very hot steamer (or inside a wok on a rack) and steam vigorously, under cover, for 12–15 minutes.

4 Heat the vegetable oil until hot. Remove the platter from the steamer, place the shredded spring onions on top of the fish, then pour the hot oil along the whole length of the fish. Serve immediately.

Fried Monkfish Coated with Rice Noodles

These marinated medallions of fish are coated in rice vermicelli and deep fried – they taste as good as they look.

INGREDIENTS

Serves 4

450g/1lb monkfish
5ml/1 tsp grated fresh root ginger
1 garlic clove, finely chopped
30ml/2 tbsp soy sauce
175g/6oz rice vermicelli
50g/2oz cornflour
2 eggs, beaten
salt and freshly ground black pepper
oil for deep frying
banana leaves, to serve (optional)

For the dipping sauce

30ml/2 tbsp soy sauce
30ml/2 tbsp rice vinegar
15ml/1 tbsp sugar
2 red chillies, thinly sliced
1 spring onion, thinly sliced

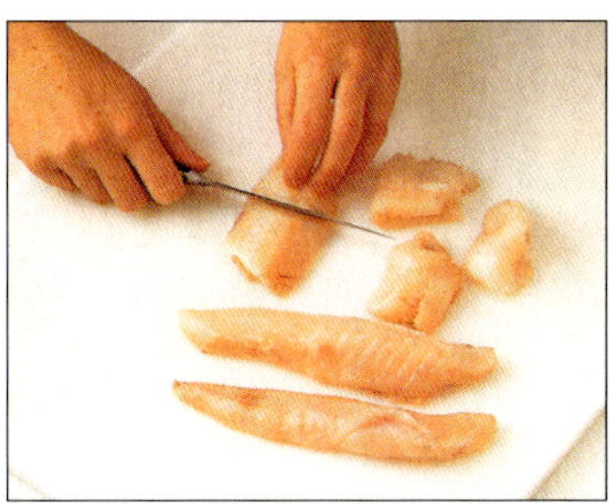

1 Trim the monkfish and cut into 2.5cm/1in thick medallions. Place in a dish and add the ginger, garlic and soy sauce. Mix lightly and leave to marinate for 10 minutes.

2 Meanwhile, make the dipping sauce. Combine the soy sauce, vinegar and sugar in a small saucepan. Bring to the boil. Add salt and pepper to taste. Remove from the heat, add the chillies and spring onion and set aside until required.

3 Using kitchen scissors, cut the noodles into 4cm/1½in lengths. Spread them out in a shallow bowl.

4 Coat the fish medallions in cornflour, dip in beaten egg and cover with noodles, pressing them on to the fish so that they stick.

5 Deep fry the coated fish in hot oil, 2–3 pieces at a time, until the noodle coating is fluffy, crisp and light golden brown. Drain and serve hot on banana leaves, if you like, accompanied by the dipping sauce.

Fish with Sweet-and-sour Sauce

Another name for this dish is Five-willow Fish, after the five shredded vegetables in the sweet-and-sour sauce.

Ingredients

Serves 4–6

1 carp, bream, sea bass, trout, grouper or grey mullet, weighing about 675g/1½lb, gutted
5ml/1 tsp salt
about 30ml/2 tbsp plain flour
vegetable oil, for deep-frying
fresh coriander leaves, to garnish

For the sauce

15ml/1 tbsp vegetable oil
50g/2oz carrot, thinly shredded
50g/2oz bamboo shoots, shredded
25g/1oz green pepper, seeded and thinly shredded
25g/1oz red pepper, seeded and thinly shredded
2–3 spring onions, finely shredded
15ml/1 tbsp finely chopped fresh root ginger
15ml/1 tbsp light soy sauce
30ml/2 tbsp light brown sugar
30–45ml/2–3 tbsp rice vinegar
about 120ml/4fl oz/½ cup Basic Stock
15ml/1 tbsp cornflour paste

1 Clean and dry the fish well. Using a sharp knife, score both sides of the fish as deep as the bone with diagonal cuts at intervals of about 2.5cm/1in.

2 Rub the whole fish with salt both inside and out, then coat it from head to tail with flour.

3 Heat the oil in a wok or frying pan and deep-fry the fish for about 3–4 minutes on both sides, or until golden brown. Remove the fish and drain, then place on a warmed serving platter.

4 For the sauce, heat the oil in a preheated pan or wok and stir-fry all the vegetables for about 1 minute, then add the ginger, soy sauce, sugar and rice vinegar. Blend well, add the stock and bring to the boil. Add the cornflour paste, stirring well until the sauce thickens. Pour over the fish and serve garnished with coriander.

Sesame Baked Fish with a Hot Ginger Marinade

Although tropical varieties of fish are found increasingly frequently in supermarkets, oriental food stores usually have a wider selection suitable for this Malaysian dish.

Ingredients

Serves 4–6

- 2 red snapper, parrot fish or monkfish tails, each weighing about 350g/12oz
- 30ml/2 tbsp vegetable oil, plus extra for greasing
- 10ml/2 tsp sesame oil
- 30ml/2 tbsp sesame seeds
- 2.5cm/1in fresh root ginger, thinly sliced
- 2 garlic cloves, crushed
- 2 small fresh red chillies, seeded and finely chopped
- 4 shallots or 1 medium onion, halved and sliced
- 30ml/2 tbsp water
- 1cm/½in square shrimp paste or 15ml/1 tbsp fish sauce
- 10ml/2 tsp sugar
- 2.5ml/½ tsp cracked black pepper
- juice of 2 limes
- 3–4 banana leaves (optional)

1 Clean and dry the fish well. Slash both sides of the fish deeply with a sharp knife. If using parrot fish, rub with fine salt and leave to stand for 15 minutes to remove the rather chalky coral flavour.

2 To make the marinade, heat the vegetable and sesame oils in a preheated wok. Add the sesame seeds and fry until golden. Add the ginger, garlic, chillies and shallots or onion and stir-fry 1–2 minutes, until softened. Add the water, shrimp paste or fish sauce, sugar, pepper and lime juice and simmer for 2–3 minutes. Remove from the heat and allow to cool.

Cook's Tip

Banana leaves are available from Indian and South-east Asian food stores.

3 If using banana leaves, remove and discard the central stems. Soften the leaves by dipping them in boiling water. To keep them supple, rub the surfaces with vegetable oil. Spread the sesame seed marinade over the fish, then wrap them separately in the banana leaves, secured with a skewer, or enclose them in foil. Set aside in a cool place to allow the flavours to mingle, for up to 3 hours.

4 Place the fish parcels on a baking sheet and cook in a preheated oven at 180°C/350°F/Gas 4 or on a glowing barbecue for 35–40 minutes. Serve hot.

Sizzling Chinese Steamed Fish

Steamed whole fish is very popular in China, and the wok is used as a steamer. In this recipe the fish is flavoured with garlic, ginger and spring onions cooked in sizzling hot oil.

Ingredients

Serves 4

- 4 rainbow trout, about 250g/9oz each
- 1.5ml/¼ tsp salt
- 2.5ml/½ tsp sugar
- 2 garlic cloves, finely chopped
- 15ml/1 tbsp finely diced fresh root ginger
- 5 spring onions, cut into 5cm/2in lengths and finely shredded
- 60ml/4 tbsp groundnut oil
- 5ml/1 tsp sesame oil
- 45ml/3 tbsp light soy sauce
- thread egg noodles and stir-fried vegetables, to serve

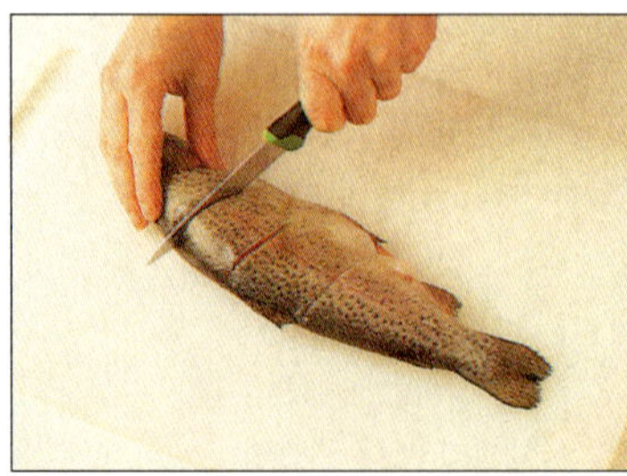

1 Make three diagonal slits on both sides of each fish and lay them on a heatproof plate. Place a small rack or trivet in a wok half-filled with water, cover and heat until just simmering.

2 Sprinkle the fish with the salt, sugar, garlic and ginger. Place the plate securely on the rack or trivet and cover. Steam gently for about 10–12 minutes, or until the flesh has turned pale pink and feels quite firm.

3 Turn off the heat, remove the lid and scatter the spring onions over the fish. Replace the lid.

4 Heat the groundnut and sesame oils in a small pan over a high heat until just smoking, then quickly pour a quarter over the spring onions on each of the fish – the shredded onions will sizzle and cook in the hot oil. Sprinkle the soy sauce over the top. Serve the fish and juices immediately with boiled noodles and stir-fried vegetables.

Chinese-spiced Fish Fillets

Ingredients

Serves 4

65g/2½oz/generous ½ cup plain flour
5ml/1 tsp Chinese five-spice powder
8 skinless fillets of fish, such as plaice or lemon sole, about 800g/1¾lb in total
1 egg, lightly beaten
40–50g/1½–2oz/scant 1 cup fine fresh breadcrumbs
groundnut oil, for frying
25g/1oz/2 tbsp butter
4 spring onions, cut diagonally into thin slices
350g/12oz tomatoes, seeded and diced
30ml/2 tbsp soy sauce
salt and ground black pepper
red pepper strips and chives, to garnish

1 Sift the flour together with the Chinese five-spice powder and salt and pepper to taste on to a plate. Dip the fish fillets first in the seasoned flour, then in the beaten egg and finally in breadcrumbs.

2 Pour oil into a large frying pan to a depth of 1cm/½ in. Heat until it is very hot and starting to sizzle. Add the coated fillets, a few at a time, and fry for 2–3 minutes on each side, depending on their thickness, until just cooked and golden brown. Do not crowd the pan, or the temperature of the oil will drop and the fish will absorb too much of it.

3 Drain the fillets on kitchen paper, then transfer to serving plates and keep warm. Pour off all the oil from the frying pan and wipe it out with kitchen paper.

4 Cook the spring onions and tomatoes in the butter for 1 minute, then add the soy sauce.

5 Spoon the tomato mixture over the fish, garnish with red pepper strips and chives and serve.

Fish with a Cashew Ginger Marinade

To capture the sweet, spicy flavour of this Indonesian favourite, marinated fish are wrapped in parcels before baking. When they are unwrapped at the table, their delicious aroma will make your mouth water.

Ingredients

Serves 4

1.1kg/2½lb sea bass or pomfret, scaled and cleaned
150g/5oz/1¼ cups raw cashew nuts
2 shallots or 1 small onion, finely chopped
1cm/½in fresh root ginger, finely chopped
1 garlic clove, crushed
1 small fresh red chilli, seeded and finely chopped
30ml/2 tbsp vegetable oil
15ml/1 tbsp shrimp paste
10ml/2 tsp sugar
30ml/2 tbsp tamarind sauce
30ml/2 tbsp tomato ketchup
juice of 2 limes
salt

1 Slash the fish 3–4 times on each side with a sharp knife. Set aside.

2 Grind the cashew nuts, shallots or onion, ginger, garlic and chilli to a fine paste in a mortar with a pestle or in a food processor. Add the vegetable oil, shrimp paste and sugar and season to taste with salt. Blend, then add the tamarind sauce, tomato ketchup and lime juice and blend again.

3 Cover both sides of the fish with the paste and set aside in the refrigerator for up to 8 hours to allow the flavours to mingle.

4 Wrap the fish in foil, securing the parcels carefully. Bake in a preheated oven at 180°C/350°F/Gas 4 for 30–35 minutes.

Whole Fish with Sweet-and-sour Sauce

INGREDIENTS

Serves 4

1 whole fish, such as red snapper or carp, about 1kg/2¼lb
30–45ml/2–3 tbsp cornflour
oil for frying
salt and freshly ground black pepper
boiled rice, to serve

For the spice paste

2 garlic cloves
2 lemon grass stems
2.5cm/1in fresh *lengkuas*
2.5cm/1in fresh root ginger
2cm/¾in fresh turmeric or 2.5ml/½ tsp ground turmeric
5 macadamia nuts or 10 almonds

For the sauce

15ml/1 tbsp brown sugar
45ml/3 tbsp cider vinegar
about 350ml/12fl oz/1½ cups water
2 lime leaves, torn
4 shallots, quartered
3 tomatoes, skinned and cut in wedges
3 spring onions, finely shredded
1 fresh red chilli, seeded and shredded

1 Ask the fishmonger to gut and scale the fish, leaving on the head and tail, or you may do this yourself. Wash and dry the fish thoroughly and then sprinkle it inside and out with salt. Set aside for 15 minutes, while preparing the other ingredients.

2 Peel and crush the garlic cloves. Use only the lower white part of the lemon grass stems and slice thinly. Peel and slice the fresh *lengkuas*, the fresh root ginger and fresh turmeric, if using. Grind the nuts, garlic, lemon grass, *lengkuas*, ginger and turmeric to a fine paste in a food processor or with a pestle and mortar.

3 Scrape the paste into a bowl. Stir in the brown sugar, cider vinegar, seasoning to taste and the water. Add the lime leaves.

4 Dust the fish with the cornflour and fry on both sides in hot oil for about 8–9 minutes or until almost cooked through. Drain the fish on kitchen paper and transfer to a serving dish. Keep warm.

5 Pour off most of the oil and then pour in the spicy liquid and allow to come to the boil. Reduce the heat and cook for 3–4 minutes. Add the shallots and tomatoes, followed a minute later by the spring onions and chilli. Taste and adjust the seasoning.

6 Pour the sauce over the fish. Serve at once, with plenty of rice.

Sea Bass with Chinese Chives

Chinese chives are widely available in oriental supermarkets but if you are unable to buy them, use half a large Spanish onion, finely sliced, instead.

Ingredients

Serves 4

2 sea bass, about 450g/1lb in total
15ml/1 tbsp cornflour
45ml/3 tbsp vegetable oil
175g/6oz Chinese chives
15ml/1 tbsp Chinese rice wine or dry sherry
5ml/1 tsp caster sugar
salt and ground black pepper
Chinese chives with flowerheads, to garnish

1 Remove the scales from the bass by scraping them with the back of a knife, working from the tail end towards the head end. Fillet the fish.

2 Cut the fillets into large chunks and dust them lightly with cornflour, salt and pepper.

3 Heat 30ml/2 tbsp of the oil in a preheated wok. When the oil is hot, toss the chunks of fish in the wok briefly to seal, then set aside. Wipe out the wok with kitchen paper.

4 Cut the Chinese chives into 5cm/2in lengths and discard the flowers. Reheat the wok and add the remaining oil, then stir-fry the Chinese chives for 30 seconds. Add the fish and rice wine or dry sherry, then bring to the boil and stir in the sugar. Serve hot, garnished with some flowering Chinese chives.

Salt-grilled Mackerel

In Japan salt is applied to oily fish before cooking to draw out the flavours. Mackerel, snapper and garfish are the most popular choices for this treatment, known as *Shio-yaki* in Japanese. All of them develop a unique flavour and texture when treated with salt. The salt is washed away before cooking.

Ingredients

Serves 2

2 small or 1 large mackerel, snapper or garfish, gutted and cleaned, with head on
30ml/2 tbsp fine table salt
1 medium carrot, shredded, to serve

For the soy ginger dip

60ml/4 tbsp dark soy sauce
30ml/2 tbsp sugar
2.5cm/1in piece fresh root ginger

For the Japanese horseradish

45ml/3 tbsp *wasabi* powder
10ml/2 tsp water

1 To make the soy ginger dip, put the soy sauce, sugar and ginger in a stainless steel saucepan. Bring to the boil, lower the heat and simmer for 2–3 minutes. Strain and set aside to cool. To make the Japanese horseradish, put the *wasabi* powder into a small bowl and stir in the water to make a stiff paste. Shape the mixture into a neat ball and set aside.

2 Rinse the fish under cold, running water and pat thoroughly dry with kitchen paper. Slash the fish several times on both sides, cutting down as far as the bone. Sprinkle the salt inside the fish and rub it well into the skin. Set aside on a plate for 40 minutes.

3 Wash the fish in plenty of cold water to remove all traces of salt. Shape the fish into a gentle curve and secure in position with two bamboo skewers inserted along the length of the body, one above and one below the eye.

4 Cook the fish under a preheated grill or on a barbecue for 10–12 minutes, turning once. The skin can be basted with a little of the soy ginger dip part way through cooking, if liked. Transfer the fish to a serving plate and arrange carrot, Japanese horseradish and soy ginger dip decoratively around it.

Cook's Tip

Wasabi is the ground root of an oriental type of horseradish. It is very sharp and aromatic and often served with raw fish and shellfish. In the West, it is usually available only as a powder, which has to be mixed with water to make a paste.

Gingered Seafood Stir-fry

This cornucopia of scallops, prawns and squid in an aromatic sauce makes a refreshing summer supper, served with plenty of crusty bread to mop up the juices – together with a glass of chilled dry white wine. It would also make a great dinner-party starter for four people.

INGREDIENTS

Serves 2

15ml/1 tbsp sunflower oil
5ml/1 tsp sesame oil
2.5cm/1in fresh root ginger, finely chopped
1 bunch spring onions, sliced
1 red pepper, seeded and finely chopped
115g/4 oz small queen scallops
8 large raw prawns, peeled
115g/4oz squid rings
15ml/1 tbsp lime juice
15ml/1 tbsp light soy sauce
60ml/4 tbsp coconut milk
salt and ground black pepper
mixed salad leaves and lime slices, to serve

1 Heat the sunflower and sesame oils in a preheated wok or large frying pan and cook the ginger and spring onions for 2–3 minutes, or until golden. Stir in the red pepper and cook for a further 3 minutes.

2 Add the scallops, prawns and squid rings and cook over a medium heat for about 3 minutes, until the seafood is just cooked.

3 Stir in the lime juice, soy sauce and coconut milk. Simmer, uncovered, for 2 minutes, until the juices begin to thicken slightly.

4 Season well. Arrange the salad leaves on 2 serving plates and spoon over the seafood mixture with the juices. Serve with lime slices for squeezing over the seafood.

Spiced Scallops in their Shells

Scallops are excellent steamed. When served with this spicy sauce, they make a delicious, yet simple, starter for four people or a light lunch for two. Each person spoons sauce on to the scallops before eating them.

Ingredients

Serves 2

8 scallops, shelled (ask the fishmonger to reserve the cupped side of 4 shells)
2 slices fresh root ginger, shredded
½ garlic clove, shredded
2 spring onions, green parts only, shredded
salt and ground black pepper

For the sauce

1 garlic clove, crushed
15ml/1 tbsp grated fresh root ginger
2 spring onions, white parts only, chopped
1–2 fresh green chillies, seeded and finely chopped
15ml/1 tbsp light soy sauce
15ml/1 tbsp dark soy sauce
10ml/2 tsp sesame oil

1 Remove the dark beard-like fringe and tough muscle from the scallops.

2 Place 2 scallops in each shell. Season lightly with salt and pepper, then scatter the ginger, garlic and spring onions on top. Place the shells in a bamboo steamer in a wok and steam for about 6 minutes, until the scallops look opaque (you may have to do this in batches).

3 Meanwhile, make the sauce. Mix together the garlic, ginger, spring onions, chillies, soy sauces and sesame oil and pour into a small serving bowl.

4 Carefully remove each shell from the steamer, taking care not to spill the juices, and arrange them on a serving plate with the sauce bowl in the centre. Serve at once.

Chilli Prawns

This delightful, spicy combination makes a lovely, light main course for a casual supper. Serve with rice, noodles or even freshly cooked pasta and a leafy green salad.

Ingredients

Serves 3–4

45ml/3 tbsp olive oil
2 shallots, chopped
2 garlic cloves, chopped
1 fresh red chilli, chopped
450g/1lb ripe tomatoes, skinned, seeded and chopped
15ml/1 tbsp tomato purée
1 bay leaf
1 thyme sprig
90ml/6 tbsp dry white wine
450g/1lb cooked large prawns, peeled
salt and ground black pepper
roughly torn basil leaves, to garnish

1 Heat the oil in a pan, then add the shallots, garlic and chilli and fry until the garlic starts to brown.

2 Add the tomatoes, tomato purée, bay leaf, thyme, wine and seasoning. Bring to the boil, then reduce the heat and cook gently for about 10 minutes, stirring occasionally, until the sauce has thickened. Discard the herbs.

3 Stir the prawns into the sauce and heat through for a few minutes. Taste and adjust the seasoning. Scatter over the basil leaves and serve at once.

Cook's Tip

For a milder flavour, remove all the seeds from the chilli.

Scallops with Ginger

Scallops are at their best in the winter, but are available frozen throughout the year. Rich and creamy, this dish is very simple to make and utterly scrumptious.

Ingredients

Serves 4

8–12 scallops, shelled
40g/1½oz/3 tbsp butter
2.5cm/1in fresh root ginger, finely chopped
1 bunch spring onions, sliced diagonally
60ml/4 tbsp white vermouth
250ml/8fl oz/1 cup crème fraîche
salt and ground black pepper
chopped fresh parsley, to garnish

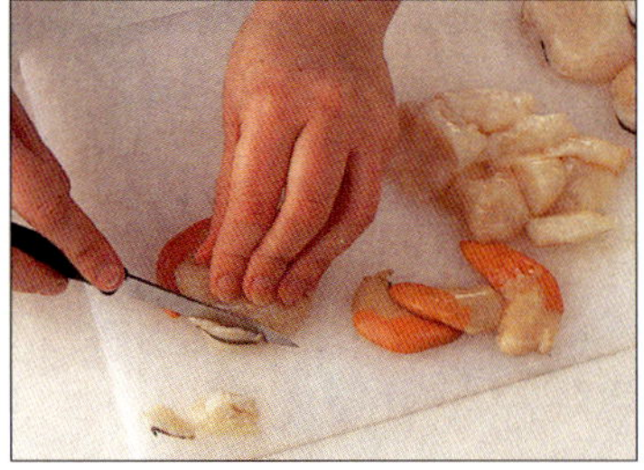

1 Remove the tough muscle opposite the coral on each scallop. Separate the coral and cut the white part of the scallop in half horizontally.

2 Melt the butter in a frying pan. Add the scallops, including the corals, and sauté for about 2 minutes until lightly browned. Take care not to overcook the scallops as this will make them tough.

3 Lift out the scallops with a slotted spoon and transfer to a warmed serving dish. Keep warm.

4 Add the ginger and spring onions to the pan and stir-fry for 2 minutes. Pour in the vermouth and allow to bubble until it has almost evaporated. Stir in the crème fraîche and cook for a few minutes until the sauce has thickened. Taste and adjust the seasoning.

5 Pour the sauce over the scallops, sprinkle with parsley and serve immediately.

Salmon Teriyaki

Marinating the salmon makes it so wonderfully tender, it just melts in the mouth, and the crunchy condiment provides an excellent foil.

Ingredients

Serves 4

675g/1½lb salmon fillet
30ml/2 tbsp sunflower oil
watercress, to garnish

For the teriyaki sauce

5ml/1 tsp caster sugar
5ml/1 tsp dry white wine
5ml/1 tsp sake, rice wine or dry sherry
30ml/2 tbsp dark soy sauce

For the condiment

5cm/2in fresh root ginger, grated
pink food colouring (optional)
50g/2oz mooli, grated

1 For the teriyaki sauce, mix together the sugar, white wine, sake or rice wine or dry sherry and soy sauce, stirring until the sugar dissolves.

2 Remove the skin from the salmon using a very sharp filleting knife.

3 Cut the fillet into strips, then place in a non-metallic dish. Pour over the teriyaki sauce and set aside to marinate for 10–15 minutes.

4 To make the condiment, place the ginger in a bowl and add a little pink food colouring if you wish. Stir in the mooli.

5 Lift the salmon from the teriyaki sauce and drain.

6 Heat the oil in a preheated wok. Add the salmon in batches and stir-fry for 3–4 minutes, until it is cooked. Transfer to serving plates, garnish with the watercress and serve with the mooli and ginger condiment.

Lemon-grass-and-basil-scented Mussels

The classic Thai flavourings of lemon grass and basil are used in this fragrant dish.

INGREDIENTS

Serves 4

1.75kg/4–4½lb fresh mussels in their shells
2 lemon grass stalks
5–6 fresh basil sprigs
5cm/2in fresh root ginger
2 shallots, finely chopped
150ml/¼ pint/⅔ cup fish stock

1 Scrub the mussels under cold running water, scraping off any barnacles with a small, sharp knife. Pull or cut off the hairy "beards". Discard any mussels with damaged shells and any that remain open when they are sharply tapped.

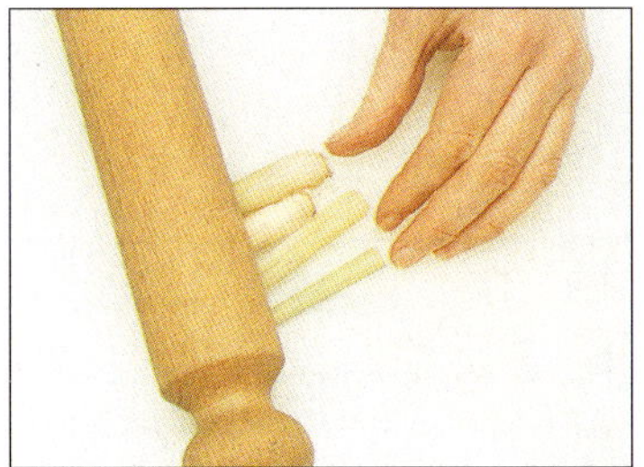

2 Cut each lemon grass stalk in half and bruise with a rolling pin.

3 Pull the basil leaves off the stems and roughly chop half of them. Reserve the remainder.

4 Put the mussels, lemon grass, chopped basil, ginger, shallots and stock in a wok. Bring to the boil, cover and simmer for 5 minutes. Discard the lemon grass and any mussels that remain closed, scatter over the reserved basil leaves and serve immediately.

Baked Crab with Spring Onions and Ginger

This recipe is far less complicated than it looks and will delight the eyes as much as the taste buds.

Ingredients

Serves 4

1 large or 2 medium crabs, about 675g/1½lb in total
30ml/2 tbsp Chinese rice wine or dry sherry
1 egg, lightly beaten
15ml/1 tbsp cornflour
45–60ml/3–4 tbsp vegetable oil
15ml/1 tbsp finely chopped fresh root ginger
3–4 spring onions, cut into short lengths
30ml/2 tbsp soy sauce
5ml/1 tsp light brown sugar
about 75ml/5 tbsp Basic Stock
few drops of sesame oil

1 Cut the crab in half from the underbelly. Break off the claws and crack them with the back of a cleaver. Discard the legs and crack the shell, breaking it into several pieces. Discard the feathery gills and the sac. Put the pieces of crab in a bowl.

2 Mix together the rice wine or dry sherry, egg and cornflour and pour over the crab. Leave to marinate for 10–15 minutes.

3 Heat the oil in a preheated wok. Add the crab pieces, ginger and spring onions and stir-fry for about 2–3 minutes.

4 Add the soy sauce, sugar and stock and blend well. Bring to the boil, reduce the heat, cover and braise for 3–4 minutes. Transfer the crab to a serving dish, sprinkle with the sesame oil and serve.

Cook's Tip

For the very best flavour, buy a live crab and cook it yourself. However, if you prefer to buy a cooked crab, look for one that feels heavy for its size. This is an indication that it has fully grown into its shell and that there will be plenty of meat. Male crabs have larger claws, so will yield a greater proportion of white meat. However, females – identifiable by a broader, less-pointed tail flap – may contain coral, which many people regard as a delicacy.

Pan-steamed Mussels with Thai Herbs

Another simple dish to prepare. The lemon grass adds a refreshing tang to the mussels.

Ingredients

Serves 4–6

1kg/2¼lb mussels, cleaned and beards removed
2 stalks lemon grass, finely chopped
4 shallots, chopped
4 kaffir lime leaves, roughly torn
2 red chillies, sliced
15ml/1 tbsp fish sauce
30ml/2 tbsp lime juice
2 spring onions, chopped, to garnish
coriander leaves, to garnish

1 Place all the ingredients, except for the spring onions and coriander, in a large saucepan and stir thoroughly.

2 Cover and steam for 5–7 minutes, shaking the saucepan occasionally, until the mussels open. Discard any mussels that do not open.

3 Transfer the cooked mussels to a serving dish.

4 Garnish the mussels with chopped spring onions and coriander leaves. Serve immediately.

Pineapple Curry with Prawns and Mussels

The delicate sweet and sour flavour of this curry comes from the pineapple and although it seems an odd combination, it is rather delicious. Use the freshest shellfish that you can find.

Ingredients

Serves 4–6

600ml/1 pint/2½ cups coconut milk
30ml/2 tbsp red curry paste
30ml/2 tbsp fish sauce
15ml/1 tbsp granulated sugar
225g/8oz king prawns, shelled and deveined
450g/1lb mussels, cleaned and beards removed
175g/6oz fresh pineapple, finely crushed or chopped
5 kaffir lime leaves, torn
2 red chillies, chopped, to garnish
coriander leaves, to garnish

1 In a large saucepan, bring half the coconut milk to the boil and heat, stirring, until it separates.

2 Add the red curry paste and cook until fragrant. Add the fish sauce and sugar and continue to cook for a few moments.

3 Stir in the rest of the coconut milk and bring back to the boil. Add the king prawns, mussels, pineapple and kaffir lime leaves.

4 Reheat until boiling and then simmer for 3–5 minutes, until the prawns are cooked and the mussels have opened. Remove any mussels that have not opened and discard. Serve garnished with chopped red chillies and coriander leaves.

Curried Prawns in Coconut Milk

A curry-like dish where the prawns are cooked in a spicy coconut gravy.

Ingredients

Serves 4–6

600ml/1 pint/2½ cups coconut milk
30ml/2 tbsp yellow curry paste (see Cook's Tip)
15ml/1 tbsp fish sauce
2.5ml/½ tsp salt
5ml/1 tsp granulated sugar
450g/1lb king prawns, shelled, tails left intact and deveined
225g/8oz cherry tomatoes
juice of ½ lime, to serve
2 red chillies, cut into strips, to garnish
coriander leaves, to garnish

1 Put half the coconut milk into a pan or wok and bring to the boil.

2 Add the yellow curry paste to the coconut milk, stir until it disperses, then simmer for about 10 minutes.

3 Add the fish sauce, salt, sugar and remaining coconut milk. Simmer for another 5 minutes.

4 Add the prawns and cherry tomatoes. Simmer very gently for about 5 minutes until the prawns are pink and tender.

5 Serve sprinkled with lime juice and garnish with chillies and coriander.

Cook's Tip

To make yellow curry paste, process together 6–8 yellow chillies, 1 chopped lemon grass stalk, 4 peeled shallots, 4 garlic cloves, 15ml/1 tbsp peeled chopped fresh root ginger, 5ml/1 tsp coriander seeds, 5ml/1 tsp mustard powder, 5ml/1 tsp salt, 2.5ml/½ tsp ground cinnamon, 15ml/1 tbsp light brown sugar and 30ml/2 tbsp oil in a blender or food procesor. When a paste has formed, transfer to a glass jar and keep in the fridge.

Baked Lobster with Black Beans

The term "baked", as used on most Chinese restaurant menus, is not strictly correct – "pot-roasted" or "pan-baked" is more accurate.

Ingredients

Serves 4–6

- 1 large or 2 medium lobsters, about 800g/1¾lb in total
- vegetable oil, for deep-frying
- 1 garlic clove, finely chopped
- 5ml/1 tsp finely chopped fresh root ginger
- 2–3 spring onions, chopped
- 30ml/2 tbsp black bean sauce
- 30ml/2 tbsp Chinese rice wine or dry sherry
- 120ml/4fl oz/½ cup Basic Stock
- fresh coriander leaves, to garnish

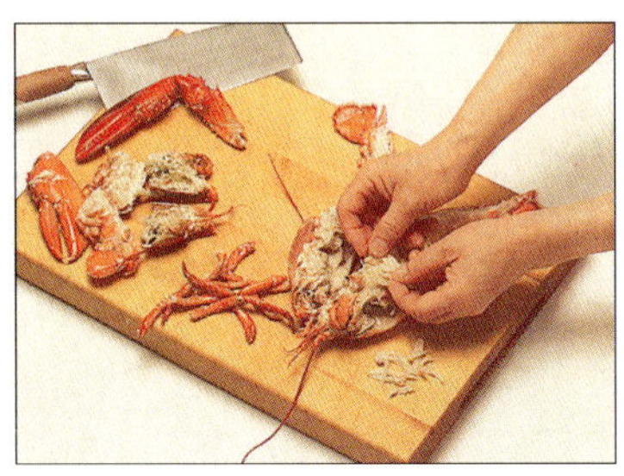

1 Starting from the head, cut the lobster in half lengthways. Discard the legs, remove the claws and crack them with the back of a cleaver. Discard the feathery lungs and intestine. Cut each half into 4–5 pieces.

2 Heat the oil in a preheated wok and deep-fry the lobster pieces for about 2 minutes, or until the shells turn bright orange. Remove the pieces from the wok and drain on kitchen paper.

3 Pour off the excess oil, leaving about 15ml/1 tbsp in the wok. Add the garlic, ginger, spring onions and black bean sauce and stir-fry for 1 minute.

4 Add the lobster pieces to the sauce and blend well. Add the rice wine or dry sherry and stock, bring to the boil, cover and cook for 2–3 minutes. Serve garnished with coriander leaves.

Cook's Tip

Ideally, buy live lobsters and cook them yourself. Ready-cooked ones have usually been boiled for far too long and have lost much of their delicate flavour and texture.

Prawn Curry with Quail's Eggs

This luscious Indonesian recipe is characterized by the mix of flavours – galangal, chillies, turmeric and coconut milk.

INGREDIENTS

Serves 4

12 quail's eggs
30ml/2 tbsp vegetable oil
4 shallots or 1 medium onion, finely chopped
2.5cm/1in fresh galangal or root ginger, chopped
2 garlic cloves, crushed
5cm/2in lemon grass, finely shredded
1–2 small, fresh red chillies, seeded and finely chopped
2.5ml/½ tsp ground turmeric
1cm/½in square shrimp paste or 15ml/1 tbsp fish sauce
900g/2lb raw prawn tails, peeled and deveined
400ml/14fl oz/1⅔ cups coconut milk
300ml/½ pint/1¼ cups chicken stock
115g/4oz Chinese leaves, roughly shredded
10ml/2 tsp sugar
salt
2 spring onions, green part only, shredded, and 30ml/2 tbsp shredded fresh coconut, to garnish

1 Put the quail's eggs in a saucepan, cover with water and boil for 8 minutes. Refresh in cold water, peel by dipping in cold water to release the shells and set aside.

2 Heat the oil in a preheated wok. Add the shallots or onion, galangal or ginger and garlic and stir-fry for 1 minute, until soft but not coloured. Add the lemon grass, chillies, turmeric and shrimp paste or fish sauce and stir-fry for 1 minute.

3 Add the prawns to the wok and stir-fry for 1 minute. Strain the coconut milk and add the thin liquid to the wok, together with the chicken stock. Add the Chinese leaves and sugar and season to taste with salt. Bring to the boil, reduce the heat and simmer for 6–8 minutes.

4 Turn the curry out on to a serving dish. Halve the quail's eggs and toss them in the sauce. Scatter over the spring onions and shredded coconut and serve immediately.

Cook's Tip

Quail's eggs are available from speciality grocers and delicatessens. If you cannot find them, use hens' eggs – one hen's egg is the equivalent of four quail's eggs.

Ragout of Shellfish with Sweet-scented Basil

Green curry paste, so called because it is made with green chillies, is an essential part of Thai cuisine. It can be used to accompany many other dishes and will keep for up to three weeks in the refrigerator. Ready-made curry pastes are available, but they are not as full of flavour as the home-made variety.

Ingredients

Serves 4–6

450g/1lb mussels in their shells
60ml/4 tbsp water
225g/8oz medium cuttlefish or squid
400ml/14fl oz/1⅔ cups coconut milk
300ml/½ pint/1¼ cups chicken or vegetable stock
350g/12oz monkfish, hoki or red snapper, skinned
150g/5oz raw or cooked prawn tails, peeled and deveined
4 scallops, shelled and sliced
75g/3oz French beans, trimmed and cooked
50g/2oz canned bamboo shoots, drained
1 tomato, skinned, seeded and roughly chopped
4 sprigs large leaf basil, torn, to garnish
boiled rice, to serve

For the green curry paste

10ml/2 tsp coriander seeds
2.5ml/½ tsp caraway or cumin seeds
3–4 medium fresh green chillies, finely chopped
20ml/4 tsp sugar
10ml/2 tsp salt
7.5cm/3in lemon grass stalk
2cm/¾in fresh galangal or ginger root, peeled and finely chopped
3 garlic cloves, crushed
4 shallots or 1 medium onion, finely chopped
2cm/¾in square shrimp paste
50g/2oz fresh coriander leaves, finely chopped
45ml/3 tbsp finely chopped fresh basil
2.5ml/½ tsp grated nutmeg
30ml/2 tbsp vegetable oil

1 Scrub the mussels in cold running water and pull off the "beards". Discard any that do not shut when sharply tapped. Put them in a saucepan with the water, cover and cook for 6–8 minutes. Discard any mussels that remain closed and remove three-quarters of the mussels from their shells. Set aside. Strain the cooking liquid and set aside.

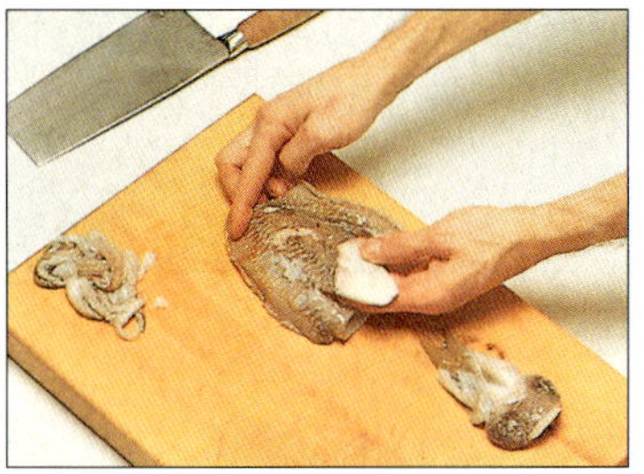

2 To prepare the cuttlefish or squid, trim off the tentacles and discard the gut. Remove the cuttle shell from inside the body and rub off the skin. Cut the body open and score in a criss-cross pattern with a sharp knife. Cut into strips and set aside.

3 To make the green curry paste, dry-fry the coriander and caraway or cumin seeds in a wok. Grind the chillies with the sugar and salt in a pestle with a mortar or in a food processor. Add the coriander and caraway or cumin seeds, lemon grass, galangal or ginger, garlic and shallots or onion and grind. Add the shrimp paste, fresh coriander, chopped basil, nutmeg and oil and combine thoroughly.

4 Strain the coconut milk and pour the thin liquid into a wok with the chicken or vegetable stock and reserved cooking liquid from the mussels. Reserve the thick part of the coconut milk. Add 60–75ml/4–5 tbsp of the green curry paste to the wok and bring the mixture to the boil. Boil rapidly for a few minutes, until the liquid has reduced completely.

5 Add the thick part of the coconut milk, then add the cuttlefish or squid and monkfish, hoki or red snapper. Simmer for 15–20 minutes. Then add the prawns, scallops, mussels, beans, bamboo shoots and tomato. Simmer for 2–3 minutes until heated through. Transfer to a warmed serving dish, garnish with torn basil leaves and serve immediately with boiled rice.

Battered Fish, Prawns and Vegetables

This is a recipe for tempura, one of the few dishes that was brought to Japan from the West. The idea came from Spanish and Portuguese missionaries who settled in southern Japan in the late sixteenth century.

Ingredients

Serves 4–6

1 sheet nori
8 large raw prawn tails
175g/6oz whiting or monkfish fillet, cut into fingers
1 small aubergine
4 spring onions, trimmed
6 fresh shiitake mushrooms
vegetable oil, for deep-frying
flour, for dusting
fine salt
75ml/5 tbsp soy or tamari sauce, to serve

For the batter

2 egg yolks
300ml/½ pint/1¼ cups iced water
225g/8oz/2 cups flour
2.5ml/½ tsp salt

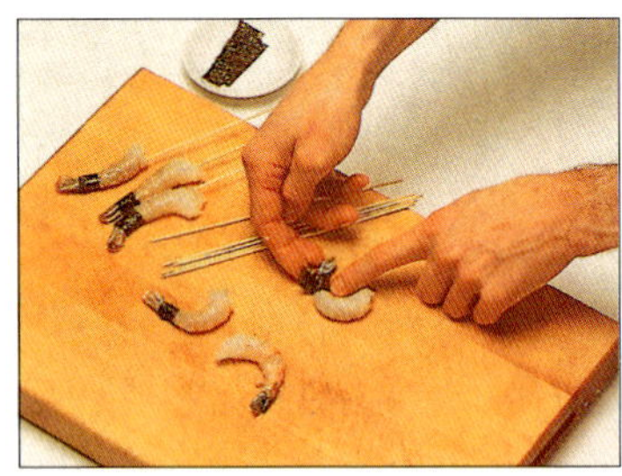

1 Cut the nori into strips 1cm/½in wide and 5cm/2in long. Moisten one end of each strip with water and wrap it round the tail end of each prawn. Skewer the prawns along their length to straighten them. Skewer the fingers of white fish and set aside.

2 Slice the aubergine into neat sections, sprinkle with salt and arrange in layers on a plate. Press lightly with your hand to expel the bitter juices, then leave for 20–30 minutes. Rinse thoroughly under cold water, dry well and place on bamboo skewers. Skewer the spring onions and shiitake mushrooms.

3 Make the batter just before using. Beat together the egg yolks and half the iced water. Sift in the flour and salt and stir lightly with chopsticks without mixing to a dry paste. Add the remaining water and stir to make a smooth batter. Avoid over-mixing.

4 Heat the oil to 180°C/350°F in a wok fitted with a wire draining rack. Dust the vegetables and fish in flour, not more than three at a time. Dip them into the batter to coat, then fry for 1–2 minutes, until crisp and golden. Drain well, sprinkle with salt and drain on kitchen paper. Serve with soy or tamari sauce for dipping.

Prawn Satés

For *Saté Udang*, king prawns look spectacular and taste wonderful. The spicy coconut marinade marries beautifully with the prawns and is also excellent when used with firm cubes of monkfish or halibut and cooked in the same way.

Ingredients

Makes 4 skewers

12 uncooked king prawns

For the marinade

5mm/¼in cube *terasi*
1 garlic clove, crushed
1 lemon grass stem, lower 6cm/2½in sliced, top reserved
3–4 macadamia nuts or 6–8 almonds
2.5ml/½ tsp chilli powder
salt
oil for frying
120ml/4fl oz/½ cup coconut milk
2.5ml/½ tsp tamarind pulp, soaked in 30ml/2 tbsp water, then strained and juice reserved

To serve

Peanut Sauce
cucumber cubes (optional)
lemon wedges

1 Remove the heads from the prawns. Peel the prawns and remove the spinal cord, if liked. Using a small sharp knife, make an incision along the underbody of each prawn, without cutting it completely in half and open it up like a book. Thread 3 of the prawns on to each skewer.

2 Make the marinade. Grind the *terasi*, garlic, lemon grass slices, nuts, chilli powder and a little salt to a paste in a food processor or with a pestle and mortar.

3 Fry the paste in oil, for 1 minute. Add the coconut milk and tamarind juice. Simmer for 1 minute. Cool. Pour over the prawns and leave for 1 hour.

4 Cook the prawns under a hot grill or on the barbecue for 3 minutes or until cooked through. Beat the top part of the lemon grass with the end of a rolling pin, to make it into a brush. Use this to brush the prawns with the marinade during cooking.

5 Serve on a platter, with the Peanut Sauce, cucumber cubes, if using, and lemon wedges.

Prawns with Chayote in Turmeric Sauce

This delicious, attractively coloured dish is called *Gule Udang Dengan Labu Kuning*.

Ingredients

Serves 4

1–2 chayotes or 2–3 courgettes
2 fresh red chillies, seeded
1 onion, quartered
5mm/¼in fresh *lengkuas*, peeled
1 lemon grass stem, lower 5cm/2in sliced, top bruised
2.5cm/1in fresh turmeric, peeled
200ml/7fl oz/scant 1 cup water
lemon juice
400ml/14fl oz can coconut milk
450g/1lb cooked, peeled prawns
salt
red chilli shreds, to garnish (optional)
boiled rice, to serve

1 Peel the chayotes, remove the seeds and cut into strips. If using courgettes, cut into 5cm/2in strips.

2 Grind the fresh red chillies, onion, sliced *lengkuas*, sliced lemon grass and the fresh turmeric to a paste in a food processor or with a pestle and mortar. Add the water to the paste mixture, with a squeeze of lemon juice and salt to taste.

3 Pour into a pan. Add the top of the lemon grass stem. Bring to the boil and cook for 1–2 minutes. Add the chayote or courgette pieces and cook for 2 minutes. Stir in the coconut milk. Taste and adjust the seasoning.

4 Stir in the prawns and cook gently for 2–3 minutes. Remove the lemon grass stem. Garnish with shreds of chilli, if using, and serve with rice.

Doedoeh of Fish

Haddock or cod fillet may be substituted in this recipe.

Ingredients

Serves 6–8

1kg/2¼lb fresh mackerel fillets, skinned
30ml/2 tbsp tamarind pulp, soaked in 200ml/7fl oz/scant 1 cup water
1 onion
1cm/½in fresh *lengkuas*
2 garlic cloves
1–2 fresh red chillies, seeded, or 5ml/1 tsp chilli powder
5ml/1 tsp ground coriander
5ml/1 tsp ground turmeric
2.5ml/½ tsp ground fennel seeds
15ml/1 tbsp dark brown sugar
90–105ml/6–7 tbsp oil
200ml/7fl oz/scant 1 cup coconut cream
salt and freshly ground black pepper
fresh chilli shreds, to garnish

1 Rinse the fish fillets in cold water and dry them well on kitchen paper. Put into a shallow dish and sprinkle with a little salt. Strain the tamarind and pour the juice over the fish fillets. Leave for 30 minutes.

2 Quarter the onion, peel and slice the *lengkuas* and peel the garlic. Grind the onion, *lengkuas*, garlic and chillies or chilli powder to a paste in a food processor or with a pestle and mortar. Add the ground coriander, turmeric, fennel seeds and sugar.

3 Heat half of the oil in a frying pan. Drain the fish fillets and fry for 5 minutes, or until cooked. Set aside.

4 Wipe out the pan and heat the remaining oil. Fry the spice paste, stirring all the time, until it gives off a spicy aroma. Do not let it brown. Add the coconut cream and simmer gently for a few minutes. Add the fish fillets and gently heat through.

5 Taste for seasoning and serve scattered with shredded chilli.

Red and White Prawns with Green Vegetables

The Chinese name for this dish is *Yuan Yang* prawns. Pairs of mandarin ducks are also known as *yuan yang*, or love birds, because they are always seen together. They symbolize affection and happiness.

INGREDIENTS

Serves 4–6

450g/1lb raw prawns
½ egg white
15ml/1 tbsp cornflour paste
175g/6oz mangetouts
about 600ml/1 pint/2½ cups vegetable oil
5ml/1 tsp light brown sugar
15ml/1 tbsp finely chopped spring onion
5ml/1 tsp finely chopped fresh root ginger
15ml/1 tbsp light soy sauce
15ml/1 tbsp Chinese rice wine or dry sherry
5ml/1 tsp chilli bean sauce
15ml/1 tbsp tomato purée
salt

1 Peel and devein the prawns and mix with the egg white, cornflour paste and a pinch of salt. Top and tail the mangetouts.

2 Heat 30–45ml/2–3 tbsp of the oil in a preheated wok and stir-fry the mangetouts for about 1 minute. Add the sugar and a little salt and continue stirring for 1 more minute. Remove and place in the centre of a warmed serving platter.

3 Add the remaining oil to the wok and cook the prawns for 1 minute. Remove and drain.

4 Pour off all but about 15ml/1 tbsp of the oil. Add the spring onion and ginger to the wok.

5 Return the prawns to the wok and stir-fry for 1 minute, then add the soy sauce and rice wine or dry sherry. Blend the mixture thoroughly. Transfer half the prawns to one end of the serving platter.

6 Add the chilli bean sauce and tomato purée to the remaining prawns in the wok, blend well and place the "red" prawns at the other end of the platter. Serve.

COOK'S TIP

All raw prawns have an intestinal tract that runs just beneath the outside curve of the tail. The tract is not poisonous, but it can taste unpleasant. It is, therefore, best to remove it – devein. To do this, peel the prawns, leaving the tail intact. Score each prawn lightly along its length to expose the tract. Remove the tract with a small knife or Chinese cleaver.

Vietnamese Stuffed Squid

The smaller the squid, the sweeter the dish will taste. Be very careful not to overcook the flesh, as it becomes tough extremely quickly.

Ingredients

Serves 4

8 small squid
50g/2oz cellophane noodles
30ml/2 tbsp groundnut oil
2 spring onions, finely chopped
8 shiitake mushrooms, halved if large
250g/9oz minced pork
1 garlic clove, chopped
30ml/2 tbsp fish sauce
5ml/1 tsp caster sugar
15ml/1 tbsp finely chopped fresh coriander
5ml/1 tsp lemon juice
salt and ground black pepper

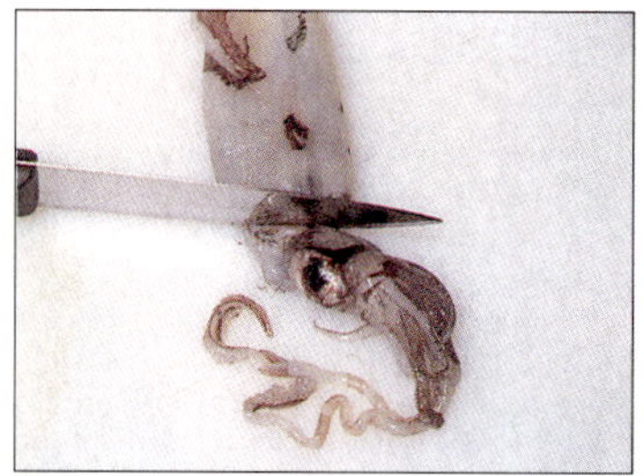

1 Cut off the tentacles of the squid just below the eye. Remove the transparent "quill" from inside the body and rub off the skin on the outside. Wash thoroughly in cold water and set aside.

2 Bring a saucepan of water to the boil and add the noodles. Remove from the heat and set aside to soak for 20 minutes.

3 Heat 15ml/1 tbsp of the oil in a preheated wok and stir-fry the spring onions, shiitake mushrooms, pork and garlic for 4 minutes until the meat is golden.

4 Drain the noodles and add to the wok, with the fish sauce, sugar, coriander, lemon juice and salt and pepper to taste.

5 Stuff the squid with the mixture and secure with cocktail or satay sticks. Arrange the squid in an ovenproof dish, drizzle over the remaining oil and prick each squid twice. Bake in a preheated oven at 200°C/400°F/Gas 6 for 10 minutes. Serve hot.

Stir-fried Five-spice Squid

Squid is perfect for stir-frying as it should be cooked quickly. The spicy sauce makes the ideal accompaniment.

INGREDIENTS

Serves 6

450g/1lb small squid, cleaned
45ml/3 tbsp oil
2.5cm/1 in fresh root ginger, grated
1 garlic clove, crushed
8 spring onions, cut diagonally into 2.5cm/1in lengths
1 red pepper, seeded and cut into strips
1 fresh green chilli, seeded and thinly sliced
6 mushrooms, sliced
5ml/1 tsp Chinese five-spice powder
30ml/2 tbsp black bean sauce
30ml/2 tbsp soy sauce
5ml/1 tsp sugar
15ml/1 tbsp Chinese rice wine or dry sherry

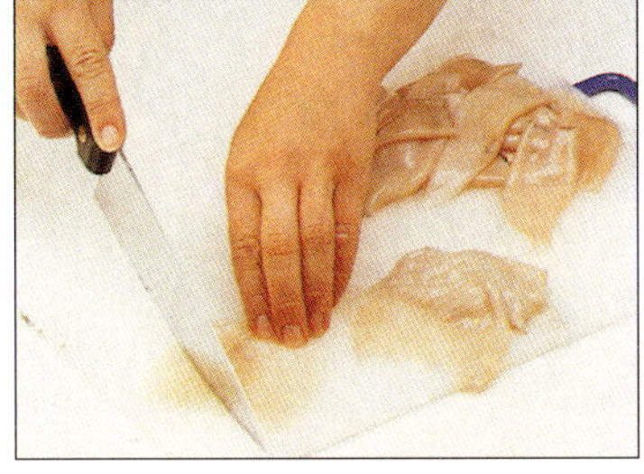

1 Rinse the squid and pull away the outer skin. Dry on kitchen paper. Slit the squid open and score the inside into diamonds with a sharp knife. Cut the squid into strips.

2 Heat the oil in a preheated wok. Stir-fry the squid quickly. Remove the squid strips from the wok with a slotted spoon and set aside. Add the ginger, garlic, spring onions, red pepper, chilli and mushrooms to the oil remaining in the wok and stir-fry for 2 minutes.

3 Return the squid to the wok and stir in the five-spice powder. Stir in the black bean sauce, soy sauce, sugar and rice wine or dry sherry. Bring to the boil and cook, stirring, for 1 minute. Serve immediately.

Clay Pot of Chilli Squid and Noodles

INGREDIENTS

Serves 4

675g/1½lb fresh squid
30ml/2 tbsp vegetable oil
3 slices fresh root ginger, finely shredded
2 garlic cloves, finely chopped
1 red onion, finely sliced
1 carrot, finely sliced
1 celery stick, diagonally sliced
50g/2oz sugar snap peas, topped and tailed
5ml/1 tsp sugar
15ml/1 tbsp chilli bean paste
2.5ml/½ tsp chilli powder
75g/3oz cellophane noodles, soaked in hot water until soft
120ml/4fl oz/½ cup chicken stock or water
15ml/1 tbsp soy sauce
15ml/1 tbsp oyster sauce
5ml/1 tsp sesame oil
pinch of salt
coriander leaves, to garnish

1 Prepare the squid. Holding the body in one hand, gently pull away the head and tentacles. Discard the head; trim and reserve the tentacles. Remove the transparent "quill" from inside the body of the squid. Peel off the brown skin on the outside of the body. Rub a little salt into the squid and wash thoroughly under cold running water. Cut the body of the squid into rings or split it open lengthways, score criss-cross patterns on the inside of the body and cut it into 5 x 4cm/2 x 1½in pieces.

2 Heat the oil in a large clay pot or flameproof casserole. Add the ginger, garlic and onion, and fry for 1–2 minutes. Add the squid, carrot, celery and sugar snap peas. Fry until the squid curls up. Season with salt and sugar, and stir in the chilli bean paste and powder. Transfer the mixture to a bowl and set aside until required.

3 Drain the soaked noodles and add them to the clay pot or casserole. Stir in the stock or water, soy sauce and oyster sauce. Cover and cook over a medium heat for about 10 minutes or until the noodles are tender.

4 Return the squid and vegetables to the pot. Cover and cook for about 5–6 minutes more, until all the flavours are combined. Season to taste.

5 Just before serving, drizzle with the sesame oil and sprinkle with the coriander leaves.

COOK'S TIP

These noodles have a smooth, light texture that readily absorbs the other flavours in the dish. To vary the flavour, the vegetables can be altered according to what is available.

Squid with Green Pepper and Black Bean Sauce

This dish is a product of the Cantonese school and makes an attractive meal that is just as delicious as it looks.

Ingredients

Serves 4

350–400g/12–14oz squid
1 medium green pepper, cored and seeded
45–60ml/3–4 tbsp vegetable oil
1 garlic clove, finely chopped
2.5ml/½ tsp finely chopped fresh root ginger
15ml/1 tbsp finely chopped spring onion
5ml/1 tsp salt
15ml/1 tbsp black bean sauce
15ml/1 tbsp Chinese rice wine or dry sherry
few drops of sesame oil

1 To clean the squid, cut off the tentacles just below the eye. Remove the "quill" from inside the body. Peel off and discard the skin, then wash the squid and dry well. Cut open the squid and score the inside of the flesh in a criss-cross pattern.

2 Cut the squid into pieces each about the size of an oblong postage stamp. Blanch the squid in a pan of boiling water for a few seconds. Remove and drain. Dry well.

3 Cut the green pepper into small triangular pieces. Heat the oil in a preheated wok and stir-fry the green pepper for about 1 minute.

4 Add the garlic, ginger, spring onion, salt and squid, then stir for 1 minute. Add the black bean sauce, rice wine or dry sherry and sesame oil and serve.

MEAT

Satisfying beef curries, quick and easy stir-fried steak, fragrant lamb dishes and, of course, sweet-and-sour pork – the range of Chinese and Asian meat recipes is immense, offering something special for all tastes and budgets. The recipes in this chapter include inexpensive and easy-to-prepare weekday family meals, such as Braised Beef in a Rich Peanut Sauce and Pork and Vegetable Stir-fry, as well as impressive and unusual dinner party dishes, such as Beef and Vegetables in Table-top Broth and Braised Birthday Noodles with Hoisin Lamb.

Peking Beef and Pepper Stir-fry

This quick and easy stir-fry is perfect for today's busy cook and tastes superb.

INGREDIENTS

Serves 4

350g/12oz rump or sirloin steak, sliced into strips
30ml/2 tbsp soy sauce
30ml/2 tbsp medium sherry
15ml/1 tbsp cornflour
5ml/1 tsp brown sugar
15ml/1 tbsp sunflower oil
15ml/1 tbsp sesame oil
1 garlic clove, finely chopped
15ml/1 tbsp grated fresh root ginger
1 red pepper, seeded and sliced
1 yellow pepper, seeded and sliced
115g/4oz sugar snap peas
4 spring onions, cut into 5cm/2in lengths
30ml/2 tbsp oyster sauce
60ml/4 tbsp water
cooked noodles, to serve

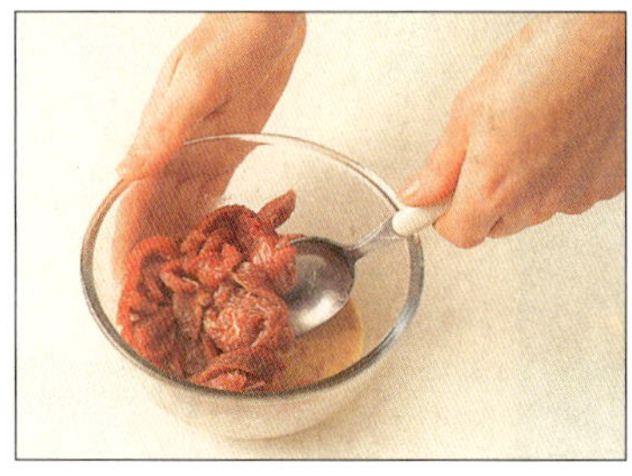

1 In a bowl, mix together the steak strips, soy sauce, sherry, cornflour and brown sugar. Cover and leave to marinate for 30 minutes.

2 Heat the sunflower and sesame oils in a preheated wok or large frying pan. Add the garlic and ginger and stir-fry for about 30 seconds. Add the peppers, sugar snap peas and spring onions and stir-fry for 3 minutes.

3 Add the beef, together with the marinade juices, to the wok or frying pan and stir-fry for a further 3–4 minutes. Pour in the oyster sauce and water and stir until the sauce has thickened slightly. Serve immediately with cooked noodles.

Stir-fried Beef and Broccoli

This spicy beef may be served with noodles or on a bed of boiled rice for a speedy and low-calorie Chinese meal.

INGREDIENTS

Serves 4

350g/12oz rump steak
15ml/1 tbsp cornflour
5ml/1 tsp sesame oil
350g/12oz broccoli, cut into small florets
4 spring onions, sliced diagonally
1 carrot, cut into matchstick strips
1 garlic clove, crushed
2.5cm/1in fresh root ginger, cut into very fine strips
120ml/4fl oz/½ cup beef stock
30ml/2 tbsp soy sauce
30ml/2 tbsp dry sherry
10ml/2 tsp soft light brown sugar
spring onion tassels, to garnish (optional)
noodles or rice, to serve

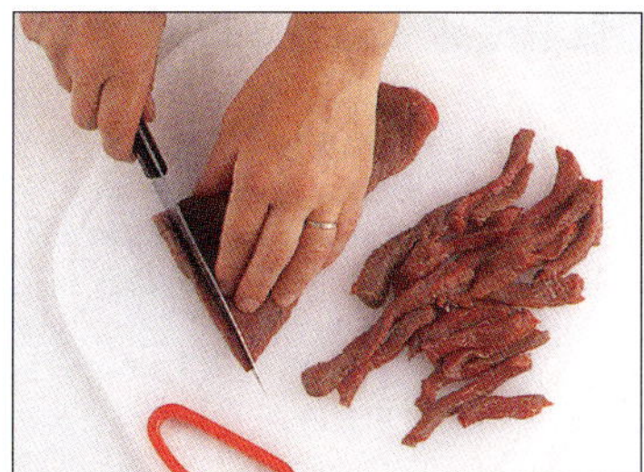

1 Trim the beef and cut into thin slices across the grain. Cut each slice into thin strips. Toss in the cornflour to coat thoroughly.

2 Heat the sesame oil in a preheated wok or large non-stick frying pan. Add the beef strips and stir-fry over a brisk heat for 3 minutes. Remove and set aside.

3 Add the broccoli, spring onions, carrot, garlic, ginger and stock to the wok or frying pan. Cover and simmer for 3 minutes. Uncover and cook, stirring, until all the stock has reduced entirely.

4 Mix the soy sauce, dry sherry and brown sugar together and add to the wok or frying pan with the beef. Cook for 2–3 minutes, stirring continuously. Spoon into a warmed serving dish and garnish with spring onion tassels, if liked. Serve on a bed of noodles or rice.

COOK'S TIP

To make spring onion tassels, trim the bulb base, then cut the green shoot so that the onion is 7.5cm/3in long. Shred to within 2.5cm/1in of the base and put into iced water for 1 hour.

Beef Stir-fry with Crisp Parsnips

Wonderful crisp shreds of parsnip add extra crunchiness to this unusual stir-fry – a great supper dish to share with friends.

INGREDIENTS

Serves 4

350g/12oz parsnips
450g/1lb rump steak
450g/1lb trimmed leeks
2 red peppers, seeded
350g/12oz courgettes
90ml/6 tbsp vegetable oil
2 garlic cloves, crushed
45ml/3 tbsp hoisin sauce
salt and ground black pepper

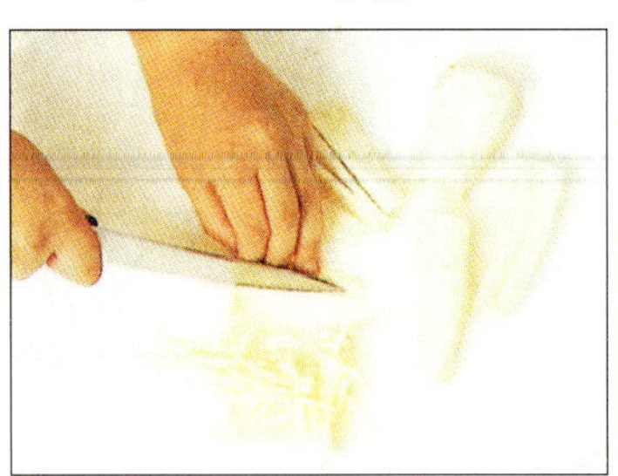

1 Peel the parsnips and cut in half lengthways. Place the flat surface on a chopping board and cut them into thin strips. Finely shred each piece. Rinse in cold water and drain thoroughly. Dry the parsnips on kitchen paper, if necessary.

2 Cut the steak into thin strips. Split the leeks in half lengthways and thickly slice at an angle. Roughly chop the peppers and thinly slice the courgettes.

3 Heat the oil in a preheated wok or large frying pan. Fry the parsnips until crisp and golden. You may need to do this in batches, adding a little more oil if necessary. Remove with a slotted spoon and drain on kitchen paper.

4 Stir-fry the steak in the wok or frying pan until golden and cooked through. You may need to do this in batches, adding more oil if necessary. Remove and drain on kitchen paper.

5 Stir-fry the garlic, leeks, peppers and courgettes for about 10 minutes, or until golden brown and beginning to soften but still retaining a little bite. Season the mixture well.

6 Return the meat to the pan with the hoisin sauce. Stir-fry for 2–3 minutes, or until piping hot. Adjust the seasoning and serve with the crisp parsnips piled on top.

Beef with Cantonese Oyster Sauce

This is a classic Cantonese recipe in which any combination of vegetables can be used. Broccoli may be used instead of mangetouts, bamboo shoots instead of baby corn cobs, and white or black mushrooms instead of straw mushrooms, for example.

INGREDIENTS

Serves 4

275–350g/10–12oz rump steak
5ml/1 tsp light brown sugar
15ml/1 tbsp light soy sauce
10ml/2 tsp Chinese rice wine or dry sherry
10ml/2 tsp cornflour paste
115g/4oz mangetouts
115g/4oz baby corn cobs
115g/4oz straw mushrooms
1 spring onion
300ml/½ pint/1¼ cups vegetable oil
few small pieces of fresh root ginger
2.5ml/½ tsp salt
30ml/2 tbsp oyster sauce

1 Cut the beef into thin strips. Place in a bowl and add the sugar, soy sauce, rice wine or dry sherry and cornflour paste. Mix well and set aside to marinate for 25–30 minutes.

2 Top and tail the mangetouts and cut the baby corn cobs in half. If using canned straw mushrooms, drain them. If the straw mushrooms are large, cut them in half, but leave whole if they are small. Cut the spring onion into short sections.

3 Heat the oil in a preheated wok and stir-fry the beef until the colour changes. Remove with a perforated spoon and drain.

4 Pour off the excess oil, leaving about 30ml/2 tbsp in the wok, then add the spring onion, ginger and the vegetables. Stir-fry for about 2 minutes with the salt, then add the beef and the oyster sauce. Blend well and serve.

Beef Strips with Orange and Ginger

Stir-frying is one of the best ways to cook with the minimum of fat. This recipe is ideal for people trying to lose weight, those requiring a low-fat and low-cholesterol diet or, in fact, anyone who wants to eat healthily.

INGREDIENTS

Serves 4

450g/1lb lean rump, fillet or sirloin steak, cut into thin strips
finely grated rind and juice of 1 orange
15ml/1 tbsp light soy sauce
5ml/1 tsp cornflour
2.5cm/1in fresh root ginger, finely chopped
10ml/2 tsp sesame oil
1 large carrot, cut into matchstick strips
2 spring onions, thinly sliced
rice noodles or boiled rice, to serve

1 Place the steak strips in a bowl and sprinkle over the orange rind and juice. Set aside to marinate for about 30 minutes.

2 Drain the liquid from the steak and reserve. Mix together the steak, soy sauce, cornflour and ginger.

3 Heat the oil in a preheated wok or large frying pan, then add the steak and stir-fry for 1 minute, until lightly coloured. Add the carrot and stir-fry for a further 2–3 minutes.

4 Stir in the spring onions and reserved marinade liquid. Cook, stirring constantly, until boiling and thickened. Serve hot with rice noodles or plain boiled rice.

Sizzling Steak

This Malaysian method of sizzling richly marinated meat on a cast iron grill can be applied with equal success to sliced chicken or pork.

INGREDIENTS

Serves 4–6

1 garlic clove, crushed
2.5cm/1in fresh root ginger, finely chopped
10ml/2 tsp black peppercorns
15ml/1 tbsp sugar
30ml/2 tbsp tamarind sauce
45ml/3 tbsp dark soy sauce
15ml/1 tbsp oyster sauce
4 slices rump steak, each about 200g/7oz
vegetable oil, for brushing

For the dipping sauce

75ml/5 tbsp beef stock
30ml/2 tbsp tomato ketchup
5ml/1 tsp chilli sauce
juice of 1 lime

1 Pound together the garlic, ginger, peppercorns, sugar and tamarind sauce in a mortar with a pestle. Mix in the soy sauce and oyster sauce, then spoon over the steaks. Set aside in the refrigerator to marinate for up to 8 hours.

2 Heat a cast iron grilling plate over high heat until very hot. Scrape the marinade from the meat and reserve. Brush the meat with oil and grill for 2 minutes on each side for rare and 3–4 minutes on each side for medium, depending on thickness.

3 Meanwhile, make the sauce. Pour the marinade into a saucepan and add the stock, tomato ketchup, chilli sauce and lime juice. Set over a low heat and simmer to heat through. Serve the steak and hand the dipping sauce separately.

Thick Beef Curry in Sweet Peanut Sauce

This curry is deliciously rich and thicker than most other Thai curries. Serve with boiled jasmine rice and salted duck's eggs, if liked.

INGREDIENTS

Serves 4–6

600ml/1 pint/2½ cups coconut milk
45ml/3 tbsp red curry paste
45ml/3 tbsp fish sauce
30ml/2 tbsp palm sugar
2 stalks lemon grass, bruised
450g/1lb rump steak, cut into thin strips
75g/3oz roasted ground peanuts
2 red chillies, sliced
5 kaffir lime leaves, torn
salt and freshly ground black pepper
2 salted eggs, to serve
10–15 Thai basil leaves, to garnish

1 Put half the coconut milk into a heavy-bottomed saucepan and heat, stirring, until it boils and separates.

2 Add the red curry paste and cook until fragrant. Add the fish sauce, palm sugar and lemon grass.

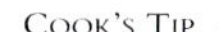

COOK'S TIP

If you don't have the time to make your own red curry paste, you can buy a ready-made Thai curry paste. There is a wide range available in most supermarkets.

3 Continue to cook until the colour deepens. Add the rest of the coconut milk. Bring back to the boil.

4 Add the beef and ground peanuts. Stir and cook for 8–10 minutes or until most of the liquid has evaporated.

5 Add the chillies and kaffir lime leaves. Adjust the seasoning to taste. Serve with salted eggs and garnish with Thai basil leaves.

Sesame Steak

Toasted sesame seeds bring their distinctive smoky aroma to this scrumptious oriental marinade.

INGREDIENTS

Serves 4

450g/1lb rump steak
30ml/2 tbsp sesame seeds
15ml/1 tbsp sesame oil
30ml/2 tbsp vegetable oil
115g/4oz small mushrooms, quartered
1 large green pepper, seeded and cut into strips
4 spring onions, chopped diagonally
boiled rice, to serve

For the marinade

10ml/2 tsp cornflour
30ml/2 tbsp Chinese rice wine or dry sherry
15ml/1 tbsp lemon juice
15ml/1 tbsp soy sauce
few drops of Tabasco sauce
2.5cm/1in fresh root ginger, grated
1 garlic clove, crushed

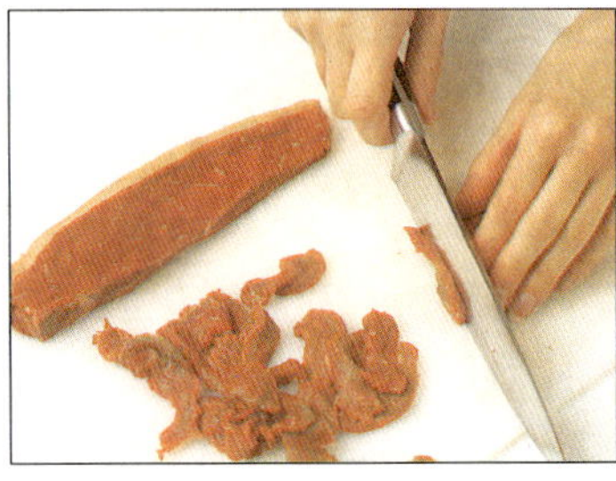

1 Trim the steak and cut into thin strips about 1 x 5cm/½ x 2in.

COOK'S TIP

This marinade would also be good with pork or chicken.

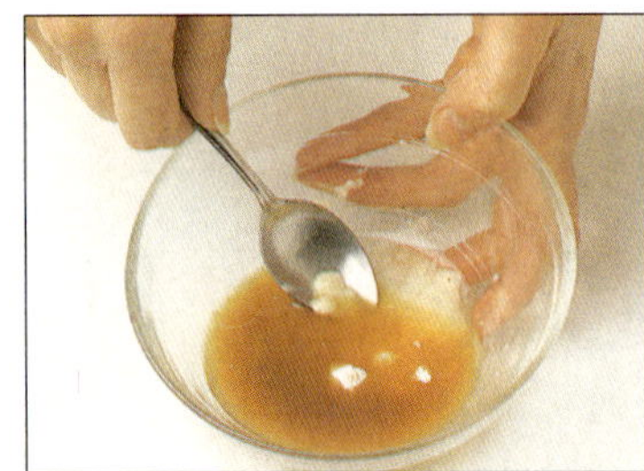

2 Make the marinade. In a bowl, blend the cornflour with the rice wine or dry sherry, then stir in the lemon juice, soy sauce, Tabasco sauce, ginger and garlic. Stir in the steak strips, cover and leave in a cool place for 3–4 hours.

3 Place the sesame seeds in a wok or large frying pan and dry-fry over a moderate heat, shaking the pan, until the seeds are golden. Set aside.

4 Heat the sesame and vegetable oils in the wok or frying pan. Drain the steak, reserving the marinade, and stir-fry a few pieces at a time until browned. Remove with a slotted spoon.

5 Add the mushrooms and green pepper and stir-fry for 2–3 minutes. Add the spring onions and cook for 1 minute more.

6 Return the steak to the wok or frying pan, together with the reserved marinade, and stir over a moderate heat for a further 2 minutes until the ingredients are evenly coated with glaze. Sprinkle over the sesame seeds and serve immediately with boiled rice.

Stir-fried Beef with Mangetouts

The crisp texture and fresh taste of mangetouts perfectly complement the melt-in-the-mouth tenderness of the steak, all served in a richly aromatic sauce.

INGREDIENTS

Serves 4

450g/1lb rump steak
45ml/3 tbsp soy sauce
30ml/2 tbsp Chinese rice wine or dry sherry
15ml/1 tbsp soft brown sugar
2.5ml/½ tsp cornflour
15ml/1 tbsp vegetable oil
15ml/1 tbsp finely chopped fresh root ginger
15ml/1 tbsp finely chopped garlic
225g/8oz mangetouts

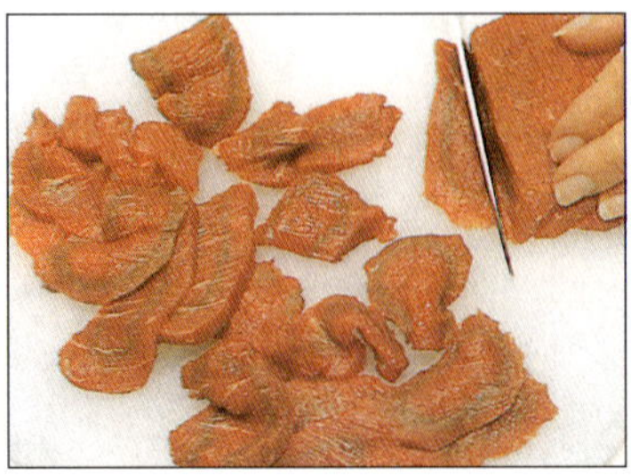

1 Cut the steak into even-sized, very thin strips.

2 Combine the soy sauce, rice wine or dry sherry, brown sugar and cornflour. Mix well and set aside.

3 Heat the oil in a preheated wok. Add the ginger and garlic and stir-fry for 30 seconds. Add the steak and stir-fry for 2 minutes, or until evenly browned.

4 Add the mangetouts and stir-fry for a further 3 minutes.

5 Stir the soy sauce mixture until smooth, then add to the wok. Bring to the boil, stirring constantly, lower the heat and simmer until the sauce is thick and smooth. Serve immediately.

Braised Beef in a Rich Peanut Sauce

Like many dishes brought to the Philippines by the Spanish, this slow-cooking stew, renamed *kari kari*, retains much of its original charm, while at the same time it has acquired a uniquely oriental flavour. Rice and peanuts are used to thicken the juices, yielding a rich, glossy sauce.

INGREDIENTS

Serves 4–6

900g/2lb braising steak
30ml/2 tbsp vegetable oil
15ml/1 tbsp annatto seeds
2 medium onions, chopped
2 garlic cloves, crushed
275g/10oz celeriac or swede, roughly chopped
475ml/16fl oz/2 cups beef stock
375g/12oz new potatoes, peeled and cut into large dice
15ml/1 tbsp fish or anchovy sauce
30ml/2 tbsp tamarind sauce
10ml/2 tsp sugar
1 bay leaf
1 fresh thyme sprig
45ml/3 tbsp long-grain rice
50g/2oz/½ cup peanuts or 30ml/2 tbsp peanut butter
15ml/1 tbsp white wine vinegar
salt and ground black pepper

1 Cut the beef into 2.5cm/1in cubes and set aside. Heat the oil in a flameproof casserole, add the annatto seeds and stir until the oil is dark red in colour. Remove the seeds with a slotted spoon and discard.

2 Add the onions, garlic and celeriac or swede to the casserole and fry for 3–5 minutes, until softened but not coloured. Add the beef and fry until lightly and evenly browned. Add the stock, potatoes, fish or anchovy sauce, tamarind sauce, sugar, bay leaf and thyme. Bring to a simmer, cover and cook for 2 hours.

3 Meanwhile, place the rice in a bowl, cover with cold water and set aside for 30 minutes. Roast the peanuts, if using, under a preheated grill for 2 minutes. Remove and rub off the skins with a clean tea towel. Drain the rice and grind with the peanuts or peanut butter in a mortar with a pestle or in a food processor.

4 When the beef is tender, add 60ml/4 tbsp of the cooking liquid to the rice and nut mixture. Blend until smooth, then stir into the casserole. Simmer gently, uncovered, for 15–20 minutes, until thickened. Stir in the wine vinegar and season to taste.

COOK'S TIP

Annatto seeds have little flavour, although they are edible. They are used to colour oil or lard to a rich reddish-orange shade. If you cannot find them, substitute 5ml/1 tsp paprika and a pinch of turmeric, adding these to the casserole with the beef.

Beef and Vegetables in a Table-top Broth

In Japanese, this dish is called *Shabu Shabu*, which refers to the swishing sound made as wafer-thin slices of beef, tofu and vegetables cook in a special broth. This is a delicious and easy all-in-one main course for a dinner party.

INGREDIENTS

Serves 4–6

450g/1lb sirloin steak, trimmed
1.75 litres/3 pints/7½ cups water
½ sachet instant *dashi* powder or ½ vegetable stock cube
150g/5oz carrots
6 spring onions, sliced
150g/5oz Chinese leaves, roughly chopped
225g/8oz mooli, shredded
115g/4oz canned bamboo shoots, drained and sliced
175g/6oz tofu, cut into large dice
10 shiitake mushrooms, fresh or dried
salt
275g/10oz udon noodles, cooked, to serve

For the sesame dipping sauce

50g/2oz sesame seeds or 30ml/2 tbsp tahini paste
120ml/4fl oz/½ cup instant *dashi* stock or vegetable stock
60ml/4 tbsp dark soy sauce
10ml/2 tsp sugar
30ml/2 tbsp sake (optional)
10ml/2 tsp *wasabi* powder (optional)

For the ponzu dipping sauce

45ml/3 tbsp lemon juice
15ml/1 tbsp rice vinegar or white wine vinegar
45ml/3 tbsp dark soy sauce
15ml/1 tbsp tamari sauce
15ml/1 tbsp mirin or 5ml/1 tsp sugar
1.5ml/¼ tsp instant *dashi* powder or ¼ vegetable stock cube

1 Place the beef in the freezer for 30 minutes, or until firm but not frozen. Slice it very thinly using a cleaver or large, sharp knife. Arrange it decoratively on a serving plate, cover and set aside. Bring the water to the boil in a Japanese *donabe*, a fondue pot or any other covered flameproof casserole with an unglazed outside. Stir in the *dashi* powder or stock cube, cover and simmer for 8–10 minutes. Transfer the container to a heat source (its own stand or a hot plate) at the dining table.

2 Meanwhile, prepare the vegetables and bring a saucepan of lightly salted water to the boil. With a canelle knife, cut a series of grooves along the length of the carrots, then slice thinly. Blanch the carrots, spring onions, Chinese leaves and mooli, separately, for 2–3 minutes each and drain thoroughly. Arrange the vegetables decoratively on serving dishes, together with the bamboo shoots and tofu. If using dried mushrooms, put them in a bowl, cover with hot water and leave to soak for 3–4 minutes, then drain. Slice the shiitake mushrooms.

3 To make the sesame dipping sauce, dry-fry the sesame seeds, if using, in a heavy frying pan over medium heat. Grind them in a mortar with a pestle or in a food processor.

4 Mix together the ground sesame seeds or tahini paste, stock, soy sauce, sugar, sake and *wasabi* powder, if using. Combine thoroughly and pour into a shallow dish.

5 To make the ponzu dipping sauce, put all the ingredients in a screw-top jar and shake vigorously. Pour into a shallow dish.

6 To serve, arrange the plates of vegetables and dishes of sauce around the broth and provide your guests with chopsticks and individual bowls so that they can help themselves to what they want, cook it in the broth and then serve themselves. Towards the end of the meal, each guest can take a portion of noodles and ladle a little stock over them before eating.

COOK'S TIP

Tahini paste is a purée of toasted sesame seeds that is used mainly in Greek, Turkish and some Middle Eastern cooking. It makes a quick alternative to using sesame seeds in this recipe and is readily available from large supermarkets and delicatessens.

Sukiyaki Beef

This Japanese dish, with its mixture of meat, vegetables, noodles and tofu, is a meal in itself. If you want to do it properly, eat the meal with chopsticks and then use a spoon to collect the stock juices.

INGREDIENTS

Serves 4

450g/1lb thick rump steak
200g/7oz Japanese rice noodles
15ml/1 tbsp shredded suet
200g/7oz firm tofu, cut into cubes
8 shiitake mushrooms, hard stems trimmed
2 medium leeks, sliced into 2.5cm/1in lengths
90g/3½oz baby spinach, to serve

For the stock

15ml/1 tbsp caster sugar
90ml/6 tbsp sake, Chinese rice wine or dry sherry
45ml/3 tbsp dark soy sauce
120ml/4fl oz/½ cup water

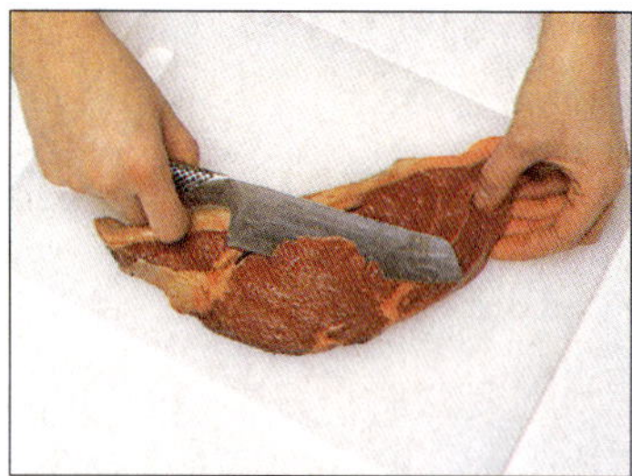

1 Cut the steak into thin slices using a cleaver or sharp knife.

2 Blanch the noodles in boiling water for 2 minutes. Drain thoroughly and set aside.

3 Make the stock: mix together the sugar, sake, rice wine or dry sherry, soy sauce and water.

4 Melt the suet in a preheated wok. Add the steak and stir-fry for 2–3 minutes, or until cooked through but still pink.

5 Pour the stock over the beef.

6 Add the tofu, mushrooms and leeks and cook for 4 minutes, or until the leeks are tender. Serve a selection of the different ingredients, together with a few baby spinach leaves, to each person.

Beef Saté with Hot Mango Dip

Aromatic beef is served with a spicy fruit sauce. Just add a green salad and plain boiled rice for the perfect balance of flavours and textures.

INGREDIENTS

Serves 4
450g/1lb sirloin steak
15ml/1 tbsp coriander seeds
5ml/1 tsp cumin seeds
50g/2oz/½ cup raw cashew nuts
15ml/1 tbsp vegetable oil
2 shallots or 1 small onion, finely chopped
1cm/½in fresh root ginger, finely chopped
1 garlic clove, crushed
30ml/2 tbsp tamarind sauce
30ml/2 tbsp dark soy sauce
10ml/2 tsp sugar
5ml/1 tsp rice vinegar or white wine vinegar
salad leaves, to serve

For the hot mango dip
1 ripe mango
1–2 small fresh red chillies, seeded and finely chopped
15ml/1 tbsp fish sauce
juice of 1 lime
10ml/2 tsp sugar
30ml/2 tbsp chopped fresh coriander
salt

1 Slice the beef into long, narrow strips and thread, zig-zag style, on to 12 bamboo skewers. Put them on a flat plate and set aside.

2 Dry-fry coriander seeds, cumin seeds and cashew nuts in a preheated wok until evenly brown. Transfer to a mortar and crush with a pestle or crush finely in a food processor. Mix together the crushed spices and nuts, vegetable oil, shallots or onion, ginger, garlic, tamarind sauce, soy sauce, sugar and vinegar. Spoon this mixture over the beef and set aside to marinate for up to 8 hours.

3 Cook the steak skewers under a preheated grill for 6–8 minutes, turning occasionally to ensure an even colour.

4 Meanwhile, make the mango dip. Peel the mango and cut the flesh from the stone. Place in a food processor with the chillies, fish sauce, lime juice and sugar and process until smooth. Stir in the coriander and season with salt to taste. Serve the skewers on a bed of salad leaves, with the sauce separately.

Paper-thin Lamb with Spring Onions

Spring onions lend a delicious flavour to the lamb in this simple supper dish.

INGREDIENTS

Serves 3–4

450g/1lb lamb neck fillet
30ml/2 tbsp Chinese rice wine or dry sherry
10ml/2 tsp light soy sauce
2.5ml/½ tsp roasted and ground Szechuan peppercorns
2.5ml/½ tsp salt
2.5ml/½ tsp dark brown soft sugar
20ml/4 tsp dark soy sauce
15ml/1 tbsp sesame oil
30ml/2 tbsp groundnut oil
2 garlic cloves, thinly sliced
2 bunches spring onions, cut into 7.5cm/3 in lengths, then shredded
30ml/2 tbsp chopped fresh coriander

1 Wrap the lamb and place in the freezer for about 1 hour until just frozen. Cut the meat across the grain into paper-thin slices. Put the lamb slices in a bowl, add 10ml/2 tsp of the rice wine or sherry, the soy sauce and ground Szechuan peppercorns. Mix well and set aside to marinate for 15–30 minutes.

2 Make the sauce: in a bowl mix together the remaining rice wine or sherry, the salt, brown sugar, soy sauce and 10ml/2 tsp of the sesame oil. Set aside.

3 Heat the groundnut oil in a preheated wok. Add the garlic and let it sizzle for a few seconds, then add the lamb. Stir-fry for about 1 minute, until the lamb is no longer pink. Pour in the sauce and stir briefly to mix.

4 Add the spring onions and coriander and stir-fry for 15–20 seconds, until the spring onions just wilt. The finished dish should be slightly dry in appearance. Serve at once, sprinkled with the remaining sesame oil.

COOK'S TIP

Some large supermarkets sell very thinly sliced lean lamb ready for stir-frying, which makes this dish even quicker to prepare.

Minted Lamb Stir-fry

Lamb and mint have a long-established partnership that works particularly well in this full-flavoured stir-fry. Serve with plenty of crusty bread.

INGREDIENTS

Serves 2

275g/10oz lamb neck fillet
30ml/2 tbsp sunflower oil
10ml/2 tsp sesame oil
1 onion, roughly chopped
2 garlic cloves, crushed
1 fresh red chilli, seeded and finely chopped
75g/3oz fine green beans, halved
225g/8oz fresh spinach
30ml/2 tbsp oyster sauce
30ml/2 tbsp fish sauce
15ml/1 tbsp lemon juice
5ml/1 tsp caster sugar
45ml/3 tbsp chopped fresh mint
salt and ground black pepper
fresh mint sprigs, to garnish
crusty bread, to serve

1 Trim the lamb of any excess fat and cut into thin slices. Heat the sunflower and sesame oils in a preheated wok or large frying pan and stir-fry the lamb over a high heat until browned. Remove with a slotted spoon and drain on kitchen paper.

2 Add the onion, garlic and chilli to the wok and cook for 2–3 minutes. Add the beans to the wok and stir-fry for 3 minutes.

3 Stir in the spinach with the browned lamb, oyster sauce, fish sauce, lemon juice and sugar. Stir-fry for a further 3–4 minutes, or until the lamb is cooked through.

4 Sprinkle over the mint, adjust the seasoning and garnish with mint sprigs. Serve piping hot, with plenty of crusty bread to mop up all the juices.

Stir-fried Lamb with Spring Onions

This is a classic Beijing "meat and veg" recipe, in which the lamb can be replaced with either beef or pork, and the spring onions by other strongly flavoured vegetables, such as leeks or onions.

INGREDIENTS

Serves 4
350–400g/12–14oz leg of lamb fillet
5ml/1 tsp light brown sugar
15ml/1 tbsp light soy sauce
15ml/1 tbsp Chinese rice wine or dry sherry
10ml/2 tsp cornflour paste
15g/½oz dried wood ears
300ml/½ pint/1¼ cups vegetable oil
6–8 spring onions
few small pieces of fresh root ginger
30ml/2 tbsp yellow bean sauce
few drops of sesame oil

1 Slice the lamb thinly and place in a shallow dish. Mix together the sugar, soy sauce, rice wine or dry sherry and cornflour paste, pour over the lamb and set aside to marinate for 30–45 minutes. Soak the wood ears in water for 25–30 minutes, then drain and cut into small pieces. Finely chop the spring onions.

2 Heat the oil in a preheated wok and stir-fry the lamb for about 1 minute, or until the colour changes. Remove with a slotted spoon, drain and set aside.

3 Pour off all but about 15ml/1 tbsp oil from the wok, then add the spring onions, ginger, wood ears and yellow bean sauce. Blend well, then add the meat and stir for about 1 minute. Sprinkle with the sesame oil and serve.

Five-spice Lamb

This aromatic and mouth-watering lamb dish is perfect for an informal supper party.

INGREDIENTS

Serves 4

30ml/2 tbsp oil
1.5kg/3–3½lb leg of lamb, boned and cubed
1 onion, chopped
10ml/2 tsp grated fresh root ginger
1 garlic clove, crushed
5ml/1 tsp Chinese five-spice powder
30ml/2 tbsp hoisin sauce
15ml/1 tbsp light soy sauce
300ml/½ pint/1¼ cups passata
250ml/8fl oz/1 cup lamb stock
1 red pepper, seeded and diced
1 yellow pepper, seeded and diced
30ml/2 tbsp chopped fresh coriander
15ml/1 tbsp sesame seeds, toasted
salt and ground black pepper
boiled rice, to serve

1 Heat 30ml/2 tbsp of the oil in a flameproof casserole and brown the lamb in batches over a high heat. Remove and set aside.

2 Add the onion, ginger and garlic to the casserole with a little more oil, if necessary, and cook for about 5 minutes, until softened.

3 Return the lamb to the casserole. Stir in the five-spice powder, hoisin and soy sauces, passata, stock and seasoning. Bring to the boil, cover and cook in a preheated oven at 160°C/325°F/Gas 3 for 1¼ hours.

4 Remove the casserole from the oven, stir in the peppers, then cover and return to the oven for a further 15 minutes, or until the lamb is cooked and very tender.

5 Sprinkle with the coriander and sesame seeds. Serve hot with rice.

Braised Birthday Noodles with Hoisin Lamb

In China, the egg symbolizes continuity and fertility so it is frequently included in birthday dishes. The noodles traditionally served at birthday celebrations are left long: it is considered bad luck to cut them since this might shorten one's life.

Ingredients

Serves 4

350g/12oz thick egg noodles
1kg/2¼lb lean neck fillets of lamb
30ml/2 tbsp vegetable oil
115g/4oz fine green beans, topped and tailed, and blanched
salt and freshly ground black pepper
2 hard-boiled eggs, halved, and 2 spring onions, finely chopped, to garnish

For the marinade

2 garlic cloves, crushed
10ml/2 tsp grated fresh root ginger
30ml/2 tbsp soy sauce
30ml/2 tbsp rice wine
1–2 dried red chillies
30ml/2 tbsp vegetable oil

For the sauce

15ml/1 tbsp cornflour
30ml/2 tbsp soy sauce
30ml/2 tbsp rice wine
grated rind and juice of ½ orange
15ml/1 tbsp hoisin sauce
15ml/1 tbsp wine vinegar
5ml/1 tsp soft light brown sugar

1 Bring a large saucepan of water to the boil. Add the noodles and cook for 2 minutes only. Drain, rinse under cold water and drain again. Set aside.

2 Cut the lamb into 5cm/2in thick medallions. Mix the ingredients for the marinade in a large shallow dish. Add the lamb and leave to marinate for at least 4 hours or overnight.

3 Heat the oil in a heavy-based saucepan or flameproof casserole. Fry the lamb for 5 minutes until browned. Add just enough water to cover the meat. Bring to the boil, skim, then reduce the heat and simmer for 40 minutes or until the meat is tender, adding more water as necessary.

4 Make the sauce. Blend the cornflour with the remaining ingredients in a bowl. Stir into the lamb and mix well without breaking up the meat.

5 Add the noodles to the lamb with the beans. Simmer gently until both the noodles and the beans are cooked. Add salt and pepper to taste. Divide the noodles, lamb and beans among four large bowls, garnish each portion with half a hard-boiled egg, sprinkle with spring onions and serve.

Pork Chow Mein

A perfect, speedy meal, this family favourite is flavoured with sesame oil for an authentic oriental taste.

INGREDIENTS

Serves 4

175g/6oz medium egg noodles
350g/12oz pork fillet
30ml/2 tbsp sunflower oil
15ml/1 tbsp sesame oil
2 garlic cloves, crushed
8 spring onions, sliced
1 red pepper, seeded and roughly chopped
1 green pepper, seeded and roughly chopped
30ml/2 tbsp dark soy sauce
45ml/3 tbsp Chinese rice wine or dry sherry
175g/6oz beansprouts
45ml/3 tbsp chopped fresh flat-leaf parsley
15ml/1 tbsp toasted sesame seeds

1 Soak the noodles according to the packet instructions. Drain well.

2 Thinly slice the pork fillet. Heat the sunflower oil in a preheated wok or large frying pan and cook the pork over a high heat until golden brown and cooked through.

3 Add the sesame oil to the wok or frying pan, with the garlic, spring onions and peppers. Cook over a high heat for 3–4 minutes, or until the vegetables are beginning to soften.

4 Reduce the heat slightly and stir in the noodles, with the soy sauce and rice wine or dry sherry. Stir-fry for 2 minutes. Add the beansprouts and cook for a further 1–2 minutes. If the noodles begin to stick, add a splash of water. Stir in the parsley and serve sprinkled with the sesame seeds.

Hot-and-sour Pork

This tasty dish is cooked in the oven and uses less oil than a stir-fry. Trim all visible fat from the pork before cooking, for a healthy, low-fat recipe.

INGREDIENTS

Serves 4

350g/12oz pork fillet
5ml/1 tsp sunflower oil
2.5cm/1in fresh root ginger, grated
1 fresh red chilli, seeded and finely chopped
5ml/1 tsp Chinese five-spice powder
15ml/1 tbsp sherry vinegar
15ml/1 tbsp soy sauce
225g/8oz can pineapple chunks in natural juice
175ml/6fl oz/¾ cup chicken stock
20ml/4 tsp cornflour
15ml/1 tbsp water
1 small green pepper, seeded and sliced
115g/4oz baby sweetcorn, halved
salt and ground black pepper
sprig of flat-leaf parsley, to garnish
boiled rice, to serve

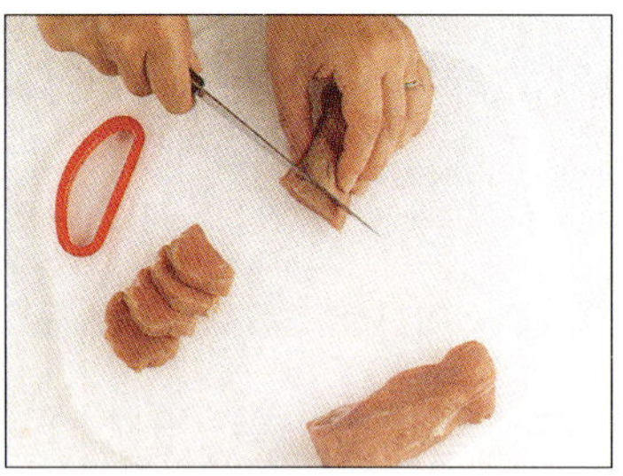

1 Trim away any visible fat from the pork and cut into 1cm/½in-thick slices using a sharp knife.

2 Brush the sunflower oil over the base of a flameproof casserole. Heat over a medium heat, then fry the pork for about 2 minutes on each side or until lightly browned.

3 Blend together the ginger, chilli, Chinese five-spice powder, sherry vinegar and soy sauce.

4 Drain the pineapple chunks, reserving the juice. Make the stock up to 300ml/½ pint/1¼ cups with the reserved juice, mix together with the spices and pour over the pork.

5 Slowly bring the stock to the boil. Blend the cornflour with the water and gradually stir into the pork. Add the green pepper and baby sweetcorn and season to taste.

6 Cover and cook in a preheated oven at 160°C/325°F/Gas 3 for 30 minutes or until the pork is tender. Stir in the pineapple and cook for a further 5 minutes. Garnish with flat-leaf parsley and serve with boiled rice.

COOK'S TIP

Chinese five-spice powder is available from oriental food stores and some large supermarkets. However, if you cannot find it, you can use ground mixed spice instead, although the flavour will be slightly different.

Chinese Sweet-and-sour Pork

Sweet-and-sour pork must be one of the most popular dishes served in Chinese restaurants and take-aways in the Western world. Unfortunately, it is often spoiled by cooks who use too much tomato ketchup in the sauce. Here is a classic recipe from Canton, the city of its origin.

INGREDIENTS

Serves 4

350g/12oz lean pork
1.5ml/¼ tsp salt
2.5ml/½ tsp ground Szechuan peppercorns
15ml/1 tbsp Chinese rice wine or dry sherry
115g/4oz bamboo shoots
30ml/2 tbsp plain flour
1 egg, lightly beaten
vegetable oil, for deep-frying

For the sauce

15ml/1 tbsp vegetable oil
1 garlic clove, finely chopped
1 spring onion, cut into short sections
1 small green pepper, seeded and diced
1 fresh red chilli, seeded and thinly shredded
15ml/1 tbsp light soy sauce
30ml/2 tbsp light brown sugar
30–45ml/2–3 tbsp rice vinegar
15ml/1 tbsp tomato purée
about 120ml/4fl oz/½ cup Basic Stock or water

1 Cut the pork into small bite-sized cubes and place in a shallow dish. Add the salt, peppercorns and rice wine or dry sherry and set aside to marinate for 15–20 minutes.

2 Drain the bamboo shoots, if canned, and cut them into small cubes the same size as the pork.

3 Dust the pork with flour, dip in the beaten egg and coat with more flour. Heat the oil in a preheated wok and deep-fry the pork in moderately hot oil for 3–4 minutes, stirring to separate the pieces. Remove and drain.

4 Reheat the oil until hot, return the pork to the wok and add the bamboo shoots. Fry for about 1 minute, or until the pork is golden. Remove and drain well.

5 To make the sauce, heat the oil in a clean wok or frying pan and add the garlic, spring onion, green pepper and red chilli. Stir-fry for 30–40 seconds, then add the soy sauce, sugar, rice vinegar, tomato purée and stock or water. Bring to the boil, then add the pork and bamboo shoots. Heat through and stir to mix, then serve.

Pork and Vegetable Stir-fry

A quick and easy stir-fry of pork and a mixture of vegetables, this makes an excellent family lunch or supper dish.

INGREDIENTS

Serves 4

225g/8oz can pineapple chunks
15ml/1 tbsp cornflour
30ml/2 tbsp light soy sauce
15ml/1 tbsp Chinese rice wine or dry sherry
15ml/1 tbsp soft brown sugar
15ml/1 tbsp white wine vinegar
5ml/1 tsp Chinese five-spice powder
10ml/2 tsp olive oil
1 red onion, sliced
1 garlic clove, crushed
1 fresh red chilli, seeded and chopped
2.5cm/1in fresh root ginger
350g/12oz lean pork tenderloin, cut into thin strips
175g/6oz carrots
1 red pepper, seeded and sliced
175g/6oz mangetouts, halved
115g/4oz beansprouts
200g/7oz can sweetcorn kernels
30ml/2 tbsp chopped fresh coriander
salt
15ml/1 tbsp toasted sesame seeds, to garnish

1 Drain the pineapple, reserving the juice. In a small bowl, blend the cornflour with the reserved pineapple juice. Add the soy sauce, rice wine or dry sherry, sugar, vinegar and five-spice powder, stir to mix and set aside.

2 Heat the oil in a preheated wok or large, non-stick frying pan. Add the onion, garlic, chilli and ginger and stir-fry for 30 seconds. Add the pork and stir-fry for 2–3 minutes.

3 Cut the carrots into matchstick strips. Add to the wok with the red pepper and stir-fry for 2–3 minutes. Add the mangetouts, beansprouts and sweetcorn and stir-fry for 1–2 minutes.

4 Pour in the sauce mixture and the reserved pineapple and stir-fry until the sauce thickens. Reduce the heat and stir-fry for a further 1–2 minutes. Stir in the coriander and season to taste. Sprinkle with sesame seeds and serve immediately.

Sweet-and-sour Pork and Prawn Soup

This main-course soup has a sour, rich flavour.

INGREDIENTS

Serves 4–6

225g/8oz raw or cooked prawns, peeled
30ml/2 tbsp tamarind sauce
juice of 2 limes
350g/12oz lean pork, diced
1 small green guava, peeled, halved and seeded
1 small under-ripe mango, peeled, stoned and chopped
1.5 litres/2½ pints/6¼ cups chicken stock
15ml/1 tbsp fish sauce or soy sauce
275g/10oz sweet potato, peeled and cut into even-sized pieces
225g/8oz unripe tomatoes, quartered
115g/4oz green beans, halved
1 star fruit, thickly sliced
75g/3oz green cabbage, shredded
salt and ground black pepper
lime wedges, to garnish

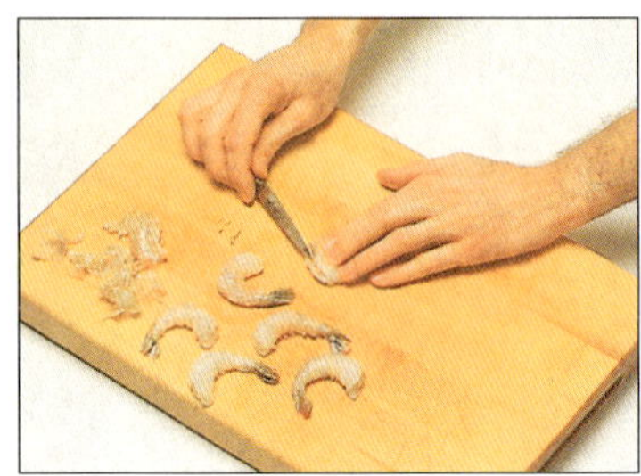

1 Devein the prawns and set aside. Put the tamarind sauce and lime juice into a saucepan.

2 Add the pork, guava and mango to the pan and pour in the stock. Add the fish sauce or soy sauce, bring to the boil, reduce the heat and simmer for 30 minutes.

3 Add the remaining fruit and vegetables and the prawns and simmer for a further 10–15 minutes. Season to taste. Transfer to a serving dish and garnish with lime wedges.

Savoury Pork Pies

This recipe from the Philippines is a legacy of sixteenth-century Spanish colonialism, with a unique Eastern touch.

INGREDIENTS

Serves 6

15ml/1 tbsp vegetable oil
1 medium onion, chopped
1 garlic clove, crushed
5ml/1 tsp chopped fresh thyme
115g/4oz minced pork
5ml/1 tsp paprika
1 hard-boiled egg, chopped
1 medium gherkin, chopped
30ml/2 tbsp chopped fresh parsley
350g/12oz frozen pastry, thawed
salt and ground black pepper
vegetable oil, for deep-frying

1 To make the filling, heat the oil in a saucepan, add the onions, garlic and thyme and fry for 3–4 minutes. Add the pork and paprika and stir-fry until the meat is evenly browned. Season and turn the mixture into a bowl. Set aside to cool. Add the hard-boiled egg, gherkin and parsley.

2 Lightly knead the pastry on a floured surface, then roll out to a 38cm/15in square. Cut out 12 circles, 13cm/5in in diameter. Place 15ml/1 tbsp of the filling on each circle, moisten the edges with a little water, fold over into a half-moon shape and press the edges together to seal.

3 Heat the vegetable oil in a deep-fryer to 196°C/385°F. Deep-fry the pies, three at a time, for 1–2 minutes, until golden brown. Drain on kitchen paper and keep warm while you fry the remaining pies. Serve warm.

Lion's Head Casserole

The name of this dish – *Shi Zi Tou* in Chinese – derives from the rather strange idea that the meatballs look like a lion's head and the Chinese leaves resemble its mane.

INGREDIENTS

Serves 4–6

450g/1lb minced pork
10ml/2 tsp finely chopped spring onion
5ml/1 tsp finely chopped fresh root ginger
50g/2oz mushrooms, chopped
50g/2oz cooked prawns, peeled, or crab meat, finely chopped
15ml/1 tbsp light soy sauce
5ml/1 tsp light brown sugar
15ml/1 tbsp Chinese rice wine or dry sherry
15ml/1 tbsp cornflour
675g/1½lb Chinese leaves
45–60ml/3–4 tbsp vegetable oil
5ml/1 tsp salt
300ml/½ pint/1¼ cups Basic Stock or water

1 Mix together the pork, spring onion, ginger, mushrooms, prawns or crab meat, soy sauce, brown sugar, rice wine or dry sherry and cornflour. Shape the mixture into 4–6 meatballs.

2 Cut the Chinese leaves into large pieces, all about the same size.

3 Heat the oil in a preheated wok or large frying pan. Add the Chinese leaves and salt and stir-fry for 2–3 minutes. Add the meatballs and the stock, bring to the boil, cover and simmer gently for 30–45 minutes. Serve immediately.

Stir-fried Pork with Vegetables

This dish is a perfect example of the Chinese way of balancing and harmonizing colours, flavours and textures.

INGREDIENTS

Serves 4

225g/8oz pork fillet, thinly sliced
15ml/1 tbsp light soy sauce
5ml/1 tsp light brown sugar
5ml/1 tsp Chinese rice wine or dry sherry
10ml/2 tsp cornflour paste
115g/4oz firm tomatoes, skinned
175g/6oz courgettes
1 spring onion
60ml/4 tbsp vegetable oil
5ml/1 tsp salt (optional)
Basic Stock or water, if necessary

1 Put the pork in a bowl with 5ml/1 tsp of the soy sauce, the sugar, rice wine or dry sherry and cornflour paste. Set aside to marinate. Cut the tomatoes and courgettes into wedges. Slice the spring onion.

2 Heat the oil in a preheated wok and stir-fry the pork for 1 minute, or until it colours. Remove with a slotted spoon, set aside and keep warm.

3 Add the vegetables to the wok and stir-fry for 2 minutes. Add the salt, if using, the pork and a little stock or water, if necessary, and stir-fry for 1 minute. Add the remaining soy sauce, mix well and serve.

Poultry

The versatility of chicken has never been so apparent – stir-fried with ginger, baked with spices, braised in coconut milk and even barbecued Thai-style – and, of course, this chapter also includes mouth-watering recipes for other types of poultry. Some dishes are familiar favourites, such as Chicken Teriyaki, Duck and Ginger Chop Suey and Peking Duck, while others offer new and exciting combinations of ingredients. Try Chilli Duck with Crab and Cashew Sauce, Green Curry Coconut Chicken or Honey-glazed Quail with a Five-spice Marinade.

Chicken Curry with Rice Vermicelli

Lemon grass gives this South East Asian curry a wonderful lemony flavour and fragrance.

INGREDIENTS

Serves 4

1 chicken, about 1.5kg/3–3½lb
225g/8oz sweet potatoes
60ml/4 tbsp vegetable oil
1 onion, finely sliced
3 garlic cloves, crushed
30–45ml/2–3 tbsp Thai curry powder
5ml/1 tsp sugar
10ml/2 tsp fish sauce
600ml/1 pint/2½ cups coconut milk
1 lemon grass stalk, cut in half
350g/12oz rice vermicelli, soaked in hot water until soft
1 lemon, cut into wedges, to serve

For the garnish
115g/4oz beansprouts
2 spring onions, finely sliced diagonally
2 red chillies, seeded and finely sliced
8–10 mint leaves

1 Skin the chicken. Cut the flesh into small pieces and set aside. Peel the sweet potatoes and cut them into large chunks, about the size of the chicken pieces.

2 Heat half the oil in a large heavy saucepan. Add the onion and garlic and fry until the onion softens.

3 Add the chicken pieces and stir-fry until they change colour. Stir in the curry powder. Season with salt and sugar and mix thoroughly, then stir in the fish sauce.

4 Pour in the coconut milk and add the lemon grass. Cook over a low heat for 15 minutes.

5 Meanwhile, heat the remaining oil in a large frying pan. Fry the sweet potatoes until lightly golden. Using a slotted spoon, add them to the chicken. Cook for 10–15 minutes more, or until both the chicken and sweet potatoes are tender.

6 Drain the rice vermicelli and cook it in a saucepan of boiling water for 3–5 minutes. Drain well. Place in shallow bowls, with the chicken curry. Garnish with beansprouts, spring onions, chillies and mint leaves and serve with lemon wedges.

Gingered Chicken Noodles

A blend of ginger, spices and coconut milk flavours this delicious supper dish, which is made in minutes. For a real oriental touch, add a little fish sauce to taste, just before serving.

INGREDIENTS

Serves 4

350g/12oz boneless chicken breasts, skinned
225g/8oz courgettes
275g/10oz aubergine
30ml/2 tbsp vegetable oil
5cm/2in fresh root ginger, finely chopped
6 spring onions, sliced
10ml/2 tsp Thai green curry paste
400ml/14fl oz/$1\frac{2}{3}$ cups coconut milk
475ml/16fl oz/2 cups chicken stock
115g/4oz medium egg noodles
45ml/3 tbsp chopped fresh coriander
15ml/1 tbsp lemon juice
salt and ground black pepper
chopped fresh coriander, to garnish

1 Cut the chicken into bite-sized pieces. Halve the courgettes lengthways and roughly chop them. Roughly chop the aubergine.

2 Heat the oil in a large saucepan and cook the chicken until golden. Remove with a slotted spoon and drain on kitchen paper.

3 Add a little more oil, if necessary, and cook the ginger and spring onions for 3 minutes. Add the courgettes and cook for 2–3 minutes, or until beginning to turn golden. Stir in the Thai curry paste and cook for 1 minute.

4 Add the coconut milk, stock, aubergine and chicken and simmer for 10 minutes. Add the noodles and cook for a further 5 minutes, or until the chicken is cooked and the noodles are tender. Stir in the coriander and lemon juice and adjust the seasoning. Serve immediately garnished with chopped fresh coriander.

Spicy Chicken Stir-fry

The chicken is marinated in an aromatic blend of spices and stir-fried with crisp vegetables. If you find it too spicy, serve with a spoonful of soured cream or yogurt. It's delicious hot or cold.

INGREDIENTS

Serves 4
2.5ml/½ tsp ground turmeric
2.5ml/½ tsp ground ginger
5ml/1 tsp salt
5ml/1 tsp ground black pepper
10ml/2 tsp ground cumin
15ml/1 tbsp ground coriander
15ml/1 tbsp caster sugar
450g/1lb boneless chicken breasts, skinned
1 bunch spring onions
4 celery sticks
2 red peppers, seeded
1 yellow pepper, seeded
175g/6oz courgettes
175g/6oz mangetouts or sugar snap peas
sunflower oil, for frying
15ml/1 tbsp lime juice
15ml/1 tbsp clear honey

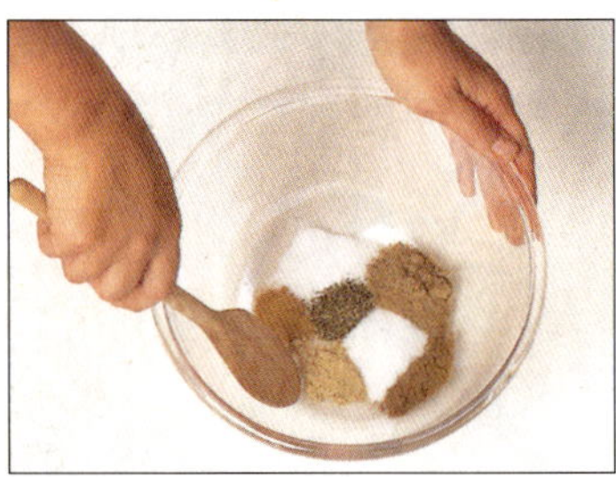

1 Mix together the turmeric, ginger, salt, pepper, cumin, coriander and sugar in a bowl until well combined.

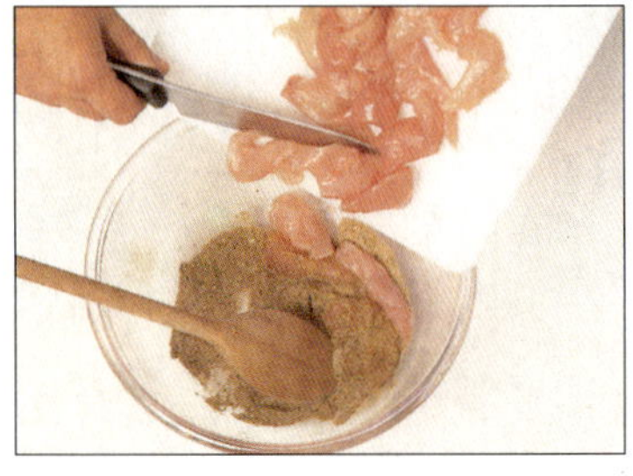

2 Cut the chicken into bite-sized strips. Add to the spice mixture and stir to coat the chicken pieces thoroughly. Set aside.

3 Prepare the vegetables. Cut the spring onions, celery and peppers into 5cm/2in-long, thin strips. Cut the courgettes at a slight angle into thin rounds and top and tail the mangetouts or sugar snap peas.

4 Heat 30ml/2 tbsp of oil in a preheated wok or large frying pan. Stir-fry the chicken in batches until cooked through and golden brown, adding a little more oil if necessary. Remove from the pan and keep warm.

5 Add a little more oil to the pan and cook the spring onions, celery, peppers and courgettes over a medium heat for about 8–10 minutes, until beginning to soften and turn golden. Add the mangetouts or sugar snap peas and cook for a further 2 minutes.

6 Return the chicken to the pan, with the lime juice and honey. Cook for 2 minutes. Serve immediately.

Spicy Clay-pot Chicken

Clay-pot cooking stems from the practice of burying a glazed pot in the embers of an open fire. The gentle heat surrounds the base and keeps the liquid inside at a slow simmer, similar to the modern-day casserole.

INGREDIENTS

Serves 4–6

1.5kg/3–3½lb chicken
45ml/3 tbsp freshly grated coconut
30ml/2 tbsp vegetable oil
2 shallots or 1 small onion, finely chopped
2 garlic cloves, crushed
5cm/2in lemon grass stalk
2.5cm/1in galangal or fresh root ginger, thinly sliced
2 small fresh green chillies, seeded and finely chopped
1cm/½ in square shrimp paste or 15ml/1 tbsp fish sauce
400ml/14fl oz/1⅔ cups canned coconut milk
300ml/½ pint/1¼ cups chicken stock
2 kaffir lime leaves (optional)
15ml/1 tbsp sugar
15ml/1 tbsp rice vinegar or white wine vinegar
2 ripe tomatoes, to garnish and 30ml/2 tbsp chopped coriander leaves, to garnish

1 To joint the chicken, remove the legs and wings with a chopping knife. Skin the pieces and divide the drumsticks from the thighs and, using a pair of kitchen scissors, remove the lower part of the chicken, leaving the breast piece. Remove as many of the bones as you can, to make the dish easier to eat. Cut the breast piece into four and set aside.

2 Dry-fry the coconut in a large wok until evenly brown. Add the vegetable oil, shallots or onion, garlic, lemon grass, galangal or ginger, chillies and shrimp paste or fish sauce. Fry briefly to release the flavours. Add the chicken pieces to the wok and brown evenly with the spices for 2–3 minutes.

3 Strain the coconut milk and reserve the thick part. Add the thin part to the wok, together with the chicken stock, lime leaves, if using, sugar and vinegar. Transfer to a glazed clay pot, cover and bake in a preheated oven at 180°C/350°F/Gas 4 for 50–55 minutes or until the chicken is tender. Stir in the thick part of the coconut milk and return to the oven for 5–10 minutes to simmer and thicken.

4 Place the tomatoes in a bowl and cover with boiling water to loosen and remove the skins. Halve the tomatoes, discard the seeds and cut into large dice. Add the tomatoes to the finished dish, scatter with the chopped coriander and serve.

Green Curry Coconut Chicken

The recipe given here for green curry paste takes time to make properly. Pork, prawns and fish can all be used instead of chicken, but cooking times must be adjusted accordingly.

INGREDIENTS

Serves 4–6
1.1kg/2½lb chicken
600ml/1 pint/2½ cups canned coconut milk
450ml/¾ pint/1¾ cups chicken stock
2 kaffir lime leaves
350g/12oz sweet potatoes, roughly chopped
350g/12oz winter squash, seeded and roughly chopped
115g/4oz French beans, halved
1 small bunch fresh coriander, shredded, to garnish

For the green curry paste
10ml/2 tsp coriander seeds
2.5ml/½ tsp caraway or cumin seeds
3–4 medium fresh green chillies, finely chopped
20ml/4 tsp sugar
10ml/2 tsp salt
7.5cm/3in lemon grass stalk
2cm/¾in galangal or fresh root ginger, finely chopped
3 garlic cloves, crushed
4 shallots or 1 medium onion, finely chopped
2cm/¾in square shrimp paste
45ml/3 tbsp finely chopped fresh coriander
45ml/3 tbsp finely chopped fresh mint
2.5ml/½ tsp ground nutmeg
30ml/2 tbsp vegetable oil

1 To prepare the chicken, remove the legs, then separate the thighs from the drumsticks. Separate the lower part of the chicken carcass by cutting through the rib section with kitchen scissors. Divide the breast part in half down the middle, then chop each half in two. Remove the skin from all the pieces and discard.

2 Strain the coconut milk into a bowl, reserving the thick part. Place the chicken in a stainless steel or enamel saucepan, pour in the thin part of the coconut milk and the stock. Add the lime leaves and simmer, uncovered, for 40 minutes. Remove the chicken from the saucepan and allow to cool. Reserve the cooking liquid. Remove the cooled meat from the bone and set aside.

3 To make the curry paste, dry-fry the coriander seeds and caraway or cumin seeds. Grind the chillies with the sugar and salt in a mortar with a pestle to make a smooth paste. Combine the seeds from the wok with the chilli paste, the lemon grass, galangal or ginger, garlic and shallots or onion, then grind smoothly. Add the shrimp paste, coriander leaves, mint, nutmeg and vegetable oil.

4 Place 250ml/8fl oz/1 cup of the reserved cooking liquid in a large wok. Add 60–75ml/4–5 tbsp of the curry paste to the liquid, according to taste. Boil rapidly until the liquid has reduced completely. Add the chicken stock, chicken meat, sweet potatoes, squash and beans. Simmer for 10–15 minutes until the potatoes are cooked. Stir in the thick part of the coconut milk and simmer gently to thicken. Serve garnished with coriander.

Chicken Cooked in Coconut Milk

Traditionally, the chicken pieces would be part-cooked by frying, but I think that roasting in the oven is a better option. *Ayam Opor* is an unusual recipe in that the sauce is white as it does not contain chillies or turmeric, unlike many other Indonesian dishes. The dish is served with crisp Deep-fried Onions.

Ingredients

Serves 4

1.5kg/3–3½ lb chicken or 4 chicken quarters
4 garlic cloves
1 onion, sliced
4 macadamia nuts or 8 almonds
15ml/1 tbsp coriander seeds, dry-fried, or 5ml/1 tsp ground coriander
45ml/3 tbsp oil
2.5cm/1in fresh *lengkuas*, peeled and bruised
2 lemon grass stems, fleshy part bruised
3 lime leaves
2 bay leaves
5ml/1 tsp sugar
600ml/1 pint/2½ cups coconut milk
salt
boiled rice and deep-fried onions, to serve

1 Preheat the oven to 190°C/375°F/Gas 5. Cut the chicken into four or eight pieces. Season with salt. Put in an oiled roasting tin and cook in the oven for 25–30 minutes. Meanwhile prepare the sauce.

2 Grind the garlic, onion, nuts and coriander to a fine paste in a food processor or with a pestle and mortar. Heat the oil and fry the paste to bring out the flavour. Do not allow it to brown.

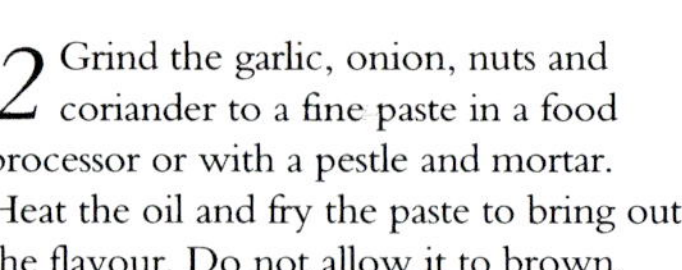

3 Add the part-cooked chicken pieces to a wok together with the *lengkuas*, lemon grass, lime and bay leaves, sugar, coconut milk and salt to taste. Mix well to coat in the sauce.

4 Bring to the boil and then reduce the heat and simmer gently for 30–40 minutes, uncovered, until the chicken is tender and the coconut sauce is reduced and thickened. Stir the mixture occasionally during cooking.

5 Just before serving remove the bruised *lengkuas* and lemon grass. Serve with boiled rice sprinkled with crisp deep-fried onions.

Chicken Teriyaki

A simple bowl of boiled rice is the ideal accompaniment to this subtle Japanese chicken dish.

INGREDIENTS

Serves 4

450g/1lb boneless chicken breasts, skinned
orange segments and mustard and cress, to garnish

For the marinade

5ml/1 tsp sugar
15ml/1 tbsp sake
15 ml/1 tbsp dry sherry
30ml/2 tbsp dark soy sauce
grated rind of 1 orange

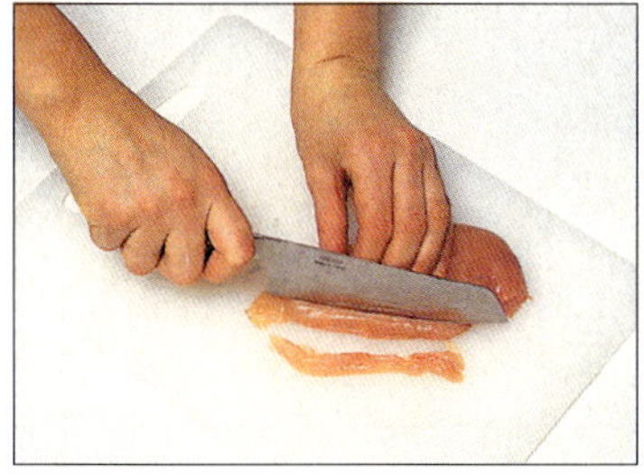

1 Slice the chicken into long, thin strips using a cleaver or sharp knife.

2 Mix together the sugar, sake, dry sherry, soy sauce and grated orange rind in a bowl.

3 Place the chicken in a separate bowl, pour over the marinade and set aside to marinate for 15 minutes.

4 Add the chicken and the marinade to a preheated wok and stir-fry for 4–5 minutes. Serve garnished with orange segments and mustard and cress.

Shredded Chicken with Celery

The tender chicken breast contrasts with the crunchy texture of the celery, and the red chillies add colour and flavour.

INGREDIENTS

Serves 4

275g/10oz boneless chicken breast, skinned
5ml/1 tsp salt
½ egg white, lightly beaten
10ml/2 tsp cornflour paste
475ml/16fl oz/2 cups vegetable oil
1 celery heart, thinly shredded
1–2 fresh red chillies, seeded and thinly shredded
1 spring onion, thinly shredded
few strips of fresh root ginger, thinly shredded
5ml/1 tsp light brown sugar
15ml/1 tbsp Chinese rice wine or dry sherry
few drops of sesame oil

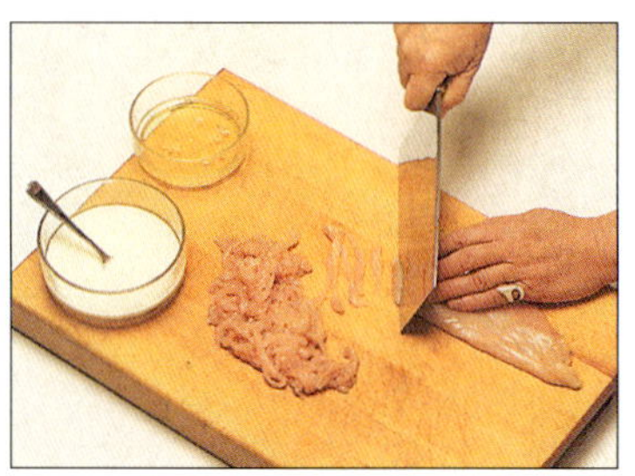

1 Using a sharp knife, thinly shred the chicken. In a bowl, mix together a pinch of the salt, the egg white and cornflour paste. Stir in the chicken.

2 Heat the oil in a preheated wok, add the chicken and stir to separate the shreds. When the chicken turns white, remove with a strainer and drain. Keep warm.

3 Pour off all but 30ml/2 tbsp of the oil. Add the celery, chillies, spring onion and ginger to the wok and stir-fry for 1 minute. Add the chicken, remaining salt, sugar and rice wine or dry sherry. Cook for 1 minute, then add the sesame oil. Serve hot.

Chicken with Chinese Vegetables

This dish makes an excellent family main course served with rice or noodles, but also combines with a selection of other dishes to serve as part of a dinner party menu.

INGREDIENTS

Serves 4

225–275g/8–10oz boneless chicken, skinned
5ml/1 tsp salt
½ egg white, lightly beaten
10ml/2 tsp cornflour paste
60ml/4 tbsp vegetable oil
6–8 small dried shiitake mushrooms, soaked in hot water
115g/4oz canned sliced bamboo shoots, drained
115g/4oz mangetouts
1 spring onion, cut into short sections
few small pieces of fresh root ginger
5ml/1 tsp light brown sugar
15ml/1 tbsp light soy sauce
15ml/1 tbsp Chinese rice wine or dry sherry
few drops of sesame oil

1 Cut the chicken into thin slices, each about the size of an oblong postage stamp. Place it in a bowl and mix with a pinch of the salt, the egg white and the cornflour paste.

2 Heat the oil in a preheated wok, add the chicken and stir-fry over medium heat for about 30 seconds, then remove with a slotted spoon and keep warm.

3 Add the vegetables to the wok and stir-fry over high heat for about 1 minute. Add the remaining salt, the sugar and chicken. Blend, then add the soy sauce and rice wine or dry sherry. Stir for a further 1 minute. Sprinkle with the sesame oil and serve.

Thai-style Chicken Livers

Chicken liver is a good source of iron and is a popular meat, especially in the north-east of Thailand. Serve this dish as a starter with salad, or as part of a main course with jasmine rice.

INGREDIENTS

Serves 4–6

45ml/3 tbsp vegetable oil
450g/1lb chicken livers, trimmed
4 shallots, chopped
2 garlic cloves, chopped
15ml/1 tbsp roasted ground rice
45ml/3 tbsp fish sauce
45ml/3 tbsp lime juice
5ml/1 tsp sugar
2 stalks lemon grass, bruised and finely chopped
30ml/2 tbsp chopped coriander
10–12 mint leaves, to garnish
2 red chillies, chopped, to garnish

1 Heat the oil in a wok or large frying pan. Add the livers and fry over a medium-high heat for about 4 minutes, until the liver is golden brown and cooked, but still pink inside.

2 Move the liver to one side of the pan and add the shallots and garlic. Fry for about 1–2 minutes.

3 Add the roasted ground rice, fish sauce, lime juice, sugar, lemon grass and coriander. Stir to combine. Remove from the heat and serve garnished with mint leaves and chillies.

Barbecued Chicken

Barbecued chicken is served almost everywhere in Thailand, from portable roadside stalls to sports stadiums and beaches.

INGREDIENTS

Serves 4–6

1 chicken, about 1.5kg/3–3½ lb, cut into 8–10 pieces
2 limes, cut into wedges, to garnish
2 red chillies, finely sliced, to garnish

For the marinade

2 stalks lemon grass, chopped
2.5cm/1in piece fresh root ginger
6 garlic cloves
4 shallots
½ bunch coriander roots
15ml/1 tbsp palm sugar
120ml/4fl oz/½ cup coconut milk
30ml/2 tbsp fish sauce
30ml/2 tbsp soy sauce

1 To make the marinade, put all the ingredients into a food processor and process until smooth.

2 Put the chicken pieces in a dish and pour over the marinade. Leave in a cool place to marinate for at least 4 hours or overnight.

3 Barbecue the chicken over glowing coals, or place on a rack over a baking tray and bake at 200°C/400°F/Gas 6 for about 20–30 minutes or until the chicken is cooked and golden brown. Turn the pieces occasionally and brush with the marinade.

4 Garnish with lime wedges and finely sliced red chillies.

Duck and Ginger Chop Suey

Chicken can also be used in this recipe, but duck gives a richer contrast of flavours.

INGREDIENTS

Serves 4

2 duck breasts, about 175g/6oz each
45ml/3 tbsp sunflower oil
1 small egg, lightly beaten
1 garlic clove
175g/6oz beansprouts
2 slices fresh root ginger, cut into matchsticks
10ml/2 tsp oyster sauce
2 spring onions, cut into matchsticks
salt and ground black pepper

For the marinade
15ml/1 tbsp clear honey
10ml/2 tsp Chinese rice wine or dry sherry
10ml/2 tsp light soy sauce
10ml/2 tsp dark soy sauce

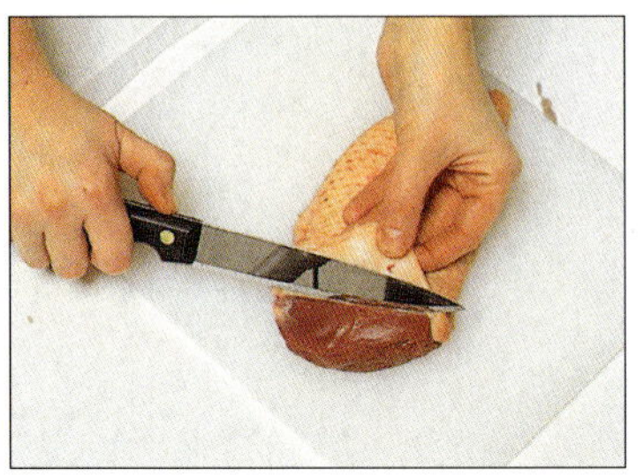

1 Remove the fat and skin from the duck, cut the breasts into thin strips and place in a bowl. Mix the marinade ingredients together, pour over the duck, cover, chill and marinate overnight.

2 Next day, make the egg omelette. Heat a small frying pan and add 15ml/1 tbsp of the oil. When the oil is hot, pour in the egg and swirl around to make an omelette. Once cooked, leave it to cool and then cut into strips. Drain the duck and discard the marinade.

3 Bruise the garlic with the flat blade of a knife. Heat 10ml/2 tsp of the oil in a preheated wok. When the oil is hot, add the garlic and fry for 30 seconds, pressing it to release the flavour. Discard. Add the beansprouts with seasoning and stir-fry for 30 seconds. Transfer to a heated dish, draining off any liquid.

4 Heat the remaining oil in a preheated wok. When the oil is hot, stir-fry the duck for 3 minutes until cooked. Add the ginger and oyster sauce and stir-fry for a further 2 minutes. Add the beansprouts, egg strips and spring onions, stir-fry briefly and serve.

Mandarin Sesame Duck

Duck is a high-fat meat but it is possible to get rid of a considerable proportion of the fat by cooking it in this way. (If you remove the skin completely, the meat can be dry.) For a special occasion, duck breasts are an excellent choice, but they are more expensive.

INGREDIENTS

Serves 4

4 duck legs or boneless breasts
30ml/2 tbsp light soy sauce
45ml/3 tbsp clear honey
15ml/1 tbsp sesame seeds
4 mandarin oranges
5ml/1 tsp cornflour
salt and ground black pepper
mixed vegetables, to serve

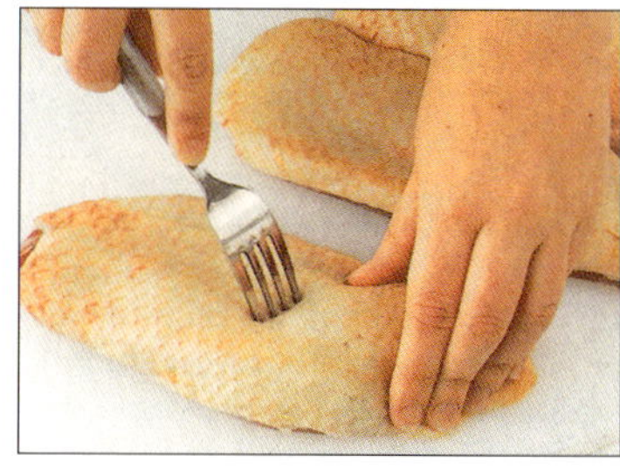

1 Prick the duck skin all over. If using breasts, slash the skin diagonally at intervals with a small, sharp knife.

2 Place the duck on a rack in a roasting tin and roast for 1 hour in a preheated oven at 180°C/350°F/Gas 4. Mix 15ml/1 tbsp of the soy sauce with 30ml/2 tbsp of the honey and brush over the duck. Sprinkle with sesame seeds. Roast for 15–20 minutes, until golden brown.

3 Meanwhile, grate the rind from 1 mandarin and squeeze the juice from 2. Mix together the rind, juice and cornflour, then stir in the remaining soy sauce and honey. Heat, stirring, until thickened and clear. Season to taste. Peel and slice the remaining mandarins. Serve the duck, with the mandarin slices and the sauce, accompanied by mixed vegetables.

Peking Duck

This has to be the *pièce de résistance* of any Chinese banquet. It is not too difficult to prepare and cook at home – the secret is to use duckling with a low fat content. Also, make sure that the skin of the duck is absolutely dry before you start to cook – the drier the skin, the crispier the duck.

INGREDIENTS

Serves 6–8

2.25kg/5–5¼lb oven-ready duckling
30ml/2 tbsp maltose or honey, dissolved in 150ml/¼ pint/⅔ cup warm water

For the duck sauce

30ml/2 tbsp sesame oil
90–120ml/6–8 tbsp yellow bean sauce, crushed
30–45ml/2–3 tbsp light brown sugar

To serve

20–24 thin pancakes
6–8 spring onions, thinly shredded
½ cucumber, thinly shredded

COOK'S TIP

If preferred, serve Peking Duck with plum sauce in place of the duck sauce. Plum sauce is available from oriental stores and larger supermarkets. Duck sauce can also be bought ready-prepared.

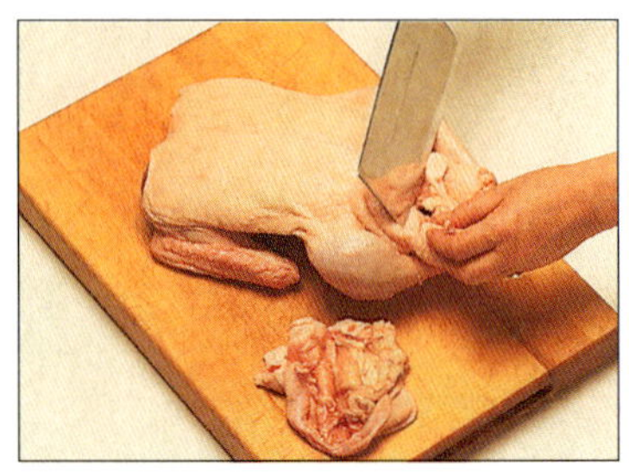

1 Remove any feather studs and any lumps of fat from inside the vent of the duck. Plunge the duck into a saucepan of boiling water for 2–3 minutes to seal the pores. This will make the skin airtight, thus preventing the fat from escaping during cooking. Remove and drain well, then dry thoroughly.

2 Brush the duck all over with the dissolved maltose or honey, then hang the bird up in a cool place for at least 4–5 hours.

3 Place the duck, breast side up, on a rack in a roasting tin and cook in a preheated oven at 200°C/400°F/Gas 6 for 1½–1¾ hours without either basting or turning.

4 Meanwhile, make the duck sauce. Heat the sesame oil in a small saucepan. Add the crushed yellow bean sauce and the light brown sugar. Stir until smooth and allow to cool.

5 To serve, peel off the crispy duck skin in small slices using a sharp carving knife or cleaver, then carve the juicy meat in thin strips. Arrange the skin and meat on separate serving plates.

6 Open a pancake on each plate, spread about 5ml/1 tsp of the chosen sauce in the middle, with a few strips of shredded spring onions and cucumber. Top with 2–3 slices each of duck skin and meat. Roll up and eat.

Crispy and Aromatic Duck

Because this dish is often served with pancakes, spring onions, cucumber and duck sauce, many people mistakenly think this is Peking Duck. This recipe, however, uses quite a different cooking method. The result is just as crispy but the delightful aroma makes this dish particularly distinctive. Plum sauce may be substituted for the duck sauce.

INGREDIENTS

Serves 6–8

1.75–2.25kg/4–5¼lb oven-ready duckling
10ml/2 tsp salt
5–6 whole star anise
15ml/1 tbsp Szechuan peppercorns
5ml/1 tsp cloves
2–3 cinnamon sticks
3–4 spring onions
3–4 slices fresh root ginger, unpeeled
75–90ml/5–6 tbsp Chinese rice wine or dry sherry
vegetable oil, for deep-frying

To serve
lettuce leaves
20–24 thin pancakes
120ml/4fl oz/½ cup duck sauce
6–8 spring onions, thinly shredded
½ cucumber, thinly shredded

1 Remove the wings from the duck. Split the body in half down the backbone.

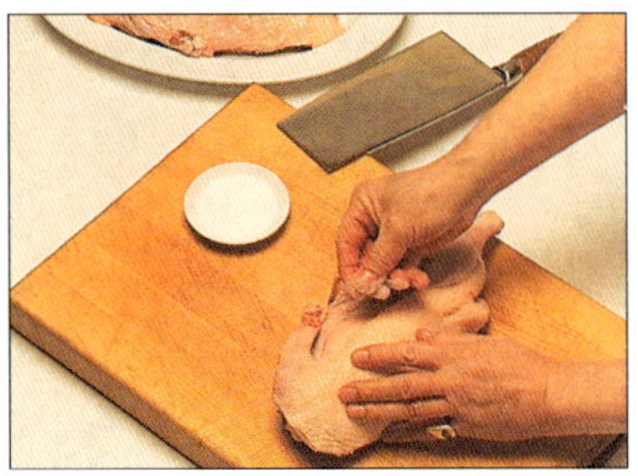

2 Rub salt all over the two duck halves, taking care to rub it well in.

3 Place the duck in a dish with the star anise, peppercorns, cloves, cinnamon, spring onions, ginger and rice wine or dry sherry and set aside to marinate for at least 4–6 hours.

4 Place the duck with the marinade in a steamer positioned in a wok partly filled with boiling water and steam vigorously for 3–4 hours (longer if possible). Remove the duck from the cooking liquid and leave to cool for at least 5–6 hours. The duck must be completely cold and dry or the skin will not become crispy.

5 Heat the oil in a preheated wok until smoking, place the duck pieces in the oil, skin side down, and deep-fry for 5–6 minutes or until crisp and brown, turning just once at the very last moment.

6 Remove, drain, take the meat off the bone and place on a bed of lettuce leaves. To serve, wrap a portion of duck in each pancake with a little sauce, shredded spring onion and cucumber. Eat with your fingers.

Chilli Duck with Crab and Cashew Sauce

This spicy dish would be delicious served with Thai rice, which is slightly aromatic.

INGREDIENTS

Serves 4–6

2.75kg/6lb duck
1.2 litres/2 pints/5 cups water
2 kaffir lime leaves
7.5ml/1½ tsp salt
2–3 small fresh red chillies, seeded and finely chopped
25ml/5 tsp sugar
30ml/2 tbsp coriander seeds
5ml/1 tsp caraway seeds
115g/4oz/1 cup raw cashew nuts, chopped
7.5cm/3in lemon grass
2.5cm/1in galangal or fresh root ginger, finely chopped
2 garlic cloves, crushed
4 shallots or 1 medium onion, finely chopped
2cm/¾in square shrimp paste
25g/1oz coriander white root or stem, finely chopped
175g/6oz frozen white crab meat, thawed
50g/2oz creamed coconut
1 small bunch fresh coriander, chopped, to garnish
boiled rice, to serve

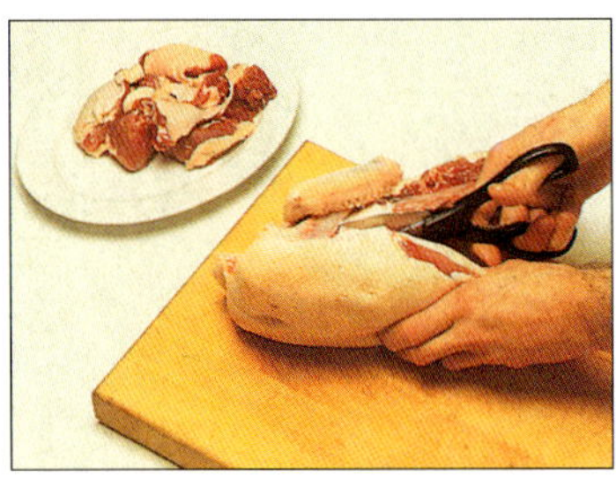

1 Remove the legs from the duck, separate the thighs from the drumsticks and chop each thigh and drumstick into two pieces. Trim away the lower half of the duck with kitchen scissors. Cut the breast piece in half down the middle, then chop each half into four pieces.

2 Put the duck flesh and bones into a large saucepan and cover with the water. Add the lime leaves and 5ml/1 tsp of the salt, bring to the boil and simmer for 30–45 minutes, until the meat is tender. Discard the duck bones. Skim off the fat from the stock and set the stock aside.

3 Grind together the chillies, sugar and remaining salt in a mortar with a pestle or in a food processor. Dry-fry the coriander seeds, caraway seeds and cashew nuts in a preheated wok for 1–2 minutes to release their flavour. Add the seeds and nuts to the chilli mixture, together with the lemon grass, galangal or ginger, garlic and shallots or onion and reduce to a smooth paste. Add the shrimp paste and coriander root or stem and mix well.

4 Add 250ml/8fl oz/1 cup of the reserved stock and blend to make a thin paste.

5 Pour the spice mixture into the saucepan with the duck and mix thoroughly. Bring to the boil, lower the heat and simmer for 20–25 minutes.

6 Add the crab meat and creamed coconut and simmer briefly to heat through. Turn out on to a warmed serving dish, garnish with the chopped coriander and accompany with boiled rice.

Stir-fried Turkey with Mangetouts

Turkey is often a rather disappointing meat with a bland flavour. Here it is enlivened with a delicious marinade and combined with crunchy nuts to provide contrasting textures.

INGREDIENTS

Serves 4
30ml/2 tbsp sesame oil
90ml/6 tbsp lemon juice
1 garlic clove, crushed
1cm/½in fresh root ginger, grated
5ml/1 tsp clear honey
450g/1lb turkey fillets, skinned and cut into strips
115g/4oz mangetouts
30ml/2 tbsp groundnut oil
50g/2oz cashew nuts
6 spring onions, cut into strips
225g/8oz can water chestnuts, drained and thinly sliced
salt
saffron rice, to serve

1 Mix together the sesame oil, lemon juice, garlic, ginger and honey in a shallow, non-metallic dish. Add the turkey and mix well. Cover and leave to marinate for 3–4 hours.

2 Blanch the mangetouts in boiling salted water for 1 minute. Drain, refresh under cold running water and set aside.

3 Drain the marinade from the turkey strips and reserve the marinade. Heat the groundnut oil in a preheated wok or large frying pan, add the cashew nuts and stir-fry for about 1–2 minutes, until golden brown. Remove the cashew nuts from the wok or frying pan, using a slotted spoon, and set aside.

4 Add the turkey to the wok or frying pan and stir-fry for 3–4 minutes, until golden brown. Add the spring onions, mangetouts, water chestnuts and reserved marinade. Cook for a few minutes, until the turkey is tender and the sauce is bubbling and hot. Stir in the cashew nuts and serve with saffron rice.

Honey-glazed Quail with a Five-spice Marinade

Although the quail is a relatively small bird – 115–150g/4–5oz – it is surprisingly meaty. One bird is usually quite sufficient for one serving.

INGREDIENTS

Serves 4

4 oven-ready quails
2 pieces star anise
10ml/2 tsp ground cinnamon
10ml/2 tsp fennel seeds
10ml/2 tsp ground Szechuan or Chinese pepper
pinch of ground cloves
1 small onion, finely chopped
1 garlic clove, crushed
60ml/4 tbsp clear honey
30ml/2 tbsp dark soy sauce
2 spring onions, roughly chopped, finely shredded rind of 1 mandarin orange or satsuma and radish and carrot "flowers", to garnish
banana leaves, to serve

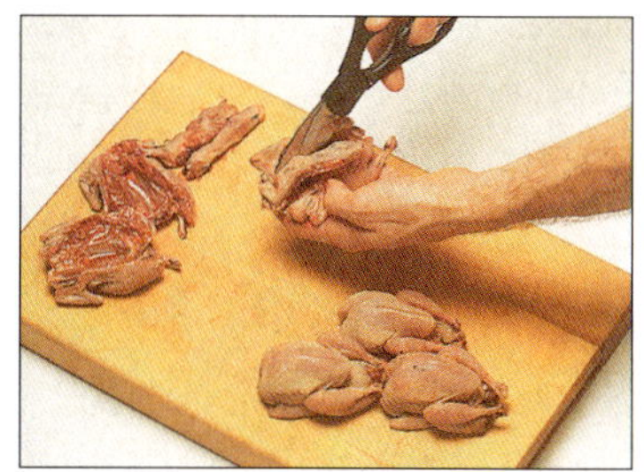

1 Remove the backbones from the quails by cutting down either side with a pair of kitchen scissors.

2 Flatten the birds with the palm of your hand and secure each one with two bamboo skewers.

3 Grind together the star anise, cinnamon, fennel seeds, pepper and cloves in a mortar with a pestle. Add the onion, garlic, honey and soy sauce and combine well.

4 Place the quails on a flat dish, cover with the spice mixture and set aside to marinate for at least 8 hours.

5 Cook the quails under a preheated grill or on a barbecue for 7–8 minutes on each side, basting from time to time with the marinade.

6 Arrange the quails on a bed of banana leaves and garnish with the spring onion, orange rind and radish and carrot "flowers".

VEGETABLES

Unusual ways of preparing familiar vegetables, as well as dishes using more exotic ingredients, can spice up Western grills and roasts or form part of an oriental meal. Stir-frying is an especially good way of cooking vegetables without losing flavour, texture, colour and valuable nutrients. There are recipes for all tastes: palate-tingling Pak Choi with Lime Dressing, Chinese Vegetable Stir-fry with its colourful, crunchy mix of ingredients, Chinese Garlic Mushrooms, the perfect vegetarian snack, and even Chinese-style Brussels sprouts!

Mooli, Beetroot and Carrot Stir-fry

This is a dazzlingly colourful dish with a crunchy texture and fragrant taste.

INGREDIENTS

Serves 4

25g/1oz/¼ cup pine nuts
115g/4oz mooli, peeled
115g/4oz raw beetroot, peeled
115g/4oz carrots, peeled
25ml/1½ tbsp vegetable oil
juice of 1 orange
30ml/2 tbsp chopped fresh coriander
salt and ground black pepper

1 Place the pine nuts in a preheated wok and toss until golden brown. Remove and set aside.

2 Cut the mooli, beetroot and carrots into long, thin strips.

3 Heat the oil in a preheated wok. When the oil is hot, stir-fry the mooli, raw beetroot and carrots for 2–3 minutes. Remove the vegetables from the wok and set aside.

4 Pour the orange juice into the wok and simmer for 2 minutes. Remove and keep warm.

5 Arrange the vegetables attractively on a warmed platter, sprinkle over the coriander and season to taste with salt and pepper.

6 Drizzle over the orange juice, sprinkle with the pine nuts, and serve immediately.

Pak Choi with Lime Dressing

For this Thai recipe, the coconut dressing is traditionally made using fish sauce, but vegetarians could use mushroom sauce instead. Beware, the red chillies make this a fiery dish!

INGREDIENTS

Serves 4

6 spring onions
2 pak choi
30ml/2 tbsp oil
3 fresh red chillies, cut into thin strips
4 garlic cloves, thinly sliced
15ml/1 tbsp crushed peanuts

For the dressing

15–30ml/1–2 tbsp fish sauce
30ml/2 tbsp lime juice
250ml/8fl oz/1 cup coconut milk

1 To make the dressing, blend together the fish sauce and lime juice, then stir in the coconut milk.

2 Trim the spring onions, then cut diagonally into slices, including all but the very tips of the green parts, but keeping the green and white parts separate.

3 Using a large sharp knife, cut the pak choi into very fine shreds.

4 Heat the oil in a preheated wok and stir-fry the chillies for 2–3 minutes until crisp. Transfer to a plate using a slotted spoon. Stir-fry the garlic for 30–60 seconds until golden brown and transfer to the plate with the chillies. Stir-fry the white parts of the spring onions for about 2–3 minutes and then add the green parts and stir-fry for a further 1 minute. Add to the plate with the chillies and garlic.

5 Bring a large pan of salted water to the boil and add the pak choi. Stir twice and then drain immediately. Place the warmed pak choi in a large bowl, add the coconut dressing and stir well. Spoon into a large serving bowl and sprinkle with the crushed peanuts and the stir-fried chilli mixture. Serve immediately.

Stir-Fried Vegetables with Pasta

This colourful Chinese-style dish is easily prepared and, for a change, uses pasta instead of Chinese noodles.

Ingredients

Serves 4

1 medium carrot
175g/6oz small courgettes
175g/6oz runner or other green beans
175g/6oz baby sweetcorn
450g/1lb ribbon pasta, such as tagliatelle
30ml/2 tbsp corn oil, plus extra for tossing the pasta
1cm/½in fresh root ginger, finely chopped
2 garlic cloves, finely chopped
90ml/6 tbsp yellow bean sauce
6 spring onions, sliced into 2.5cm/1in lengths
30ml/2 tbsp dry sherry
5ml/1 tsp toasted sesame seeds
salt

1 Slice the carrot and courgettes diagonally into chunks. Slice the beans diagonally. Cut the baby corn diagonally in half.

2 Cook the pasta in plenty of boiling salted water according to the manufacturer's instructions, drain, then rinse under hot water. Toss in a little oil to prevent sticking.

3 Heat 30ml/2 tbsp oil in a preheated wok or frying pan and add the ginger and garlic. Stir-fry for 30 seconds, then add the carrots, beans, baby sweetcorn and courgettes.

4 Stir-fry for 3–4 minutes, then stir in the yellow bean sauce. Stir-fry for 2 minutes, add the spring onions, dry sherry and pasta and stir-fry for a further 1 minute until piping hot. Sprinkle with sesame seeds and serve immediately.

Chinese Vegetable Stir-fry

This is a typical stir-fried vegetable dish popular all over China. Chinese leaves are like a cross between a cabbage and a crunchy lettuce, with a delicious peppery flavour.

INGREDIENTS

Serves 4

45ml/3 tbsp sunflower oil
15ml/1 tbsp sesame oil
1 garlic clove, chopped
225g/8oz broccoli florets, cut into small pieces
115g/4oz sugar snap peas
1 head Chinese leaves, about 450g/1lb, or Savoy cabbage, sliced
4 spring onions, finely chopped
30ml/2 tbsp soy sauce
30ml/2 tbsp Chinese rice wine or dry sherry
30–45ml/2–3 tbsp water
15ml/1 tbsp sesame seeds, lightly toasted

1 Heat the sunflower and sesame oils in a preheated wok or large frying pan, add the garlic and stir-fry for 30 seconds.

2 Add the broccoli florets and stir-fry for 3 minutes. Add the sugar snap peas and cook for 2 minutes, then toss in the Chinese leaves or cabbage and the spring onions and stir-fry for a further 2 minutes.

3 Pour on the soy sauce, rice wine or dry sherry and water and stir-fry for a further 4 minutes, or until the vegetables are just tender. Sprinkle with the toasted sesame seeds and serve hot.

Indonesian Potatoes with Onions and Chilli Sauce

This adds another dimension to potato chips, with the addition of crisply fried onions and a hot soy sauce and chilli dressing. Eat *Kentang Gula* hot, warm or cold, as a tasty snack.

INGREDIENTS

Serves 6

3 large potatoes, about 225g/8oz each, peeled and cut into chips
sunflower or groundnut oil for deep-frying
2 onions, finely sliced
salt

For the dressing

1–2 fresh red chillies, seeded and ground
45ml/3 tbsp dark soy sauce

1 Rinse the potato chips and then pat dry very well with kitchen paper. Heat the oil and deep-fry the chips, until they are golden brown in colour and crisp.

2 Put the chips in a dish, sprinkle with salt and keep warm. Fry the onion slices in the hot oil until they are similarly crisp and golden brown. Drain well on kitchen paper and then add to the potato chips.

3 Mix the chillies with the soy sauce and heat gently.

4 Pour over the potato and onion mixture and serve as suggested.

VARIATION

Alternatively, boil the potatoes in their skins. Drain, cool and slice them and then shallow-fry until golden. Cook the onions and pour over the dressing, as above.

Courgettes with Noodles

Any courgette or member of the squash family can be used in this *Oseng Oseng,* which is very similar to a dish enjoyed in Malaysia, whose cuisine has strong links with Indonesia.

INGREDIENTS

Serves 4–6

450g/1lb courgettes, sliced
1 onion, finely sliced
1 garlic clove, finely chopped
30ml/2 tbsp sunflower oil
2.5ml/½ tsp ground turmeric
2 tomatoes, chopped
45ml/3 tbsp water
115g/4oz cooked, peeled prawns (optional)
25g/1oz cellophane noodles
salt

1 Use a potato peeler to cut thin strips from the outside of each courgette. Cut them in neat slices. Set the courgettes on one side. Fry the onion and garlic in hot oil; do not allow to brown.

2 Add the turmeric, courgette slices, chopped tomatoes, water and prawns, if using.

3 Put the noodles in a pan and pour over boiling water to cover, leave for a minute and then drain. Cut the noodles in 5cm/2in lengths and add to the vegetables.

4 Cover with a lid and cook in their own steam for 2–3 minutes. Toss everything well together. Season with salt to taste and serve while still hot.

Aubergine with Sesame Chicken

Young vegetables are prized in Japan for their sweet, delicate flavour. Here, small aubergines are stuffed with seasoned chicken.

Ingredients

Serves 4

175g/6oz chicken breast or thighs, skinned
1 spring onion, green part only, finely chopped
15ml/1 tbsp dark soy sauce
15ml/1 tbsp mirin or sweet sherry
2.5ml/½ tsp sesame oil
2.5ml/½ tsp salt
4 small aubergines, about 10cm/4in long
15ml/1 tbsp sesame seeds
flour, for dusting
vegetable oil, for deep-frying

For the dipping sauce
60ml/4 tbsp dark soy sauce
60ml/4 tbsp *dashi* or vegetable stock
45ml/3 tbsp mirin or sweet sherry

1 Remove the chicken meat from the bone and mince it finely in a food processor for 1–2 minutes. Add the spring onion, soy sauce, mirin or sherry, sesame oil and salt.

2 Make four slits in each aubergine, so they remain joined at the stem. Spoon the minced chicken mixture into the aubergines, opening them slightly to accommodate it. Dip the fat end of each stuffed aubergine in the sesame seeds, then dust with flour. Set aside.

3 To make the dipping sauce, combine the soy sauce, *dashi* or stock and mirin or sherry. Pour into a shallow bowl and set aside.

4 Heat the vegetable oil in a wok or deep-fryer to 196°C/385°F. Fry the aubergines, two at a time, for 3–4 minutes. Lift out with a slotted spoon and drain on kitchen paper. Serve with the dipping sauce.

Chinese Potatoes with Chilli Beans

East meets West. An American-style dish with a Chinese flavour – the sauce is particularly tasty. Try it as a quick supper dish when you fancy a meal with a little zing!

Ingredients

Serves 4

4 medium potatoes, cut in thick chunks
30ml/2 tbsp sunflower or groundnut oil
3 spring onions, sliced
1 large fresh red chilli, seeded and sliced
2 garlic cloves, crushed
400g/14oz can red kidney beans, drained
30ml/2 tbsp soy sauce
15ml/1 tbsp sesame oil
salt and ground black pepper
15ml/1 tbsp sesame seeds and chopped fresh coriander or parsley, to garnish

1 Boil the potatoes until they are just tender. Take care not to overcook them. Drain and reserve.

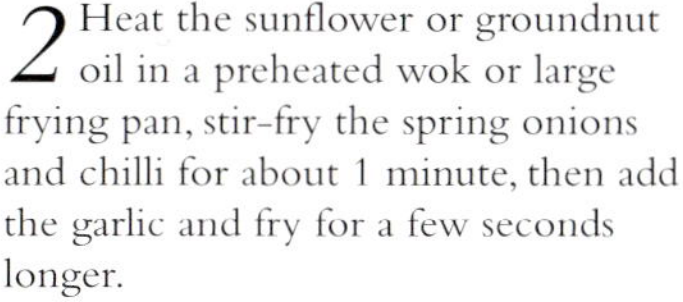

2 Heat the sunflower or groundnut oil in a preheated wok or large frying pan, stir-fry the spring onions and chilli for about 1 minute, then add the garlic and fry for a few seconds longer.

3 Add the potatoes, stirring well, then the beans and finally the soy sauce and sesame oil.

4 Season to taste and cook the vegetables until they are well heated through. Sprinkle with sesame seeds and coriander or parsley and serve.

Chinese Garlic Mushrooms

Tofu is high in protein and very low in fat, so it is an extremely useful and healthy food to keep handy for quick meals and snacks like this one.

INGREDIENTS

Serves 4

8 large open mushrooms
3 spring onions, sliced
1 garlic clove, crushed
30ml/2 tbsp oyster sauce
275g/10oz marinated tofu, cut into small dice
200g/7oz can sweetcorn kernels, drained
10ml/2 tsp sesame oil
salt and ground black pepper

1 Finely chop the mushroom stalks and mix with the spring onions, garlic and oyster sauce.

2 Stir in the diced, marinated tofu and sweetcorn, season well with salt and pepper, then spoon the filling into the mushrooms.

3 Brush the edges of the mushrooms with the sesame oil. Arrange the stuffed mushrooms in a baking dish and bake in a preheated oven at 200°C/400°F/Gas 6 for 12–15 minutes, until the mushrooms are just tender, then serve at once.

COOK'S TIP

If you prefer, omit the oyster sauce and use light soy sauce instead.

Stir-fried Mixed Vegetables

When selecting different items for a stir-fried dish, never mix the ingredients indiscriminately. The idea is to achieve a harmonious balance of colour and texture.

INGREDIENTS

Serves 4
225g/8oz Chinese leaves
115g/4oz baby corn cobs
115g/4oz broccoli
1 medium or 2 small carrots
60ml/4 tbsp vegetable oil
5ml/1 tsp salt
5ml/1 tsp light brown sugar
Basic Stock or water, if necessary
15ml/1 tbsp light soy sauce
few drops of sesame oil (optional)

1 Cut the vegetables into roughly similar shapes and sizes.

2 Heat the oil in a preheated wok and stir-fry the vegetables for about 2 minutes.

3 Add the salt and sugar and a little stock or water, if necessary, and continue stirring for another minute. Add the soy sauce and sesame oil, if using. Blend well and serve.

Chinese Leaves and Mooli with Scallops

A speedy stir-fry made using Chinese cabbage, mooli and scallops. Both the Chinese cabbage and mooli have a pleasant crunchy "bite". You need to work quickly, so have everything prepared before you start cooking.

Ingredients

Serves 4

10 prepared scallops
75ml/5 tbsp vegetable oil
3 garlic cloves, finely chopped
1 cm/½ in fresh root ginger, finely sliced
4–5 spring onions, cut lengthways into 2.5cm/1in pieces
30ml/2 tbsp Chinese rice wine or dry sherry
½ mooli, cut into 1cm/½in slices
1 Chinese cabbage, chopped lengthways into thin strips
60ml/4 tbsp water

For the marinade
5ml/1 tsp cornflour
1 egg white, lightly beaten
pinch of white pepper

For the sauce
5ml/1 tsp cornflour
60ml/4 tbsp water
45ml/3 tbsp oyster sauce

1 Rinse the scallops and separate the corals from the white meat. Cut each scallop into two pieces and slice the corals. Place them on two separate dishes. For the marinade, blend together the cornflour, egg white and white pepper. Pour half over the scallops and the rest over the corals. Set aside for 10 minutes.

2 To make the sauce, blend the cornflour with the water and the oyster sauce and set aside.

3 Heat about 30ml/2 tbsp of the oil in a preheated wok, add half the garlic and let it sizzle, then add half the ginger and half the spring onions. Stir-fry for about 30 seconds, then stir in the scallops (not the corals). Stir-fry for ½–1 minute until the scallops start to become opaque. Reduce the heat and add 15ml/1 tbsp of the rice wine or dry sherry. Cook briefly and then spoon the scallops and the cooking liquid into a bowl and set aside.

4 Heat another 30ml/2 tbsp of the oil in the wok, add the remaining garlic, ginger and spring onions and stir-fry for 1 minute. Add the corals and the remaining rice wine or dry sherry, stir-fry briefly and transfer to a dish.

5 Heat the remaining oil and add the mooli. Stir-fry for about 30 seconds, then stir in the cabbage. Stir-fry for about 30 seconds and add the oyster sauce mixture and the water. Allow the cabbage to simmer briefly. Stir in the scallops and corals, together with all their liquid, and cook briefly to heat through.

Tofu and Green Bean Red Curry

This is another curry that is simple and quick to make. This recipe uses green beans, but you can use almost any kind of vegetable such as aubergines, bamboo shoots or broccoli.

INGREDIENTS

Serves 4–6

600ml/1 pint/2½ cups coconut milk
15ml/1 tbsp red curry paste
45ml/3 tbsp fish sauce
10ml/2 tsp palm sugar
225g/8oz button mushrooms
115g/4oz green beans, trimmed
175g/6oz tofu, rinsed and cut into 2cm/¾in cubes
4 kaffir lime leaves, torn
2 red chillies, sliced
coriander leaves, to garnish

1 Put about one third of the coconut milk in a wok or saucepan. Cook until it starts to separate and an oily sheen appears.

2 Add the red curry paste, fish sauce and sugar to the coconut milk. Mix together thoroughly.

3 Add the mushrooms. Stir and cook for 1 minute.

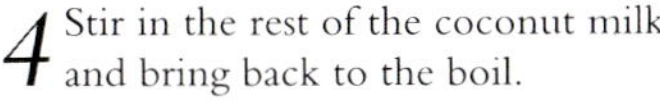

4 Stir in the rest of the coconut milk and bring back to the boil.

5 Add the green beans and cubes of tofu and simmer gently for another 4–5 minutes.

6 Stir in kaffir lime leaves and chillies. Serve garnished with the coriander leaves.

Spiced Tofu Stir-fry

You could add any quickly cooked vegetable to this stir-fry – try mangetouts, sugar snap peas, leeks or thin slices of carrot.

Ingredients

Serves 4

10ml/2 tsp ground cumin
15ml/1 tbsp paprika
5ml/1 tsp ground ginger
good pinch of cayenne pepper
15ml/1 tbsp caster sugar
275g/10oz firm tofu
oil, for frying
2 garlic cloves, crushed
1 bunch spring onions, sliced
1 red pepper, seeded and sliced
1 yellow pepper, seeded and sliced
225g/8oz brown-cap mushrooms, halved or quartered if very large
1 large courgette, sliced
115g/4oz fine green beans, halved
50g/2oz/½ cup pine nuts
15ml/1 tbsp lime juice
15ml/1 tbsp clear honey
salt and ground black pepper

1 Mix together the cumin, paprika, ginger, cayenne and sugar with plenty of seasoning. Cut the tofu into cubes and coat them thoroughly in the spice mixture.

2 Heat some oil in a preheated wok or large frying pan. Cook the tofu over a high heat for 3–4 minutes, turning occasionally. Take care not to break up the tofu too much. Remove with a slotted spoon. Wipe out the wok or pan with kitchen paper.

3 Add a little more oil to the wok or frying pan and stir-fry the garlic and spring onions for 3 minutes. Add the remaining vegetables and stir-fry over a medium heat for 6 minutes, or until beginning to soften and turn golden. Season well.

4 Return the tofu to the pan with the pine nuts, lime juice and honey. Heat through and serve.

Chinese Sprouts

If you are bored with plain boiled Brussels sprouts, try pepping them up with this unusual stir-fried method, which uses the minimum of oil.

INGREDIENTS

Serves 4
450g/1lb Brussels sprouts
5ml/1 tsp sesame or sunflower oil
2 spring onions, sliced
2.5ml/½ tsp Chinese five-spice powder
15ml/1 tbsp light soy sauce

1 Trim the Brussels sprouts, then shred them finely using a large sharp knife or shred in a food processor.

2 Heat the oil in a preheated wok or frying pan and add the sprouts and onions, then stir-fry for 2 minutes, without browning.

3 Stir in the five-spice powder and soy sauce, then cook, stirring, for a further 2–3 minutes, until just tender.

4 Serve hot, with grilled meat or fish or with Chinese dishes.

COOK'S TIP

Brussels sprouts are rich in vitamin C, and this is a good way to cook them to preserve the nutrients. Larger sprouts cook particularly well by this method, and cabbage can be cooked in the same way.

SALADS

There is much more to Asian salads than a few Chinese leaves and a bunch of beansprouts. The superb collection of recipes here includes flamboyant combinations of raw fruit and vegetables, surprisingly refreshing warm salads, startling pairings of sweet and spicy ingredients, dramatic mixtures of crunchy and melt-in-the mouth textures and daring matching of flavours. Try Thai Fruit and Vegetable Salad, Warm Stir-fried Salad, Hot Coconut Prawn and Pawpaw Salad, Sesame Noodle Salad with Hot Peanuts or Duck, Avocado and Raspberry Salad.

Chinese-style Chicken Salad

This delicious salad is a masterpiece of subtle flavours and contrasts in texture.

INGREDIENTS

Serves 4

4 boneless chicken breasts, about 175g/6oz each
60ml/4 tbsp dark soy sauce
pinch of Chinese five-spice powder
good squeeze of lemon juice
½ cucumber, peeled and cut into matchsticks
5ml/1 tsp salt
45ml/3 tbsp sunflower oil
30ml/2 tbsp sesame oil
15ml/1 tbsp sesame seeds
30ml/2 tbsp Chinese rice wine or dry sherry
2 carrots, cut into matchsticks
8 spring onions, shredded
75g/3oz beansprouts

For the sauce

60ml/4 tbsp crunchy peanut butter
10ml/2 tsp lemon juice
10ml/2 tsp sesame oil
1.5ml/¼ tsp hot chilli powder
1 spring onion, finely chopped

1 Put the chicken portions into a large pan and just cover with water. Add 15ml/1 tbsp of the soy sauce, the Chinese five-spice powder and lemon juice, cover and bring to the boil, then simmer for about 20 minutes.

2 Meanwhile, place the cucumber matchsticks in a colander, sprinkle with the salt and cover with a plate with a weight on top. Leave to drain for 30 minutes – set the colander in a bowl to catch the drips.

3 Lift out the poached chicken with a draining spoon and leave until cool enough to handle. Remove and discard the skin. Bang the chicken lightly with a rolling pin to loosen the fibres. Slice into thin strips and reserve.

4 Heat the sunflower and sesame oils in a preheated wok. Add the sesame seeds, fry for 30 seconds and then stir in the remaining soy sauce and the rice wine or dry sherry.

5 Add the carrots and stir-fry for 2–3 minutes, until just tender. Remove from the heat and reserve.

6 Rinse the cucumber well, pat dry with kitchen paper and place in a bowl. Add the spring onions, beansprouts, cooked carrots, pan juices and shredded chicken and mix together. Transfer to a shallow dish. Cover and chill for about 1 hour, turning the mixture in the juices once or twice.

7 To make the sauce, cream the peanut butter with the lemon juice, sesame oil and chilli powder, adding a little hot water to form a paste, then stir in the spring onion. Arrange the chicken mixture on a serving dish and serve with the peanut sauce.

Prawn Noodle Salad with Fragrant Herbs

A light, refreshing salad with all the tangy flavour of the sea. Instead of prawns, try squid, scallops, mussels or crab.

INGREDIENTS

Serves 4

115g/4oz cellophane noodles, soaked in hot water until soft
16 cooked prawns, peeled
1 small green pepper, seeded and cut into strips
½ cucumber, cut into strips
1 tomato, cut into strips
2 shallots, finely sliced
salt and freshly ground black pepper
coriander leaves, to garnish

For the dressing

15ml/1 tbsp rice vinegar
30ml/2 tbsp fish sauce
30ml/2 tbsp fresh lime juice
pinch of salt
2.5ml/½ tsp grated fresh root ginger
1 lemon grass stalk, finely chopped
1 red chilli, seeded and finely sliced
30ml/2 tbsp roughly chopped mint
few sprigs tarragon, roughly chopped
15ml/1 tbsp snipped chives

1 Make the dressing by combining all the ingredients in a small bowl or jug; whisk well.

2 Drain the noodles, then plunge them in a saucepan of boiling water for 1 minute. Drain, rinse under cold running water and drain again well.

3 In a large bowl, combine the noodles with the prawns, pepper, cucumber, tomato and shallots. Lightly season with salt and pepper, then toss with the dressing.

4 Spoon the noodles on to individual plates, arranging the prawns on top. Garnish with a few coriander leaves and serve at once.

COOK'S TIP

Prawns are available ready-cooked and often shelled. To cook prawns, boil them for 5 minutes. Leave them to cool in the cooking liquid, then gently pull off the tail shell and twist off the head.

Warm Stir-fried Salad

Warm salads are becoming increasingly popular because they are delicious and nutritious. Arrange the salad leaves on four individual plates, so the hot stir-fry can be served quickly on to them, ensuring the lettuce remains crisp and the chicken warm.

INGREDIENTS

Serves 4

few large sprigs of fresh tarragon
2 boneless chicken breasts, about 225g/8oz each, skinned
5cm/2in root ginger, peeled and finely chopped
45ml/3 tbsp light soy sauce
15ml/1 tbsp sugar
15ml/1 tbsp sunflower oil
1 Chinese lettuce
½ frisée lettuce, torn into bite-sized pieces
115g/4oz/1 cup unsalted cashew nuts
2 large carrots, cut into fine strips
salt and ground black pepper

1 Strip the tarragon leaves from the stems and chop the leaves.

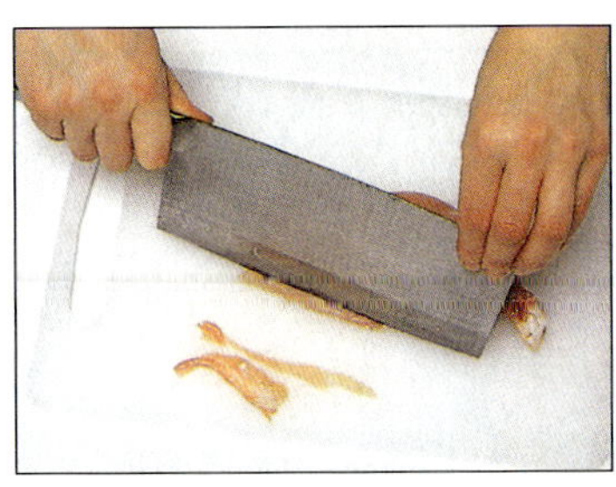

2 Cut the chicken into fine strips and place in a bowl.

3 To make the marinade, mix together in a bowl the tarragon, ginger, soy sauce, sugar and seasoning.

4 Pour the marinade over the chicken strips and leave for 2–4 hours in a cool place.

5 Strain the chicken and reserve the marinade. Heat the oil in a preheated wok. When the oil is hot, stir-fry the chicken for 3 minutes, add the marinade and allow to bubble for 2–3 minutes.

6 Slice the Chinese lettuce and arrange on a plate with the frisée. Toss the cashews and carrots together with the chicken, pile on top of the bed of lettuce and serve immediately.

Thai Beef Salad

A hearty salad of beef, laced with a chilli and lime dressing.

INGREDIENTS

Serves 4

2 x 225g/8oz sirloin steaks
1 red onion, finely sliced
½ cucumber, finely sliced into matchsticks
1 stalk lemon grass, finely chopped
juice of 2 limes
15–30ml/1–2 tbsp fish sauce
30ml/2 tbsp chopped spring onions
2–4 red chillies, finely sliced, to garnish
fresh coriander, Chinese mustard cress and mint leaves, to garnish

1 Pan-fry or grill the beef steaks to medium-rare. Allow to rest for 10–15 minutes.

2 When cool, thinly slice the beef and put the slices in a large bowl.

3 Add the sliced onion, cucumber matchsticks and lemon grass.

4 Add the spring onions. Toss and season with lime juice and fish sauce. Serve at room temperature or chilled, garnished with the chillies, coriander, mustard cress and mint.

Tangy Chicken Salad

This fresh and lively dish typifies the character of Thai cuisine. It is ideal for a starter or light lunch.

INGREDIENTS

Serves 4–6

4 skinned, boneless chicken breasts
2 garlic cloves, crushed and roughly chopped
30ml/2 tbsp soy sauce
30ml/2 tbsp vegetable oil
120ml/4fl oz/½ cup coconut cream
30ml/2 tbsp fish sauce
juice of 1 lime
30ml/2 tbsp palm sugar
115g/4oz water chestnuts, sliced
50g/2oz cashew nuts, roasted
4 shallots, finely sliced
4 kaffir lime leaves, finely sliced
1 stalk lemon grass, finely sliced
5ml/1 tsp chopped galangal
1 large red chilli, seeded and finely sliced
2 spring onions, finely sliced
10–12 mint leaves, torn
1 head of lettuce, to serve
sprigs of coriander, to garnish
2 red chillies, seeded and sliced, to garnish

1 Trim the chicken breasts of any excess fat and put them in a large dish. Rub with the garlic, soy sauce and 15ml/1 tbsp of the oil. Leave to marinate for 1–2 hours.

2 Grill or pan-fry the chicken for 3–4 minutes on both sides or until cooked. Remove and set aside to cool.

3 In a small saucepan, heat the coconut cream, fish sauce, lime juice and palm sugar. Stir until all of the sugar has dissolved and then remove from the heat.

4 Cut the cooked chicken into strips and combine with the water chestnuts, cashew nuts, shallots, kaffir lime leaves, lemon grass, galangal, red chilli, spring onions and mint leaves.

5 Pour the coconut dressing over the chicken, toss and mix well. Serve the chicken on a bed of lettuce leaves and garnish with sprigs of coriander and sliced red chillies.

Noodles with Pineapple, Ginger and Chillies

INGREDIENTS

Serves 4

275g/10oz dried udon noodles
½ pineapple, peeled, cored and sliced into 4cm/1½in rings
45ml/3 tbsp soft light brown sugar
60ml/4 tbsp fresh lime juice
60ml/4 tbsp coconut milk
30ml/2 tbsp fish sauce
30ml/2 tbsp grated fresh root ginger
2 garlic cloves, finely chopped
1 ripe mango or 2 peaches, finely diced
freshly ground black pepper
2 spring onions, finely sliced, 2 red chillies, seeded and finely shredded, plus mint leaves, to garnish

1 Cook the noodles in a large saucepan of boiling water until tender, following the directions on the packet. Drain, refresh under cold water and drain again.

2 Place the pineapple rings on a flameproof dish, sprinkle with 30ml/2 tbsp of the sugar and grill for about 5 minutes or until golden. Cool slightly and cut into small dice.

3 Mix the lime juice, coconut milk and fish sauce in a salad bowl. Add the remaining brown sugar, with the ginger and garlic, and whisk well. Add the noodles and pineapple.

4 Add the mango or peaches and toss. Scatter over the spring onions, chillies and mint leaves before serving.

Buckwheat Noodles with Smoked Salmon

Young pea sprouts are only available for a short time. You can substitute watercress, mustard cress, young leeks or your favourite green vegetable or herb in this dish.

INGREDIENTS

Serves 4

225g/8oz buckwheat or soba noodles
15ml/1 tbsp oyster sauce
juice of ½ lemon
30–45ml/2–3 tbsp light olive oil
115g/4oz smoked salmon, cut into fine strips
115g/4oz young pea sprouts
2 ripe tomatoes, peeled, seeded and cut into strips
15ml/1 tbsp snipped chives
salt and freshly ground black pepper

1 Cook the buckwheat or soba noodles in a large saucepan of boiling water, following the directions on the packet. Drain, then rinse under cold running water and drain well.

2 Tip the noodles into a large bowl. Add the oyster sauce and lemon juice and season with pepper to taste. Moisten with the olive oil.

3 Add the smoked salmon, pea sprouts, tomatoes and chives. Mix well and serve at once.

Sesame Duck and Noodle Salad

This salad is complete in itself and makes a lovely summer lunch. The marinade is a marvellous blend of spices.

INGREDIENTS

Serves 4

2 duck breasts
15ml/1 tbsp vegetable oil
150g/5oz sugar snap peas
2 carrots, cut into 7.5cm/3in sticks
225g/8oz medium egg noodles
6 spring onions, sliced
salt
fresh coriander leaves, to garnish

For the marinade

15ml/1 tbsp sesame oil
5ml/1 tsp ground coriander
5ml/1 tsp Chinese five-spice powder

For the dressing

15ml/1 tbsp garlic vinegar
5ml/1 tsp soft light brown sugar
5ml/1 tsp soy sauce
15ml/1 tbsp toasted sesame seeds
45ml/3 tbsp sunflower oil
30ml/2 tbsp sesame oil
ground black pepper

1 Slice the duck breasts thinly across and place them in a shallow dish. Mix all the ingredients for the marinade, pour over the duck and mix well to coat thoroughly. Cover and leave in a cool place for 30 minutes.

2 Heat the oil in a preheated wok or frying pan, add the slices of duck breast and stir-fry for 3–4 minutes until cooked. Set aside.

3 Bring a saucepan of lightly salted water to the boil. Place the sugar snap peas and carrots in a steamer that will fit on top of the pan. When the water boils, add the noodles, place the steamer on top and steam the vegetables while cooking the noodles for the time suggested on the packet. Set the steamed vegetables aside. Drain the noodles, refresh them under cold running water and drain again. Place them in a large serving bowl.

4 Make the dressing. Mix the vinegar, sugar, soy sauce and sesame seeds in a bowl. Season well with black pepper, then whisk in the sunflower and sesame oils.

5 Pour the dressing over the noodles and mix well. Add the sugar snap peas, carrots, spring onions and duck slices and toss to mix. Scatter over the coriander leaves and serve.

Duck, Avocado and Raspberry Salad

Rich duck breasts are roasted until crisp with a honey and soy glaze to serve warm with fresh raspberries and avocado. A delicious raspberry and redcurrant dressing adds a wonderful sweet-and-sour flavour.

INGREDIENTS

Serves 4

4 small or 2 large duck breasts, halved if large
15ml/1 tbsp clear honey
15ml/1 tbsp dark soy sauce
60ml/4 tbsp olive oil
15ml/1 tbsp raspberry vinegar
15ml/1 tbsp redcurrant jelly
selection of salad leaves, such as lamb's lettuce, red chicory and frisée
2 avocados, stoned, peeled and cut into chunks
115g/4oz raspberries
salt and ground black pepper

1 Prick the skin of each duck breast with a fork. Blend the honey and soy sauce together in a small bowl, then brush all over the skin.

2 Place the duck breasts on a rack set over a roasting tin and season with salt and pepper. Roast in a preheated oven at 220°C/425°F/Gas 7 for 15–20 minutes, until the skin is crisp and the meat is cooked.

3 Meanwhile, to make the dressing, put the oil, vinegar, redcurrant jelly and seasoning in a small bowl and whisk well until evenly blended.

4 Slice the duck breasts diagonally and arrange on individual plates with the salad leaves, avocados and raspberries. Spoon over the dressing and serve immediately.

Spicy Szechuan Noodles

INGREDIENTS

Serves 4
350g/12oz thick noodles
175g/6oz cooked chicken, shredded
50g/2oz roasted cashew nuts

For the dressing
4 spring onions, chopped
30ml/2 tbsp chopped coriander
2 garlic cloves, chopped
30ml/2 tbsp smooth peanut butter
30ml/2 tbsp sweet chilli sauce
15ml/1 tbsp soy sauce
15ml/1 tbsp sherry vinegar
15ml/1 tbsp sesame oil
30ml/2 tbsp olive oil
30ml/2 tbsp chicken stock or water
10 toasted Szechuan peppercorns, ground

1 Cook the noodles in a saucepan of boiling water until just tender, following the directions on the packet. Drain, rinse under cold running water and drain well.

2 While the noodles are cooking combine all the ingredients for the dressing in a large bowl and whisk together well.

3 Add the noodles, shredded chicken and cashew nuts to the dressing, toss gently to coat and adjust the seasoning to taste. Serve at once.

COOK'S TIP

You could substitute cooked turkey or pork for the chicken for a change.

Sesame Noodles with Spring Onions

This simple but very tasty warm salad can be prepared and cooked in just a few minutes.

INGREDIENTS

Serves 4
2 garlic cloves, roughly chopped
30ml/2 tbsp Chinese sesame paste
15ml/1 tbsp dark sesame oil
30ml/2 tbsp soy sauce
30ml/2 tbsp rice wine
15ml/1 tbsp honey
pinch of five-spice powder
350g/12oz soba or buckwheat noodles
4 spring onions, finely sliced diagonally
50g/2oz beansprouts
7.5cm/3in piece of cucumber, cut into matchsticks
toasted sesame seeds
salt and freshly ground black pepper

1 Process the garlic, sesame paste, oil, soy sauce, rice wine, honey and five-spice powder with a pinch each of salt and pepper in a blender or food processor until smooth.

2 Cook the noodles in a saucepan of boiling water until just tender, following the directions on the packet. Drain the noodles immediately and tip them into a bowl.

3 Toss the hot noodles with the dressing and the spring onions. Top with the beansprouts, cucumber and sesame seeds and serve.

COOK'S TIP

If you can't find Chinese sesame paste, then use either tahini paste or smooth peanut butter instead.

Sweet-and-sour Fruit and Vegetable Salad

Acar bening makes a perfect accompaniment to many spicy dishes, with its clean taste and bright, jewel-like colours. Any leftover salad can be covered and stored in the refrigerator for up to two days. This is an ideal dish for buffets.

INGREDIENTS

Serves 8

1 small cucumber
1 onion
1 small ripe pineapple or 425g/15oz can pineapple rings
1 green pepper, seeded and thinly sliced
3 firm tomatoes, cut into wedges
25g/1oz golden granulated sugar
45–60ml/3–4 tbsp cider vinegar or white wine vinegar
120ml/4fl oz/½ cup water
salt

1 Peel the cucumber and cut in half lengthways. Remove the seeds with a small spoon. Cut the cucumber into even-sized pieces. Sprinkle with a little salt. Thinly slice the onion and sprinkle that also with a little salt. Leave both vegetables for a few minutes, then rinse and pat dry, and mix them together in a bowl.

2 Peel the fresh pineapple, if using, removing all the "eyes". Slice the pineapple thinly, then core the slices and cut in neat pieces. If using canned pineapple, cut the rings into similarly sized pieces. Add them to the bowl, together with the green pepper and tomato wedges.

3 Heat the sugar, vinegar and water until the sugar dissolves. Remove from the heat and leave to cool. When cool, add salt to taste and then pour over the fruit and vegetables. Cover and chill until required.

Rice Vermicelli and Salad Rolls

Goi Cuor is a hearty noodle salad wrapped in rice sheets: it makes a healthy change from a sandwich and is great for a picnic.

INGREDIENTS

Makes 8

50g/2oz rice vermicelli, soaked in warm water until soft
1 large carrot, shredded
15ml/1 tbsp sugar
15–30ml/1–2 tbsp fish sauce
8 x 20cm/8in round rice sheets
8 large lettuce leaves, thick stalks removed
350g/12oz roast pork, sliced
115g/4oz beansprouts
handful of mint leaves
8 cooked king prawns, peeled, deveined and halved
½ cucumber, cut into fine strips
coriander leaves, to garnish

For the peanut sauce
15ml/1 tbsp vegetable oil
3 garlic cloves, finely chopped
1–2 red chillies, finely chopped
5ml/1 tsp tomato purée
120ml/4fl oz/½ cup water
15ml/1 tbsp smooth peanut butter
30ml/2 tbsp hoisin sauce
2.5ml/½ tsp sugar
juice of 1 lime
50g/2oz roasted peanuts, ground

1 Drain the noodles. Cook in a saucepan of boiling water for about 2–3 minutes until tender. Drain, rinse under cold running water, drain well. Tip into a bowl. Add the carrot and season with the sugar and fish sauce.

2 Assemble the rolls, one at a time. Dip a rice sheet in a bowl of warm water, then lay it flat on a surface. Place 1 lettuce leaf, 1–2 scoops of the noodle mixture, a few slices of pork, some of the beansprouts and several mint leaves on the rice sheet.

3 Start rolling up the rice sheet into a cylinder. When half the sheet has been rolled up, fold both sides of the sheet towards the centre and lay 2 pieces of prawn along the crease.

4 Add a few of strips of cucumber and some of the coriander leaves. Continue to roll up the sheet to make a tight packet. Place the roll on a plate and cover with a damp dish towel, so that it will stay moist while you make the remaining rolls.

5 Make the peanut sauce. Heat the oil in a small saucepan and fry the garlic, chillies and tomato purée for about 1 minute. Add the water and bring to the boil, then stir in the peanut butter, hoisin sauce, sugar and lime juice. Mix well. Reduce the heat and simmer for 3–4 minutes. Spoon the sauce into a bowl, add the ground peanuts and cool to room temperature.

6 To serve, cut each roll in half. Add a spoonful of the peanut sauce.

Fruit and Raw Vegetable Gado-gado

A banana leaf, which can be bought from oriental stores, can be used to line the platter for a special occasion.

INGREDIENTS

Serves 6

2 unripe pears, peeled at the last moment, or 175g/6oz wedge *bangkuang* (yambean), peeled and cut in matchsticks
1–2 eating apples
juice of ½ lemon
1 small, crisp lettuce, shredded
½ cucumber, seeded, sliced and salted, set aside for 15 minutes, then rinsed and drained
6 small tomatoes, cut in wedges
3 slices fresh pineapple, cored and cut in wedges
3 eggs or 12 quail's eggs, hard-boiled and shelled
175g/6oz egg noodles, cooked, cooled and chopped
deep-fried onions, to garnish

For the peanut sauce
2–4 fresh red chillies, seeded and ground
300ml/½ pint/1¼ cups coconut milk
350g/12oz crunchy peanut butter
15ml/1 tbsp dark soy sauce or dark brown sugar
5ml/1 tsp tamarind pulp, soaked in 45ml/3 tbsp warm water, strained and juice reserved
coarsely crushed peanuts
salt

1 To make the Peanut Sauce, put the chillies and coconut milk in a pan. Add the peanut butter and heat gently, stirring, until no lumps of peanut butter remain.

2 Allow to simmer gently until the sauce thickens, then add the soy sauce or sugar and tamarind juice. Season with salt to taste. Pour into a bowl and sprinkle with a few coarsely crushed peanuts.

3 To make the salad, peel and core the pears or *bangkuang* and apples. Slice the apples and sprinkle with lemon juice. Arrange the salad and fruit attractively on a flat platter. The lettuce can be used, instead of a banana leaf, to form a bed for the salad.

4 Add the sliced or quartered hard-boiled eggs (leave quail's eggs whole), the chopped noodles and the deep-fried onions.

5 Serve at once, accompanied with a bowl of the Peanut Sauce.

Sesame Noodle Salad with Hot Peanuts

An Eastern-inspired salad with crunchy vegetables and a light soy dressing. The hot peanuts make a surprisingly successful union with the cold noodles.

INGREDIENTS

Serves 4

350g/12oz egg noodles
2 carrots, cut into fine julienne strips
½ cucumber, peeled, seeded and cut into 1cm/½in cubes
115g/4oz celeriac, peeled and cut into fine julienne strips
6 spring onions, finely sliced
8 canned water chestnuts, drained and finely sliced
175g/6oz beansprouts
1 small fresh green chilli, seeded and finely chopped
30ml/2 tbsp sesame seeds and 115g/4oz/1 cup peanuts, to serve

For the dressing

15ml/1 tbsp dark soy sauce
15ml/1 tbsp light soy sauce
15ml/1 tbsp clear honey
15ml/1 tbsp Chinese rice wine or dry sherry
15ml/1 tbsp sesame oil

1 Cook the egg noodles in boiling water, following the instructions on the packet.

2 Drain the noodles, refresh in cold water, then drain again. Mix the noodles together with all of the prepared vegetables.

3 Combine the dressing ingredients in a small bowl, then toss into the noodle and vegetable mixture. Divide the salad between 4 plates.

4 Place the sesame seeds and peanuts on separate baking trays and place in a preheated oven at 200°C/400°F/Gas 6. Take the sesame seeds out after 5 minutes and continue to cook the peanuts for a further 5 minutes until evenly browned.

5 Sprinkle the sesame seeds and peanuts evenly over each portion and serve at once.

Thai Fruit and Vegetable Salad

This fruit salad is typically presented with the main course and serves as a cooler to counteract the heat of Thai curry.

INGREDIENTS

Serves 4–6

1 small pineapple
1 small mango, peeled, stoned and sliced
1 green apple, cored and sliced
6 ramboutans or lychees, peeled and stoned
115g/4oz French beans, halved
1 medium red onion, sliced
1 small cucumber, cut into short sticks
115g/4oz beansprouts
2 spring onions, sliced
1 ripe tomato, quartered
225g/8oz cos, Bibb or iceberg lettuce leaves, torn into pieces
salt

For the coconut dipping sauce

90ml/6 tbsp coconut cream
30ml/2 tbsp sugar
75ml/5 tbsp boiling water
1.5ml/¼ tsp chilli sauce
15ml/1 tbsp fish sauce
juice of 1 lime

1 To make the dipping sauce, place the coconut cream, sugar and boiling water in a screw-top jar. Add the chilli sauce, fish sauce and lime juice and shake to mix. Set aside.

2 Trim both ends of the pineapple with a serrated knife, then cut away the skin. Remove the central core with an apple corer, or cut the pineapple into four down the middle and remove the core with a knife. Roughly chop the pineapple and set aside with the other fruits.

3 Bring a small saucepan of lightly salted water to the boil and cook the beans for 3–4 minutes. Refresh under cold running water and set aside. To serve, arrange the fruits, vegetables and lettuce leaves in individual heaps in a serving bowl. Serve the dipping sauce separately.

COOK'S TIP

The ramboutan or rambutan, cousin to the lychee, originated in Malaysia, but is now cultivated in much of South-east Asia and the USA. It has a dark reddish-brown, hairy skin with sweet, translucent flesh and an inedible stone. It is about 5cm/2in in diameter.

Bamboo Shoot Salad

This salad, which has a hot and sharp flavour, originated in north-east Thailand. Use fresh young bamboo shoots when you can find them, otherwise substitute canned bamboo shoots.

INGREDIENTS

Serves 4

400g/14oz can whole bamboo shoots
25g/1oz glutinous rice
30ml/2 tbsp chopped shallots
15ml/1 tbsp chopped garlic
45ml/3 tbsp chopped spring onions
30ml/2 tbsp fish sauce
30ml/2 tbsp lime juice
5ml/1 tsp granulated sugar
2.5ml/½ tsp dried flaked chillies
20–25 small mint leaves
15ml/1 tbsp toasted sesame seeds

1 Rinse and drain the bamboo shoots, finely slice and set aside.

2 Dry roast the rice in a frying pan until it is golden brown. Remove and grind to fine crumbs with a pestle and mortar.

3 Tip the rice into a bowl, add the shallots, garlic, spring onions, fish sauce, lime juice, granulated sugar, chillies and half the mint leaves.

4 Mix thoroughly, then pour over the bamboo shoots and toss together. Serve sprinkled with sesame seeds and the remaining mint leaves.

Egg Pancake Salad Wrappers

One of Indonesia's favourite snack foods, pancakes are assembled according to taste and dipped in various sauces.

INGREDIENTS

Makes 12

2 eggs
2.5ml/½ tsp salt
5ml/1 tsp vegetable oil, plus extra for frying
115g/4oz/1 cup flour
300ml/½ pint/1¼ cups water
lettuce leaves, shredded, beansprouts, cucumber wedges, spring onions, shredded, cooked peeled prawns and coriander sprigs, to serve

For the filling

45ml/3 tbsp vegetable oil
1cm/½in fresh root ginger, chopped
1 garlic clove, crushed
1 small red fresh chilli, seeded and finely chopped
15ml/1 tbsp rice vinegar or white wine vinegar
10ml/2 tsp sugar
115g/4oz mooli, grated
1 medium carrot, grated
115g/4oz Chinese leaves, shredded
2 shallots or 1 small red onion, thinly sliced

1 Break the eggs into a bowl and stir in the salt, vegetable oil and flour until smooth; do not over-mix. Add the water, a little at a time, and strain into a jug. Allow the batter to stand for 15–20 minutes before use.

2 Moisten a small, non-stick frying pan with vegetable oil and heat. Pour in enough batter just to cover the base of the pan and cook for 30 seconds. Turn over and cook the other side briefly. Stack the pancakes on a plate, cover and keep warm.

3 Make the filling. Heat the oil in a preheated wok and add the ginger, garlic and chilli and stir-fry for 1–2 minutes. Add the vinegar, sugar, mooli, carrot, Chinese leaves or cabbage and shallots or onion. Cook for 3–4 minutes. Serve with the pancakes, prawns and salad ingredients.

Green Vegetable Salad with Coconut Mint Dip

This dish is usually served as an accompaniment to Singapore and Malaysian meat dishes.

INGREDIENTS

Serves 4–6

115g/4oz mangetouts, halved
115g/4oz French beans, halved
½ cucumber, peeled, halved and sliced
115g/4oz Chinese leaves, roughly shredded
115g/4oz beansprouts
salt
lettuce leaves, to serve

For the dressing

1 garlic clove, crushed
1 small fresh green chilli, seeded and finely chopped
10ml/2 tsp sugar
45ml/3 tbsp creamed coconut
75ml/5 tbsp boiling water
10ml/2 tsp fish sauce
45ml/3 tbsp vegetable oil
juice of 1 lime
30ml/2 tbsp chopped fresh mint

1 Bring a saucepan of lightly salted water to the boil. Blanch the mangetouts, French beans and cucumber for 4 minutes. Drain and refresh under cold running water. Drain and set aside.

2 To make the dressing, pound the garlic, chilli and sugar together in a mortar with a pestle. Add the creamed coconut, water, fish sauce, vegetable oil, lime juice and mint. Stir well.

3 Arrange the blanched vegetables, Chinese leaves and beansprouts on a bed of lettuce in a basket, pour the dressing into a shallow bowl and serve.

Hot Coconut Prawn and Pawpaw Salad

This Thai dish may be served as an accompaniment to beef and chicken dishes or on its own as a light lunch in the summer.

INGREDIENTS

Serves 4–6

225g/8oz raw or cooked prawn tails, peeled and deveined
2 ripe pawpaws
225g/8oz mixed salad leaves, such as Cos, Iceberg or Bib lettuce, Chinese leaves or young spinach
1 firm tomato, seeded and roughly chopped
3 spring onions, shredded

For the dressing

15ml/1 tbsp creamed coconut
30ml/2 tbsp boiling water
90ml/6 tbsp vegetable oil
juice of 1 lime
2.5ml/½ tsp hot chilli sauce
10ml/2 tsp fish sauce (optional)
5ml/1 tsp sugar
1 small bunch fresh coriander, shredded, and 1 large, fresh chilli, sliced, to garnish

1 First make the dressing: place the creamed coconut in a screw-top jar and add the boiling water. Add the vegetable oil, lime juice, chilli sauce, fish sauce, if using, and sugar. Shake well and set aside, but do not refrigerate.

2 If using raw prawns, place them in a saucepan and cover with water. Bring to the boil and simmer for 2 minutes. Drain and set aside.

3 To prepare the pawpaws, cut each in half from top to bottom and remove the black seeds with a teaspoon. Peel away the outer skin and cut the flesh into even-sized pieces. Wash the salad leaves and toss in a bowl. Add the other ingredients, pour over the dressing and serve.

Aubergine Salad with Dried Shrimps and Egg

An appetizing and unusual salad that you will find yourself making over and over again.

INGREDIENTS

Serves 4–6
2 aubergines
15ml/1 tbsp oil
30ml/2 tbsp dried shrimps, soaked and drained
15ml/1 tbsp coarsely chopped garlic
30ml/2 tbsp freshly squeezed lime juice
5ml/1 tsp palm sugar
30ml/2 tbsp fish sauce
1 hard-boiled egg, shelled and chopped
4 shallots, finely sliced into rings
coriander leaves, to garnish
2 red chillies, seeded and sliced, to garnish

COOK'S TIP

For an interesting variation, try using salted duck's or quail's eggs, cut in half, instead of chopped chicken's eggs.

1 Grill or roast the aubergines until charred and tender.

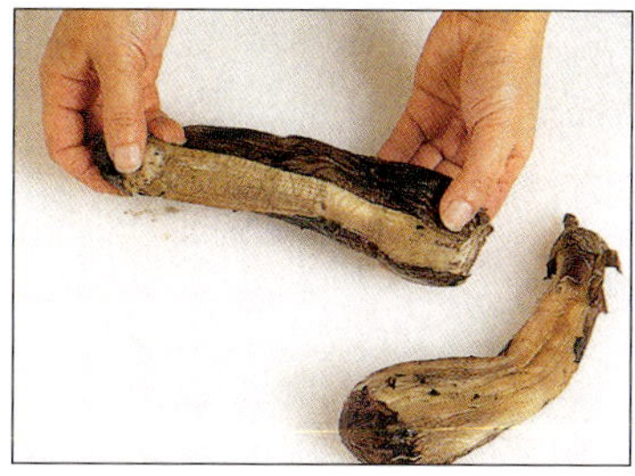

2 When cool enough to handle, peel away the skin and slice the flesh.

3 Heat the oil in a small frying pan, add the drained shrimps and garlic and fry until golden. Remove from the pan and set aside.

4 To make the dressing, put the lime juice, palm sugar and fish sauce in a small bowl and whisk together.

5 To serve, arrange the aubergine on a serving dish. Top with the egg, shallots and dried shrimp mixture. Drizzle over the dressing and garnish with coriander and red chillies.

NOODLES

Noodles are the original "fast food" throughout Asia and are eaten on almost every possible occasion, from weddings to funerals. There are numerous varieties and they are served both hot and cold, cooked in combination with vegetables, meat, poultry and seafood. They can be braised, deep-fried and stir-fried, as well as made into nests and cakes. Noodles may be served as a complete meal or as a side dish. Recipes here include Singapore Noodles, Seafood Chow Mein, Special Fried Noodles and Crisp Pork Meatballs Laced with Noodles.

Oriental Vegetable Noodles

Thin Italian egg pasta is a good alternative to oriental egg noodles; use it fresh or dried.

INGREDIENTS

Serves 6
500g/1¼lb thin tagliarini
1 red onion
115g/4oz shiitake mushrooms
45ml/3 tbsp sesame oil
45ml/3 tbsp dark soy sauce
15ml/1 tbsp balsamic vinegar
10ml/2 tsp caster sugar
salt
celery leaves, to garnish

1 Cook the tagliarini in a large pan of salted boiling water, following the instructions on the pack.

2 Thinly slice the red onion and the mushrooms, using a sharp knife.

3 Heat 15ml/1 tbsp of the sesame oil in a preheated wok. When the oil is hot, stir-fry the onion and mushrooms for 2 minutes.

4 Drain the tagliarini, then add to the wok with the soy sauce, balsamic vinegar, sugar and salt to taste. Stir-fry for 1 minute, then add the remaining sesame oil, and serve garnished with celery leaves.

Lettuce Wraps with Sesame Noodles

INGREDIENTS

Serves 4
15ml/1 tbsp vegetable oil
2 duck breasts, about 225g/8oz each, trimmed
60ml/4 tbsp saké
60ml/4 tbsp soy sauce
30ml/2 tbsp mirin
15ml/1 tbsp sugar
½ cucumber, halved, seeded and finely diced
30ml/2 tbsp chopped red onion
2 red chillies, seeded and finely chopped
30ml/2 tbsp rice vinegar
115g/4oz rice vermicelli, soaked in warm water until soft
15ml/1 tbsp dark sesame oil
15ml/1 tbsp black sesame seeds, toasted
handful of coriander leaves
12–16 large green or red lettuce leaves
handful of mint leaves
salt and freshly ground black pepper

1 Heat the oil in a large frying pan, add the duck breasts, skin side down and fry until golden. Turn each breast and fry the other side briefly. Remove the duck, rinse under hot water to remove excess oil, then drain.

2 Combine the saké, soy sauce, mirin and sugar in saucepan large enough to hold both duck breasts in a single layer. Bring to the boil, add the duck, skin side down, lower the heat and simmer for 3–5 minutes, depending on the thickness of the duck. Remove the pan from the heat and allow the duck to cool in the liquid.

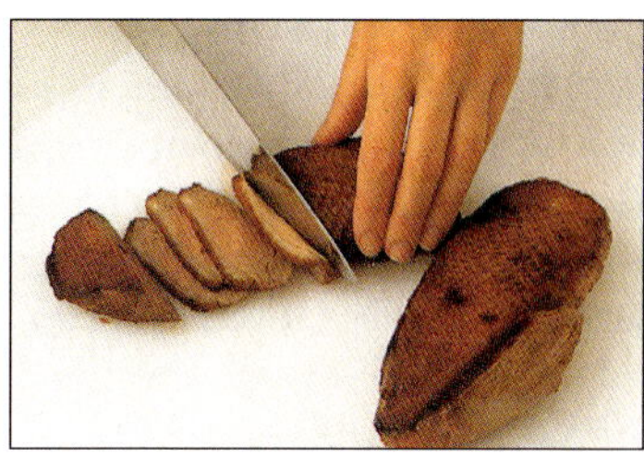

3 Using a slotted spoon, transfer the duck to a board then slice thinly using a large sharp knife. Return the pan to a low heat and cook the sauce until it reduces and thickens slightly.

4 In a serving bowl, mix the diced cucumber with the red onion, chillies and rice vinegar. Set aside.

5 Cook the noodles in a saucepan of boiling water for about 3 minutes or until tender. Drain and rinse under cold running water. Drain again, then tip into a serving bowl and toss lightly with the sesame oil and seeds. Season with salt and pepper.

6 Place the thickened sauce and coriander leaves in separate serving bowls, alongside the bowls of noodles and the cucumber mixture. Arrange the lettuce leaves and sliced duck on individual serving plates.

7 To serve, place a few slices of duck, some noodles, cucumber, herbs and sauce inside a lettuce leaf, wrap and eat.

Soft Fried Noodles

This is a very basic dish for serving as an accompaniment or for those occasions when you are feeling a little peckish and fancy something simple. Break an egg into the noodles if you want to add protein. They are also good tossed with oyster sauce and a dollop of chilli black bean sauce.

Ingredients

Serves 4–6
350g/12oz dried egg noodles
30ml/2 tbsp vegetable oil
30ml/2 tbsp finely chopped spring onions
soy sauce, to taste
salt and freshly ground black pepper

1 Cook the noodles in a large saucepan of boiling water until just tender, following the directions on the packet. Drain, rinse under cold running water and drain again thoroughly.

2 Heat the oil in a wok and swirl it around. Add the spring onions and fry for 30 seconds. Add the noodles, stirring gently to separate the strands.

3 Reduce the heat and fry the noodles until they are heated through, lightly browned and crisp on the outside, but still soft inside.

4 Season with soy sauce, salt and pepper. Serve at once.

Egg Fried Noodles

Yellow bean sauce gives these noodles a savoury flavour.

Ingredients

Serves 4–6
350g/12oz medium-thick egg noodles
60ml/4 tbsp vegetable oil
4 spring onions, cut into 1 cm/½ in rounds
juice of 1 lime
15ml/1 tbsp soy sauce
2 garlic cloves, finely chopped
175g/6oz skinless, boneless chicken breast, sliced
175g/6oz raw prawns, peeled and deveined
175g/6oz squid, cleaned and cut into rings (see page 21)
15ml/1 tbsp yellow bean sauce
15ml/1 tbsp fish sauce
15ml/1 tbsp soft light brown sugar
2 eggs
coriander leaves, to garnish

1 Cook the noodles in a saucepan of boiling water until just tender, then drain well and set aside.

2 Heat half the oil in a wok or large frying pan. Add the spring onions, stir-fry for 2 minutes, then add the noodles, lime juice and soy sauce and stir-fry for 2–3 minutes. Transfer the mixture to a bowl and keep warm.

3 Heat the remaining oil in the wok or pan. Add the garlic, chicken, prawns and squid. Stir-fry over a high heat until cooked.

4 Stir in the yellow bean paste, fish sauce and sugar, then break the eggs into the mixture, stirring gently until they set.

5 Add the noodles, toss lightly to mix, and heat through. Serve garnished with coriander leaves.

Peanut Noodles

Add any of your favourite vegetables to this recipe to make a great, quick mid-week supper – and increase the chilli, if you can take the heat!

INGREDIENTS

Serves 4
200g/7oz medium egg noodles
30ml/2 tbsp olive oil
2 garlic cloves, crushed
1 large onion, roughly chopped
1 red pepper, seeded and roughly chopped
1 yellow pepper, seeded and roughly chopped
350g/12oz courgettes, roughly chopped
150g/5oz/1¼ cups roasted unsalted peanuts, roughly chopped

For the dressing
50ml/2 fl oz/¼ cup olive oil
grated rind and juice of 1 lemon
1 fresh red chilli, seeded and finely chopped
60ml/4 tbsp chopped fresh chives
15–30ml/1–2 tbsp balsamic vinegar
salt and ground black pepper

1 Soak the noodles according to the packet instructions and drain well.

2 Meanwhile, heat the oil in a preheated wok or very large frying pan and cook the garlic and onion for 3 minutes, or until beginning to soften. Add the peppers and courgettes and cook for a further 15 minutes over a medium heat until beginning to soften and brown. Add the peanuts and cook for a further 1 minute.

3 For the dressing, whisk together the olive oil, grated lemon rind and 45ml/3 tbsp lemon juice, the chilli, 45ml/3 tbsp of the chives, plenty of seasoning and balsamic vinegar to taste.

4 Toss the noodles into the vegetables and stir-fry to heat through. Add the dressing, stir to coat and serve immediately, garnished with the remaining chopped fresh chives.

Singapore Noodles

Dried Chinese mushrooms add an intense flavour to this lightly curried dish.

INGREDIENTS

Serves 4

20g/¾oz dried Chinese mushrooms
225g/8oz fine egg noodles
10ml/2 tsp sesame oil
45ml/3 tbsp groundnut oil
2 garlic cloves, crushed
1 small onion, chopped
1 fresh green chilli, seeded and thinly sliced
10ml/2 tsp curry powder
115g/4oz green beans, halved
115g/4oz Chinese leaves, thinly shredded
4 spring onions, sliced
30ml/2 tbsp soy sauce
115g/4oz cooked prawns, peeled and deveined
salt

1 Place the mushrooms in a bowl. cover with warm water and soak for 30 minutes. Drain, reserving 30ml/2 tbsp of the soaking water, then slice.

2 Bring a saucepan of lightly salted water to the boil and cook the noodles according to the directions on the packet. Drain, tip into a bowl and toss with the sesame oil.

3 Heat the groundnut oil in a preheated wok. When it is hot, stir-fry the garlic, onion and chilli for 3 minutes. Stir in the curry powder and cook for 1 minute. Add the mushrooms, green beans, Chinese leaves and spring onions. Stir-fry for 3–4 minutes until the vegetables are tender, but still crisp.

4 Add the noodles, soy sauce, reserved mushroom soaking water and prawns. Toss over the heat for 2–3 minutes until the noodles and prawns are heated through.

COOK'S TIP

Ring the changes with the vegetables used in this dish. Try mangetouts, broccoli, peppers or baby corn cobs. The prawns can be omitted or replaced with ham or chicken, if wished.

Chinese Mushrooms with Cellophane Noodles

Red fermented bean curd adds extra flavour to this hearty vegetarian dish. It is brick red in colour, with a very strong, cheesy flavour, and is made by fermenting bean curd (tofu) with salt, red rice and rice wine. Look out for it in cans or earthenware pots at Chinese food markets.

INGREDIENTS

Serves 4

115g/4oz dried Chinese mushrooms
25g/1oz dried wood ears
115g/4oz dried bean curd
30ml/2 tbsp vegetable oil
2 garlic cloves, finely chopped
2 slices fresh root ginger, finely chopped
10 Szechuan peppercorns, crushed
15ml/1 tbsp red fermented bean curd
½ star anise
pinch of sugar
15–30ml/1–2 tbsp soy sauce
50g/2oz cellophane noodles, soaked in hot water until soft
salt

1 Soak the Chinese mushrooms and wood ears separately in bowls of hot water for 30 minutes. Break the dried bean curd into small pieces and soak in water according to the instructions on the packet.

COOK'S TIP

If you can't find Szechuan peppercorns, then use ordinary black ones instead.

2 Strain the mushrooms, reserving the liquid. Squeeze as much liquid from the mushrooms as possible, then discard the mushroom stems. Cut the cups in half if they are large.

3 The wood ears should swell to five times their original size. Drain them, rinse thoroughly and drain again. Cut off any gritty parts, then cut each wood ear into two or three pieces.

4 Heat the oil in a heavy-based pan. Add the garlic, ginger and Szechuan peppercorns. Fry for a few seconds, then add the mushrooms and red fermented bean curd. Mix lightly and fry for 5 minutes.

5 Add the reserved mushroom liquid to the pan, with sufficient water to completely cover the mushrooms. Add the star anise, sugar and soy sauce, then cover and simmer for 30 minutes.

6 Add the chopped wood ears and reconstituted bean curd pieces to the pan. Cover and cook for about 10 minutes.

7 Drain the cellophane noodles, add them to the mixture and cook for a further 10 minutes until tender, adding more liquid if necessary. Add salt to taste and serve.

Thai Noodles with Chinese Chives

This recipe requires a little time for preparation but the cooking time is very fast. Everything is cooked speedily in a hot wok and should be eaten at once.

INGREDIENTS

Serves 4

350g/12oz dried rice noodles
1cm/½ in fresh root ginger, grated
30ml/2 tbsp light soy sauce
45ml/3 tbsp vegetable oil
225g/8oz Quorn, cut into small cubes
2 garlic cloves, crushed
1 large onion, cut into thin wedges
115g/4oz fried tofu, thinly sliced
1 fresh green chilli, seeded and finely sliced
175g/6oz beansprouts
115g/4oz Chinese chives, cut into 5cm/2in lengths
50g/2oz roasted peanuts, ground
30ml/2 tbsp dark soy sauce
fresh coriander leaves, to garnish

1 Place the noodles in a large bowl, cover with warm water and soak for 20–30 minutes, then drain. Blend together the ginger, light soy sauce and 15ml/1 tbsp of the oil in a bowl. Stir in the Quorn and set aside for 10 minutes. Drain, reserving the marinade.

2 Heat 15ml/1 tbsp of the oil in a preheated wok or frying pan and fry the garlic for a few seconds. Add the Quorn and stir-fry for 3–4 minutes. Transfer to a plate and set aside.

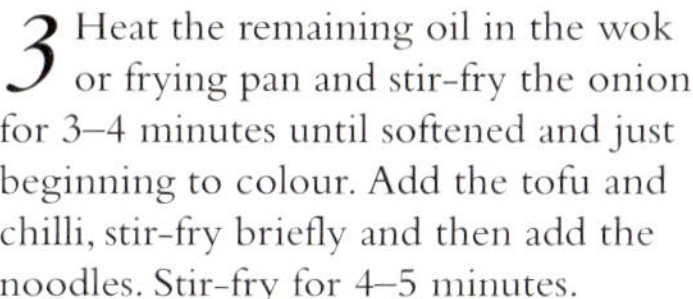

3 Heat the remaining oil in the wok or frying pan and stir-fry the onion for 3–4 minutes until softened and just beginning to colour. Add the tofu and chilli, stir-fry briefly and then add the noodles. Stir-fry for 4–5 minutes.

4 Stir in the beansprouts, Chinese chives and most of the ground peanuts, reserving a little for the garnish. Add the Quorn, the dark soy sauce and the reserved marinade.

5 When hot, spoon on to serving plates and garnish with the remaining ground peanuts and coriander leaves.

COOK'S TIP

Quorn makes this a vegetarian meal. However, thinly sliced pork or chicken could be used instead. Stir-fry them initially for 4–5 minutes.

Udon Pot

INGREDIENTS

Serves 4
350g/12oz dried udon noodles
1 large carrot, cut into bite-size chunks
225g/8oz chicken breasts or thighs, skinned and cut into bite-size pieces
8 raw king prawns, peeled and deveined
4–6 Chinese cabbage leaves, cut into short strips
8 shiitake mushrooms, stems removed
50g/2oz mange-touts, topped and tailed
1.5 litres/2½ pints/6¼ cups chicken stock or instant bonito stock
30ml/2 tbsp mirin
soy sauce, to taste
1 bunch spring onions, finely chopped, 30ml/2 tbsp grated fresh root ginger, lemon wedges, and extra soy sauce, to serve

1 Cook the noodles until just tender, following the directions on the packet. Drain, rinse under cold water and drain again. Blanch the carrot in boiling water for 1 minute, then drain.

2 Spoon the noodles and carrot chunks into a large saucepan or flameproof casserole, and arrange the chicken breasts or thighs, prawns, Chinese cabbage leaves, mushrooms and mange-touts on top.

3 Bring the stock to the boil in a saucepan. Add the mirin and enough soy sauce to taste. Pour the stock over the noodles. Cover the pan or casserole, bring to the boil over a moderate heat, then simmer gently for 5–6 minutes until all the ingredients are cooked.

4 Serve with chopped spring onions, grated ginger, lemon wedges and a little soy sauce.

Combination Chow Mein

INGREDIENTS

Serves 4–6
450g/1lb thick egg noodles
45ml/3 tbsp vegetable oil
2 garlic cloves, chopped
2 spring onions, cut into short lengths
50g/2oz pork fillet, sliced, or Chinese roast pork cut into short lengths
50g/2oz pig's liver, sliced
75g/3oz raw prawns, peeled and deveined
50g/2oz prepared squid, sliced
50g/2oz cockles or mussels
115g/4oz watercress, leaves stripped from the stems
2 red chillies, seeded and finely sliced
30–45ml/2–3 tbsp soy sauce
15ml/1 tbsp sesame oil
salt and freshly ground black pepper

1 Cook the egg noodles in a large saucepan of boiling water until just tender. Drain thoroughly.

2 Heat the oil in a wok and fry the garlic and spring onions for about 30 seconds. Add the pork fillet, if using, with the liver, prawns, squid and cockles or mussels. Stir-fry for 2 minutes over a high heat.

3 Add the watercress and chillies to the wok and stir-fry for a further 3–4 minutes, until the meat is cooked.

4 Add the drained noodles, stirring constantly but gently. Toss in the Chinese roast pork, if using, and add the soy sauce with salt and pepper to taste. Cook until the noodles are thoroughly heated through. Stir in the sesame oil, mix well and serve.

Cellophane Noodles with Pork

Unlike other types of noodles, cellophane noodles can be reheated successfully.

INGREDIENTS

Serves 3–4

115g/4oz cellophane noodles
4 dried Chinese black mushrooms
225g/8oz boneless lean pork
30ml/2 tbsp dark soy sauce
30ml/2 tbsp Chinese rice wine or dry sherry
2 garlic cloves, crushed
15ml/1 tbsp grated fresh root ginger
5ml/1 tsp chilli oil
45ml/3 tbsp groundnut oil
4–6 spring onions, chopped
5ml/1 tsp cornflour blended with 175ml/6fl oz/¾ cup chicken stock or water
30ml/2 tbsp chopped fresh coriander
salt and ground black pepper
fresh coriander sprigs, to garnish

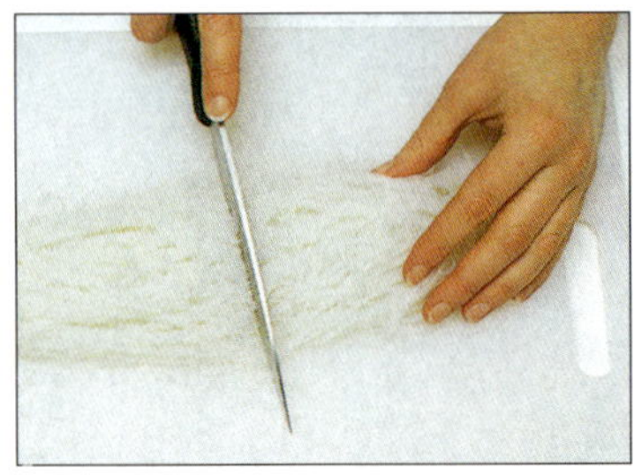

1 Put the noodles and mushrooms in separate bowls and pour over sufficient warm water to cover. Set aside to soak for 15–20 minutes, until soft. Drain well. Cut the noodles into 13cm/5in lengths using scissors or a knife. Squeeze out any excess water from the mushrooms, discard the stems and finely chop the caps.

2 Cut the pork into very small cubes and place them in a bowl. Add the soy sauce, rice wine or dry sherry, garlic, ginger and chilli oil and mix well. Set aside to marinate for 15 minutes. Drain, reserving the marinade.

3 Heat the groundnut oil in a preheated wok. Add the pork and mushrooms and stir-fry for 3 minutes. Add the spring onions and stir-fry for 1 minute. Stir in the cornflour mixture and reserved marinade and season to taste. Cook for 1 minute.

4 Add the noodles and stir-fry for about 2 minutes, until the noodles have absorbed most of the liquid and the pork is cooked through. Stir in the chopped coriander. Serve immediately, garnished with the coriander sprigs.

Noodles with Chicken, Prawns and Ham

Egg noodles can be cooked up to 24 hours in advance and kept in a bowl of cold water.

INGREDIENTS

Serves 4–6

- 275g/10oz dried egg noodles
- 15ml/1 tbsp vegetable oil
- 1 medium onion, chopped
- 1 garlic clove, crushed
- 2.5cm/1in fresh root ginger, chopped
- 50g/2oz canned water chestnuts, drained and sliced
- 15ml/1 tbsp light soy sauce
- 30ml/2 tbsp fish sauce or strong chicken stock
- 175g/6oz cooked chicken breast, sliced
- 150g/5oz cooked ham, thickly sliced and cut into short fingers
- 225g/8oz cooked prawn tails, peeled
- 175g/6oz beansprouts
- 200g/7oz canned baby corn cobs, drained
- 2 limes, cut into wedges, and 1 small bunch coriander, shredded, to garnish

1 Cook the noodles according to the packet instructions. Drain well and set aside.

2 Heat the oil in a preheated wok or frying pan. Fry the onion, garlic and ginger for 3 minutes, or until soft but not coloured. Add the chestnuts, soy sauce, fish sauce or chicken stock, chicken breast, ham and prawns.

3 Add the noodles, beansprouts and baby corn cobs and stir-fry for 6–8 minutes, until heated through. Transfer to a warmed serving dish, garnish with the lime wedges and shredded coriander and serve immediately.

Seafood Chow Mein

This basic recipe can be adapted using different items for the "dressing".

INGREDIENTS

Serves 4

75g/3oz squid, cleaned
75g/3oz raw prawns
3–4 fresh scallops
½ egg white
15ml/1 tbsp cornflour paste
250g/9oz egg noodles
75–90ml/5–6 tbsp vegetable oil
50g/2oz mangetouts
2.5ml/½ tsp salt
2.5ml/½ tsp light brown sugar
15ml/1 tbsp Chinese rice wine or dry sherry
30ml/2 tbsp light soy sauce
2 spring onions, finely shredded
Basic Stock, if necessary
few drops of sesame oil

1 Open up the squid and score the inside in a criss-cross pattern with a sharp knife. Cut the squid into pieces, each about the size of a postage stamp. Soak the squid in a bowl of boiling water until all the pieces curl up. Rinse in cold water and drain.

2 Peel and devein the prawns, then cut each in half lengthways.

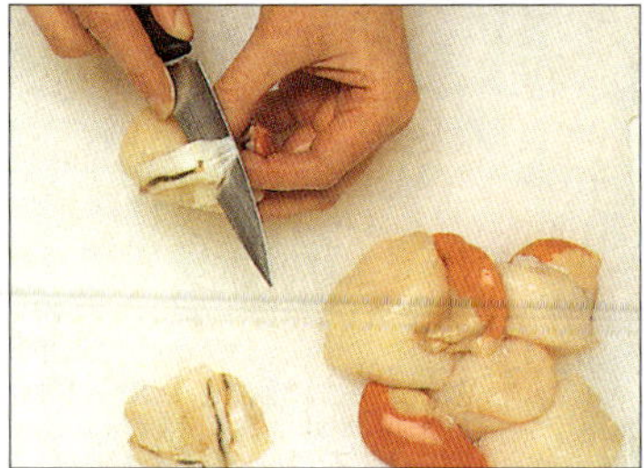

3 Cut each scallop into 3–4 slices. Mix together the scallops, prawns, egg white and cornflour paste.

4 Cook the noodles in boiling water according to the packet instructions. Drain and refresh under cold water. Mix with about 15ml/1 tbsp of the oil.

5 Heat 30–45ml/2–3 tbsp of the remaining oil in a preheated wok. Stir-fry the mangetouts, squid and prawn mixture for about 2 minutes, then add the salt, sugar, rice wine or dry sherry, half the soy sauce and the spring onions. Blend well and add a little stock, if necessary. Remove from the wok and keep warm.

6 Heat the remaining oil in the wok and stir-fry the noodles for 2–3 minutes with the remaining soy sauce. Place in a large serving dish, pour the "dressing" on top and sprinkle with a little sesame oil. Serve hot or cold.

富
貴
福

Special Fried Noodles

Mee goreng is, perhaps, the best-known dish of Singapore. It is prepared from a wide range of ingredients.

INGREDIENTS

Serves 4–6

275g/10oz egg noodles
1 boneless chicken breast, skinned
115g/4oz lean pork
30ml/2 tbsp vegetable oil
175g/6oz raw or cooked prawn tails, peeled
4 shallots or 1 medium onion, chopped
2cm/¾in fresh root ginger, thinly sliced
2 garlic cloves, crushed
45ml/3 tbsp light soy sauce
5–10ml/1-2 tsp chilli sauce
15ml/1 tbsp rice vinegar or white wine vinegar
5ml/1 tsp sugar
2.5ml/½ tsp salt
115g/4oz Chinese leaves, shredded
115g/4oz spinach, shredded
3 spring onions, shredded

1 Bring a large saucepan of lightly salted water to the boil and cook the noodles according to the instructions on the packet. Drain and set aside. Place the chicken breast and pork in the freezer for 30 minutes to firm, but not freeze.

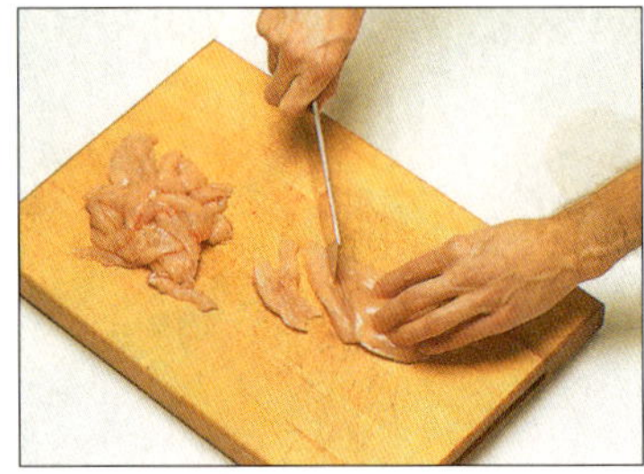

2 Slice the meat thinly against the grain. Heat the oil in a preheated wok and stir-fry the chicken, pork and prawns for 2–3 minutes. Add the shallots or onion, ginger and garlic and stir-fry for 2–3 minutes, until softened but not coloured.

3 Add the soy sauce, chilli sauce, vinegar, sugar and salt. Bring to a simmer. Add the Chinese leaves, spinach and spring onions, cover and cook for 3–4 minutes. Add the noodles, heat through and serve.

Straw Noodle Prawns in a Sweet Ginger Dip

Prawns are a popular feature in Japanese cooking. Rarely are they more delicious than when wrapped in crispy noodles.

INGREDIENTS

Serves 4–6

75g/3oz somen noodles or vermicelli
3 sheets nori
12 large raw prawn tails, peeled and deveined
vegetable oil, for deep-frying

For the dipping sauce

90ml/6 tbsp soy sauce
30ml/2 tbsp sugar
2cm/¾in fresh root ginger, grated

1 Cover the somen noodles, if using, with boiling water and leave to soak for 1–2 minutes. Drain and dry thoroughly with kitchen paper. Cut the noodles into 7.5cm/3in lengths. If using vermicelli, cover with boiling water and leave to soak for 1–2 minutes to soften. Drain and set aside. Cut the nori into 1 x 5cm/½ x 2in strips and set aside.

2 To make the dipping sauce, bring the soy sauce to the boil in a small saucepan with the sugar and ginger. Simmer for 2–3 minutes, strain and set aside to cool.

3 Line up the noodles or vermicelli on a wooden board. Straighten each prawn by pushing a bamboo skewer through its length. Roll the prawn in the noodles or vermicelli so that they adhere in neat strands.

4 Moisten one end of the nori strips and secure the noodles at the fat end of each prawn. Set aside.

5 Heat the vegetable oil in a preheated wok with a wire draining rack or in a deep-fryer to 180°C/350°F. Fry the prawns in the oil, two at a time, until the noodles or vermicelli are crisp and golden.

6 To finish, cut through the band of nori with a sharp knife, exposing a clean section of prawn. Drain on kitchen paper and serve with the dipping sauce in a small dish.

Main Course Spicy Prawn and Noodle Soup

This dish is served as a hot coconut broth with a separate platter of prawns, fish and noodles. Diners are invited to add their own choice of accompaniment to the broth.

INGREDIENTS

Serves 4–6

25g/1oz/¼ cup raw cashew nuts
3 shallots or 1 medium onion, sliced
5cm/2in lemon grass stalk, shredded
2 garlic cloves, crushed
150g/5oz laksa noodles (spaghetti-sized rice noodles), soaked for 10 minutes before cooking
30ml/2 tbsp vegetable oil
1cm/½in square shrimp paste or 15ml/1 tbsp fish sauce
15ml/1 tbsp mild curry paste
400g/14oz can coconut milk
½ chicken stock cube
3 curry leaves (optional)
450g/1lb white fish fillet, such as cod, haddock or whiting
225g/8oz raw or cooked prawn tails, peeled
1 small Cos lettuce, shredded
115g/4oz beansprouts
3 spring onions, shredded
½ cucumber, sliced and shredded
prawn crackers, to serve

1 Grind the cashew nuts with the shallots or onion, lemon grass and garlic in a mortar with a pestle or in a food processor. Cook the noodles according to the instructions on the packet.

2 Heat the oil in a large preheated wok or saucepan, add the cashew nut mixture and stir-fry for 1–2 minutes, or until the nuts are just beginning to brown.

3 Add the shrimp paste or fish sauce and curry paste, followed by the coconut milk, stock cube and curry leaves, if using. Simmer for 10 minutes.

4 Cut the white fish into bite-sized pieces. Add the fish and prawns to the simmering coconut stock and cook for 3–4 minutes.

5 To serve, line a large serving platter with the shredded lettuce leaves. Arrange the beansprouts, spring onions and cucumber in neat piles, together with the cooked fish and noodles. Serve the salad with a bowl of prawn crackers and the broth in a stoneware, closed-rim pot.

COOK'S TIP

When cooking the fish and prawns, you may find it easier to put them in a large frying basket before immersing them in the coconut stock.

Rice Noodles with Beef and Black Bean Sauce

This is an excellent combination – beef with a chilli sauce tossed with silky smooth rice noodles.

INGREDIENTS

Serves 4

450g/1lb fresh rice noodles
60ml/4 tbsp vegetable oil
1 onion, finely sliced
2 garlic cloves, finely chopped
2 slices fresh root ginger, finely chopped
225g/8oz mixed peppers, seeded and cut into strips
350g/12oz rump steak, finely sliced against the grain
45ml/3 tbsp fermented black beans, rinsed in warm water, drained and chopped
30ml/2 tbsp soy sauce
30ml/2 tbsp oyster sauce
15ml/1 tbsp chilli black bean sauce
15ml/1 tbsp cornflour
120ml/4fl oz/½ cup stock or water
2 spring onions, finely chopped, and 2 red chillies, seeded and finely sliced, to garnish

1 Rinse the noodles under hot water; drain well. Heat half the oil in a wok or large frying pan, swirling it around. Add the onion, garlic, ginger and mixed pepper strips. Stir-fry for 3–5 minutes, then remove with a slotted spoon and keep hot.

2 Add the remaining oil to the wok. When hot, add the sliced beef and fermented black beans and stir-fry over a high heat for 5 minutes or until they are cooked.

3 In a small bowl, blend the soy sauce, oyster sauce and chilli black bean sauce with the cornflour and stock or water until smooth. Add the mixture to the wok, then return the onion mixture to the wok and cook, stirring, for 1 minute.

4 Add the noodles and mix lightly. Stir over a medium heat until the noodles are heated through. Adjust the seasoning if necessary. Serve at once, garnished with the chopped spring onions and chillies.

Crisp Pork Meatballs Laced with Noodles

These little meatballs, decoratively coated with a lacing of noodles, look very impressive, but are actually extremely easy to make.

INGREDIENTS

Serves 4

400g/14oz minced pork
2 garlic cloves, finely chopped
30ml/2 tbsp chopped fresh coriander
15ml/1 tbsp oyster sauce
30ml/2 tbsp fresh breadcrumbs
1 egg, beaten
175g/6oz fresh thin egg noodles
oil, for deep-frying
salt and ground black pepper
fresh coriander leaves, to garnish
spinach leaves and chilli sauce or tomato sauce, to serve

1 Mix together the pork, garlic, chopped coriander, oyster sauce, breadcrumbs and egg. Season with salt and pepper.

2 Knead the pork mixture until it is sticky, then form into balls about the size of a walnut.

3 Blanch the noodles in a saucepan of boiling water for 2–3 minutes. Drain, rinse under cold running water and drain well.

4 Wrap 3–5 strands of noodles securely around each meatball in a criss-cross pattern.

5 Heat the oil in a deep-fryer or preheated wok. Deep-fry the meatballs in batches until golden brown and cooked through to the centre. As each batch browns, remove with a slotted spoon and drain well on kitchen paper. Serve hot on a bed of spinach leaves, garnished with fresh coriander leaves and with chilli sauce or tomato sauce in a small dish.

Noodles, Chicken and Prawns in Coconut Broth

This typical Indonesian dish has several different components from which the diners may help themselves, making a complete meal in itself.

INGREDIENTS

Serves 8

2 onions, quartered
2.5cm/1in fresh root ginger, sliced
2 garlic cloves
4 macadamia nuts or 8 almonds
1–2 fresh chillies, seeded and sliced
2 lemon grass stems, lower 5cm/2in sliced
5cm/2in fresh turmeric, peeled and sliced, or 5ml/1 tsp ground turmeric
15ml/1 tbsp coriander seeds, dry-fried
60ml/4 tbsp sunflower oil
400ml/14fl oz can coconut milk
1.5 litres/2½ pints/6¼ cups chicken stock
350g/12oz rice noodles, soaked in cold water
350
g/12oz cooked tiger prawns, peeled and deveined
salt and ground black pepper

For the garnish

4 hard-boiled eggs, shelled and quartered
225g/8oz cooked chicken, chopped
225g/8oz beansprouts
1 bunch spring onions, shredded
1 onion, finely sliced and deep-fried

1 Place the quartered onions, ginger, garlic and nuts in a food processor with the chillies, lemon grass and turmeric. Process to a paste. Alternatively, pound all the ingredients in a mortar with a pestle. Grind the coriander seeds coarsely and add to the paste.

2 Heat the oil in a preheated wok or frying pan and fry the spice paste, without allowing it to colour, to bring out the flavours. Add the coconut milk, stock and seasoning. Simmer for 5–10 minutes.

3 Meanwhile, drain the noodles and plunge them into a large pan of salted boiling water for 2 minutes. Remove from the heat and drain thoroughly. Rinse well with plenty of cold water. Add the tiger prawns to the soup just before serving and heat through for a minute or two.

4 Arrange the garnishes in separate bowls. Each person takes a helping of noodles, tops them with soup, eggs, chicken or beansprouts, then scatters shredded spring onions and fried onions on top.

Noodles in Soup

In China, noodles in soup are far more popular than fried noodles. This is a basic recipe that you can adapt by using different ingredients.

INGREDIENTS

Serves 4

225g/8oz chicken or pork fillet
3–4 dried Chinese mushrooms, soaked
115g/4oz can sliced bamboo shoots, drained
115g/4oz spinach leaves, lettuce hearts or Chinese leaves
2 spring onions
350g/12oz dried egg noodles
600ml/1 pint/2½ cups Basic Stock
30ml/2 tbsp vegetable oil
5ml/1 tsp salt
2.5ml/½ tsp light brown sugar
15ml/1 tbsp light soy sauce
10ml/2 tsp Chinese rice wine or dry sherry
few drops of sesame oil

1 Thinly shred the meat. Squeeze dry the mushrooms and discard any hard stalks. Thinly shred the mushroom caps, bamboo shoots, spinach, lettuce hearts or Chinese leaves and the spring onions. Keep the meat, the spring onions and the other ingredients in three heaps.

2 Cook the noodles in boiling water according to the instructions on the packet, then drain and rinse in cold water. Place in a serving bowl.

3 Bring the stock to the boil and pour over the noodles. Keep warm.

4 Heat the oil in a preheated wok, add the spring onions and the meat and stir-fry for about 1 minute.

5 Add the mushrooms, bamboo shoots and spinach, lettuce or Chinese leaves and stir-fry for 1 minute or until the meat is cooked through. Add the salt, sugar, soy sauce, rice wine or dry sherry and sesame oil and blend well.

6 Pour the "dressing" over the noodles and serve.

Rice Dishes

Rice is a staple food throughout much of China and Asia. While plain boiled rice is a useful accompaniment that goes well with a wide variety of dishes, it is easy to combine rice with vegetables, eggs and a range of flavourings and spices to create a rather more special meal. Rice dishes from each country and region have their own unique flavours. Try Chinese Special Fried Rice, Sushi Rice from Japan, Thai Coconut Rice or Rice Porridge with Chicken from Indonesia. Don't overlook Coconut Rice Fritters, a sweet snack from the Philippines.

Plain Rice

Use long-grain or patna rice or fragrant rice from Thailand. Allow 50g/2oz raw rice per person. If you use fragrant Thai rice, omit the salt.

INGREDIENTS

Serves 4
225g/8oz/generous 1 cup rice
about 250ml/8fl oz/1 cup water
pinch of salt
2.5ml/½ tsp vegetable oil

1 Wash and rinse the rice. Place the rice in a saucepan and add the water. There should be no more than 2cm/¾in of water above the surface of the rice.

2 Bring to the boil, add the salt and oil, then stir to prevent the rice sticking to the bottom of the pan. Reduce the heat to very, very low, cover and cook for 15–20 minutes.

3 Remove from the heat and leave to stand, still covered, for 10 minutes. Fluff up the rice with a fork or spoon just before serving.

Egg-fried Rice

Use rice with a fairly firm texture. Ideally, the raw rice should be soaked in water for a short time before cooking.

INGREDIENTS

Serves 4
3 eggs
5ml/1 tsp salt
2 spring onions, finely chopped
30–45ml/2–3 tbsp vegetable oil
450g/1lb cooked rice
115g/4oz frozen peas

1 In a bowl, lightly beat the eggs with a pinch of the salt and a few pieces of the spring onions.

2 Heat the oil in a preheated wok, and lightly scramble the eggs.

3 Add the cooked rice and stir to make sure that each grain of rice is separated. Add the remaining salt, spring onions and the peas. Blend well, allow to heat through and serve.

Chinese Special Fried Rice

This recipe combines a tasty mixture of chicken, prawns and vegetables with fried rice.

Ingredients

Serves 4

175g/6oz/scant 1 cup long-grain white rice
45ml/3 tbsp groundnut oil
350ml/12fl oz/1½ cups water
1 garlic clove, crushed
4 spring onions, finely chopped
115g/4oz cooked chicken, diced
115g/4oz cooked prawns, peeled
50g/2oz frozen peas
1 egg, lightly beaten
50g/2oz lettuce, shredded
30ml/2 tbsp light soy sauce
pinch of caster sugar
salt and ground black pepper
15ml/1 tbsp chopped roasted cashew nuts, to garnish

1 Rinse the rice in two to three changes of warm water to wash away some of the starch. Drain well.

2 Put the rice in a saucepan and add 15ml/1 tbsp of the oil and the water. Cover and bring to the boil, stir once, then cover and simmer for 12–15 minutes, until nearly all the water has been absorbed. Turn off the heat and leave, covered, to stand for 10 minutes. Fluff up with a fork and leave to cool.

3 Heat the remaining oil in a preheated wok or frying pan, add the garlic and spring onions and stir-fry for 30 seconds.

4 Add the chicken, prawns and peas and stir-fry for 1–2 minutes, then add the cooked rice and stir-fry for a further 2 minutes. Pour in the egg and stir-fry until just set. Stir in the lettuce, soy sauce, sugar and seasoning.

5 Transfer to a warmed serving bowl, sprinkle with the chopped cashew nuts and serve immediately.

Egg Foo Yung

A great way of turning a bowl of leftover cooked rice into a meal for four, this dish is tasty and full of texture.

INGREDIENTS

Serves 4
3 eggs, beaten
pinch of Chinese five-spice powder (optional)
45ml/3 tbsp groundnut or sunflower oil
4 spring onions, sliced
1 garlic clove, crushed
1 small green pepper, seeded and chopped
115g/4oz beansprouts
225g/8oz/generous 1 cup white rice, cooked
45ml/3 tbsp light soy sauce
15ml/1 tbsp sesame oil
salt and ground black pepper

1 Season the eggs with salt and pepper to taste and beat in the five-spice powder, if using.

2 Heat 15ml/1 tbsp of the oil in a preheated wok or large frying pan and, when quite hot, pour in the egg. Cook rather like an omelette, pulling the mixture away from the sides and allowing the rest to slip underneath.

3 Cook the egg until firm, then tip out. Chop the omelette into small strips and set aside.

4 Heat the remaining oil and stir-fry the onions, garlic, green pepper and beansprouts for about 2 minutes, stirring and tossing continuously.

5 Mix in the cooked rice and heat thoroughly, stirring well. Add the soy sauce and sesame oil, then return the egg strips and mix in well. Serve immediately, piping hot.

Malacca Fried Rice

There are many versions of this dish throughout the East, all of which make use of leftover rice. Ingredients vary according to what is available, but prawns are a popular addition.

Ingredients

Serves 4–6

2 eggs
45ml/3 tbsp vegetable oil
4 shallots or 1 medium onion, finely chopped
5ml/1 tsp finely chopped fresh root ginger
1 garlic clove, crushed
225g/8oz raw or cooked prawn tails, peeled and deveined
5–10ml/1–2 tsp chilli sauce (optional)
3 spring onions, green part only, roughly chopped
225g/8oz frozen peas
225g/8oz thickly sliced roast pork, diced
45ml/3 tbsp light soy sauce
350g/12oz/1⅔ cups long-grain rice, cooked
salt and ground black pepper

1 In a bowl, beat the eggs well and season to taste with salt and pepper. Heat 15ml/1 tbsp of the oil in a large, non-stick frying pan, pour in the eggs and cook for about 30 seconds, without stirring, until set. Roll up the omelette, cut into thin strips and set aside.

2 Heat the remaining oil in a large preheated wok, add the shallots or onion, ginger, garlic and prawn tails and cook for 1–2 minutes, ensuring that the garlic does not burn.

3 Add the chilli sauce, spring onions, peas, pork and soy sauce. Stir to heat through, then add the cooked rice. Fry the rice over a moderate heat for 6–8 minutes. Turn into a dish and decorate with the egg strips.

Oriental Fried Rice

This is a great way to use leftover cooked rice. Make sure the rice is very cold before attempting to fry it, as warm rice will become soggy. Some supermarkets sell frozen cooked rice.

INGREDIENTS

Serves 4–6

75ml/5 tbsp oil
115g/4oz shallots, halved and thinly sliced
3 garlic cloves, crushed
1 red chilli, seeded and finely chopped
6 spring onions, finely chopped
1 red pepper, seeded and finely chopped
225g/8oz white cabbage, finely shredded
175g/6oz cucumber, finely chopped
50g/2oz frozen peas, thawed
3 eggs, beaten
5ml/1 tsp tomato purée
30ml/2 tbsp lime juice
1.5ml/¼ tsp Tabasco sauce
675g/1½lb cooked white rice, cooled
115g/4oz/1 cup cashew nuts, roughly chopped
30ml/2 tbsp chopped fresh coriander, plus extra to garnish
salt and ground black pepper

1 Heat the oil in a large preheated wok or non-stick frying pan and cook the shallots until very crisp and golden. Remove with a slotted spoon and drain on kitchen paper.

2 Add the garlic and chilli and cook for 1 minute. Add the spring onions and red pepper and cook for 3–4 minutes, or until the onions are beginning to soften.

3 Add the cabbage, cucumber and peas and cook for a further 2 minutes.

4 Make a gap in the ingredients in the wok or frying pan and add the beaten eggs. Scramble the eggs, stirring occasionally, and then stir them into the vegetables.

5 Add the tomato purée, lime juice and Tabasco sauce and stir well to combine.

6 Increase the heat and add the cooked rice, cashew nuts, coriander and plenty of seasoning. Stir-fry for 3–4 minutes, until piping hot. Serve garnished with the crisp shallots and extra fresh coriander, if liked.

COOK'S TIP

675g/1½lb cooked rice is equivalent to 225g/8oz raw weight.

Shiitake Fried Rice

Shiitake mushrooms have a strong, meaty, mushroomy aroma and flavour. This is a very easy recipe to make, and although it is a side dish, it can almost be a meal in itself.

Ingredients

Serves 4
2 eggs
15ml/1 tbsp water
45ml/3 tbsp vegetable oil
350g/12oz shiitake mushrooms
8 spring onions, sliced diagonally
1 garlic clove, crushed
½ green pepper, seeded and chopped
25g/1oz/2 tbsp butter
175–225g/6–8oz/about 1 cup long-grain rice, cooked
15ml/1 tbsp medium-dry sherry
30ml/2 tbsp dark soy sauce
15ml/1 tbsp chopped fresh coriander
salt

1 Beat the eggs with the water and season with a little salt.

2 Heat 15ml/1 tbsp of the oil in a preheated wok or large frying pan, pour in the eggs and cook to make a large omelette. Lift the sides of the omelette and tilt the wok so that the uncooked egg can run underneath and be cooked. Roll up the omelette and slice thinly.

3 Remove and discard the mushroom stalks, if they are tough. Slice the caps thinly, halving them if they are large.

4 Heat 15ml/1 tbsp of the remaining oil in the wok and stir-fry the spring onions and garlic for 3–4 minutes until softened but not brown. Transfer them to a plate using a slotted spoon and set aside.

5 Add the green pepper and stir-fry for about 2–3 minutes, then add the butter and the remaining oil. As the butter begins to sizzle, add the mushrooms and stir-fry over a moderate heat for 3–4 minutes until both vegetables are soft.

6 Loosen the rice grains as much as possible. Pour the sherry over the mushrooms and then stir in the rice.

7 Heat the rice over a moderate heat, stirring all the time to prevent it sticking. If the rice seems very dry, add a little more oil. Stir in the cooked spring onions, garlic and omelette slices, the soy sauce and chopped coriander. Cook for a few minutes until heated through and serve.

Sushi

Ingredients

Makes 8–10

For the tuna sushi

3 sheets nori (paper-thin seaweed)
150g/5oz fresh tuna fillet, cut into fingers
5ml/1 tsp wasabi (Japanese horseradish)
6 young carrots, blanched
450g/1lb/6 cups cooked Japanese rice

For the salmon sushi

2 eggs
2.5ml/½ tsp salt
10ml/2 tsp sugar
5 sheets nori
450g/1lb/6 cups cooked Japanese rice
150g/5oz fresh salmon fillet, cut into fingers
5ml/1 tsp wasabi paste
½ small cucumber, cut into strips

1 To make the tuna sushi, spread half a sheet of nori on to a bamboo mat, lay strips of tuna across the full length and season with the thinned wasabi. Place a line of blanched carrot next to the tuna and roll tightly. Moisten the edge with water and seal.

2 Place a square of damp wax paper on to the bamboo mat, then spread evenly with sushi rice. Place the non-wrapped tuna along the centre and wrap tightly, enclosing the nori completely. Remove the paper and cut into neat rounds with a wet knife.

3 To make the salmon sushi, make a simple flat omelette by beating together the eggs, salt and sugar. Heat a large non-stick pan, pour in the egg mixture, stir briefly and allow to set. Transfer to a clean dish towel and cool.

4 Place the nori on to a bamboo mat, cover with the omelette, and trim to size. Spread a layer of rice over the omelette, then lay strips of salmon across the width. Season the salmon with the thinned wasabi, then place a strip of cucumber next to the salmon. Fold the bamboo mat in half. Cut into neat rounds with a wet knife.

Coconut Rice Fritters

These delicious fritters from the Philippines can be served at any time and go especially well with coffee or hot chocolate.

Ingredients

Makes 28

150g/5oz/⅔ cup long grain rice, cooked
30ml/2 tbsp coconut milk powder
45ml/3 tbsp sugar
2 egg yolks
juice of ½ lemon
75g/3oz desiccated coconut
oil, for deep-frying
icing sugar, for dusting

1 Place 75g/3oz of the cooked rice in a mortar and pound with a pestle until smooth and sticky. Alternatively, process in a food processor. Turn out into a bowl and mix in the remaining rice, the coconut milk powder, sugar, egg yolks and lemon juice.

2 Spread out the desiccated coconut on a tray or plate. With wet hands, divide the rice mixture into thumb-sized pieces and roll them in the coconut to make neat balls.

3 Heat the oil in a wok or deep-fryer to 180°C/350°F. Fry the coconut rice balls, three or four at a time, for 1–2 minutes, until the coconut is evenly browned. Transfer to a plate and dust with icing sugar. Place a wooden skewer in each fritter and serve in the traditional way, as an afternoon snack.

Cook's Tip

In the Philippines, hot chocolate is made by preparing a syrup with 30ml/2 tbsp sugar and 120ml/4fl oz/½ cup water and then melting 115g/4oz of best quality plain chocolate in it. Finally, 200ml/7fl oz/scant 1 cup evaporated milk is whisked in over a low heat. This luxurious drink serves 2.

Thai Rice with Bean Sprouts

Thai rice has a delicate fragrance that is delicious hot or cold.

INGREDIENTS

Serves 6

225g/8oz/1 cup Thai fragrant rice
30ml/2 tbsp sesame oil
30ml/2 tbsp fresh lime juice
1 small red chilli, seeded and chopped
1 garlic clove, crushed
10ml/2 tsp grated fresh root ginger
30ml/2 tbsp light soy sauce
5ml/1 tsp clear honey
45ml/3 tbsp pineapple juice
15ml/1 tbsp wine vinegar
2 spring onions, sliced
2 canned pineapple rings, chopped
150g/5oz/1¼ cups sprouted lentils or beansprouts
1 small red pepper, sliced
1 stick celery, sliced
50g/2oz/½ cup cashew nuts, chopped
30ml/2 tbsp toasted sesame seeds
salt and ground black pepper

1 Soak the Thai fragrant rice for 20 minutes, then rinse in several changes of water. Drain, then boil in salted water for 10–12 minutes until tender. Drain and set aside.

2 Whisk together the sesame oil, lime juice, chilli, garlic, ginger, soy sauce, honey, pineapple juice and wine vinegar in a large bowl. Stir in the rice.

3 Add the spring onions, pineapple rings, sprouted lentils or beansprouts, red pepper, celery, cashew nuts and the toasted sesame seeds and mix well. If the rice grains stick together on cooling, simply stir them with a metal spoon. This dish can be served warm or lightly chilled and is a good accompaniment to grilled or barbecued meats and fish.

COOK'S TIP

Sesame oil has a strong, nutty flavour and is used for seasoning, marinating or flavouring rather than for cooking. Because the taste is so distinctive, sesame oil can be mixed with grapeseed or other light-flavoured oils.

Coconut Rice

This rich dish is usually served with a tangy papaya salad.

Ingredients

Serves 4–6

450g/1lb/2 cups jasmine rice
250ml/8fl oz/1 cup water
475ml/16fl oz/2 cups coconut milk
2.5ml/½ tsp salt
30ml/2 tbsp granulated sugar
fresh shredded coconut, to garnish (optional)

1 Wash the rice in several changes of cold water until it runs clear. Place the water, coconut milk, salt and sugar in a heavy-bottomed saucepan.

2 Add the rice, cover and bring to the boil. Reduce the heat to low and simmer for about 15–20 minutes or until the rice is tender to the bite and cooked through.

3 Turn off the heat and allow the rice to rest in the saucepan for a further 5–10 minutes.

4 Fluff up the rice with chopsticks before serving.

Pineapple Fried Rice

When buying a pineapple, look for a sweet-smelling fruit with an even brownish/yellow skin. To test for ripeness, tap the base – a dull sound indicates that the fruit is ripe. The flesh should also give slightly when pressed.

Ingredients

Serves 4–6

1 pineapple
30ml/2 tbsp vegetable oil
1 small onion, finely chopped
2 green chillies, seeded and chopped
225g/8oz lean pork, cut into small dice
115g/4oz cooked shelled prawns
675–900g/1½–2 lb/3–4 cups cooked cold rice
50g/2oz roasted cashew nuts
2 spring onions, chopped
30ml/2 tbsp fish sauce
15ml/1 tbsp soy sauce
10–12 mint leaves, to garnish
2 red chillies, sliced, to garnish
1 green chilli, sliced, to garnish

1 Cut the pineapple in half lengthways and remove the flesh from both halves by cutting round inside the skin. Reserve the skin shells. You need 115g/4oz of fruit, chopped finely (keep the rest for a dessert).

Cook's Tip

This dish is ideal to prepare for a special occasion meal. Served in the pineapple skin shells, it is sure to be the talking point of the dinner.

2 Heat the oil in a wok or large frying pan. Add the onion and chillies and fry for about 3–5 minutes until softened. Add the pork and cook until it is brown on all sides.

3 Stir in the prawns and rice and toss well together. Continue to stir-fry until the rice is thoroughly heated.

4 Add the chopped pineapple, cashew nuts and spring onions. Season with fish sauce and soy sauce.

5 Spoon into the pineapple skin shells. Garnish with shredded mint leaves and red and green chillies.

Rice Porridge with Chicken

This dish is often served as sustaining breakfast fare. It can be served simply, with just the chicken stirred into it. Hearty eaters tuck into helpings of porridge drizzled with a little soy sauce, with strips of chicken, prawns, garlic and strips of fresh chilli, topped with a lightly fried egg and garnished with celery leaves and fried onion.

INGREDIENTS

Serves 6

1kg/2¼lb chicken, cut into 4 pieces, or 4 chicken quarters
1.75 litres/3 pints/7½ cups water
1 large onion, quartered
2.5cm/1in fresh root ginger, halved and bruised
350g/12oz Thai fragrant rice, rinsed
salt and ground black pepper
cooked peeled prawns, strips of fresh chilli, deep-fried onion and celery leaves, to garnish (optional)

1 Place the chicken pieces in a large saucepan with the water, onion quarters and ginger. Season with salt and pepper, bring to the boil and simmer for 45–50 minutes, until the chicken is tender. Remove the chicken from the pan and reserve the stock. Remove the skin from the chicken pieces. Cut the meat from the bones and then into bite-sized pieces.

2 Strain and measure the reserved chicken stock. Make the quantity up to 1.75 litres/3 pints/7½ cups with water and transfer to a clean saucepan.

3 Add the rice to the stock and bring to the boil, stirring constantly. Lower the heat and simmer gently for 20 minutes. Stir, cover and cook for a further 20 minutes, stirring from time to time, until the rice is soft.

4 Stir the chicken pieces into the porridge and heat through for 5 minutes. Serve as it is or with any of the garnishes suggested.

Spicy Peanut Rice Cakes

Serve these spicy, Indonesian rice cakes with a crisp green salad and a dipping sauce, such as Hot Tomato Sambal.

INGREDIENTS

Makes 16

1 garlic clove, crushed
1cm/½in fresh root ginger, finely chopped
1.5ml/¼ tsp ground turmeric
5ml/1 tsp sugar
2.5ml/½ tsp salt
5ml/1 tsp chilli sauce
10ml/2 tsp fish sauce or soy sauce
30ml/2 tbsp chopped fresh coriander
juice of ½ lime
115g/4oz/generous ½ cup long-grain rice, cooked
75g/3oz/¾ cup raw peanuts, chopped
vegetable oil, for deep-frying

1 Pound together the garlic, ginger and turmeric in a mortar with a pestle or in a food processor. Add the sugar, salt, chilli sauce, fish or soy sauce, coriander and lime juice.

2 Add 75g/3oz of the cooked rice and pound until smooth and sticky. Stir the mixture into the remaining rice and mix well. With wet hands, shape 16 thumb-sized balls.

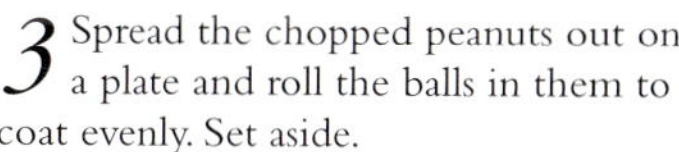

3 Spread the chopped peanuts out on a plate and roll the balls in them to coat evenly. Set aside.

4 Heat the oil in a preheated wok or deep frying pan. Deep-fry the rice cakes, three at a time, until crisp and golden. Remove and drain on kitchen paper. Serve immediately.

DESSERTS

Surprise the family with something completely different with these melt-in-the-mouth dessert recipes collected from all over China and Asia. Exotic Fruit Salad from Vietnam tastes just as wonderful – and refreshing – as it looks. Old or young, few can resist the delicious little Japanese Sweet Potato and Chestnut Candies. Thailand offers an intriguing variation on an international favourite with Steamed Coconut Custard, and the combination of crisp batter and soft, warm fruit in Indonesian Deep-fried Bananas is quite simply magical.

Chinese Fruit Salad

For an unusual fruit salad with an oriental flavour, try this mixture of fruits in a tangy lime and lychee syrup, topped with a light sprinkling of toasted sesame seeds.

INGREDIENTS

Serves 4

115g/4oz/½ cup caster sugar
300ml/½ pint/1¼ cups water
thinly pared rind and juice of 1 lime
400g/14oz can lychees in syrup
1 ripe mango, peeled, stoned and sliced
1 eating apple, cored and sliced
2 bananas, chopped
1 star fruit, sliced (optional)
5ml/1 tsp sesame seeds, toasted

1 Place the sugar in a saucepan with the water and the lime rind. Heat gently until the sugar dissolves, then increase the heat and boil gently for about 7–8 minutes. Remove from the heat and set aside to cool.

2 Drain the lychees and reserve the juice. Pour the juice into the cooled lime syrup with the lime juice. Place all the prepared fruit in a bowl and pour over the lime and lychee syrup. Chill for about 1 hour. Just before serving, sprinkle with toasted sesame seeds.

COOK'S TIP

To prepare a mango, cut through the fruit lengthways, about 1cm/½in either side of the centre. Then, using a sharp knife, cut the flesh from the central piece from the stone. Make even criss-cross cuts in the flesh of both side pieces. Hold one side piece in both hands, bend it almost inside out and remove the cubes of flesh with a spoon. Repeat with the other side piece.

Sweet Potato and Chestnut Candies

It is customary in Japan to offer special bean paste candies with tea. The candies tend to be very sweet by themselves, but contrast well with Japanese green tea. They also make an unusual dessert at the end of a special evening meal.

INGREDIENTS

Makes 18

450g/1lb sweet potatoes, peeled and chopped
1.5ml/¼ tsp salt
2 egg yolks
200g/7oz/1 cup sugar
60ml/4 tbsp water
75ml/5 tbsp rice flour or plain flour
5ml/1 tsp orange flower or rose water (optional)
200g/7oz can chestnuts in heavy syrup, drained
caster sugar, for dusting
2 strips candied angelica
10ml/2 tsp plum or apricot preserve
3–4 drops red food colouring

1 Place the sweet potatoes in a heavy saucepan, cover with cold water and add the salt. Bring to the boil and simmer for 20–25 minutes, until the sweet potatoes are tender. Drain and return to the pan. Mash until smooth or rub through a wire strainer. Place the egg yolks, sugar and water in a bowl, then mix in the flour and orange flower or rose water, if using. Add the potato purée and stir over a gentle heat for about 3–4 minutes. Turn the paste out on to a tray and allow to cool.

2 To shape the paste, place 10ml/2 tsp of the mixture in the centre of a wet, cotton napkin. Enclose the paste in the napkin and twist into a nut shape. Make sure the napkin is properly wet or the mixture will stick to it.

3 To prepare the chestnuts, rinse off the syrup and dry well. Roll the chestnuts in caster sugar and decorate with strips of angelica. To finish the sweet potato candies, colour the plum or apricot preserve with red food colouring and decorate each candy with a spot of colour.

COOK'S TIP

Sugar-coated chestnuts will keep for up to 5 days in a sealed container at room temperature. Store sweet potato candies in a sealed container in the refrigerator.

Thin Pancakes

Thin pancakes are not too difficult to make, but quite a lot of practice and patience are needed to achieve the perfect result. Nowadays, even restaurants buy frozen, ready-made ones from Chinese supermarkets. If you decide to use ready-made pancakes, or are reheating home-made ones, steam them for about 5 minutes, or microwave on high (650 watts) for 1–2 minutes.

INGREDIENTS

Makes 24–30

450g/1lb/4 cups plain flour, plus extra for dusting
about 300ml/½ pint/1¼ cups boiling water
5ml/1 tsp vegetable oil

1 Sift the flour into a mixing bowl, then pour in the boiling water very gently, stirring as you pour. Mix with the oil and knead the mixture into a firm dough. Cover with a damp cloth and let stand for about 30 minutes.

2 Lightly dust a work surface with flour. Knead the dough for about 5–8 minutes, or until smooth, then divide it into 3 equal portions. Roll out each portion into a long "sausage", cut each into 8–10 pieces and roll each into a ball. Using the palm of your hand, press each piece into a flat pancake. With a rolling pin, gently roll each into a 15cm/6in circle.

3 Heat an ungreased frying pan until hot, then reduce the heat to low and place the pancakes, one at a time, in the pan. Remove the pancakes when small brown spots appear on the underside. Keep under a damp cloth until all the pancakes are cooked.

Red Bean Paste Pancakes

If you are unable to find red bean paste, sweetened chestnut purée or mashed dates are possible substitutes.

INGREDIENTS

Serves 4

about 120ml/8 tbsp sweetened red bean paste
8 Thin Pancakes
30–45ml/2–3 tbsp vegetable oil
granulated or caster sugar, to serve

1 Spread about 15ml/1 tbsp of the red bean paste over about three-quarters of each pancake, then roll the pancake over three or four times.

2 Heat the oil in a preheated wok or frying pan and fry the pancake rolls until golden brown, turning once.

3 Cut each pancake roll into three or four pieces and sprinkle with sugar to serve.

Almond Curd Junket

Also known as almond float, this is usually made from agar-agar or isinglass, although gelatine can also be used.

INGREDIENTS

Serves 4–6

10g/¼oz agar-agar or isinglass or 25g/1oz gelatine powder
about 600ml/1 pint/2½ cups water
60ml/4 tbsp granulated or caster sugar
300ml/½ pint/1¼ cups milk
5ml/1 tsp almond essence
fresh or canned mixed fruit salad with syrup, to serve

1 In a saucepan, dissolve the agar-agar or isinglass in about half the water over a gentle heat. This will take at least 10 minutes. If using gelatine, follow the packet instructions.

2 In a separate saucepan, dissolve the sugar in the remaining water over a medium heat. Add the milk and the almond essence, blending well. Do not allow the mixture to boil.

3 Mix the milk and sugar with the agar-agar, isinglass or gelatine mixture in a serving bowl. When cool, place in the refrigerator for 2–3 hours to set.

4 To serve, cut the junket into small cubes and spoon into a serving dish or into individual bowls. Pour the fruit salad, with the syrup, over the junket and serve.

Stewed Pumpkin in Coconut Cream

Stewed fruit is a popular dessert in Thailand. Use the firm-textured Japanese kabocha pumpkin for this dish, if you can. Bananas and melons can also be prepared in this way and you can even stew sweetcorn kernels or pulses such as mung beans and black beans in coconut milk.

INGREDIENTS

Serves 4–6

1kg/2¼lb kabocha pumpkin
750ml/1¼ pint/3 cups coconut milk
175g/6oz granulated sugar
pinch of salt
pumpkin seed kernels, toasted, and mint sprigs, to decorate

1 Wash the pumpkin skin and cut off most of it. Scoop out the seeds.

2 Using a sharp knife, cut the flesh into pieces about 5cm/2in long and 2cm/¾in thick.

COOK'S TIP

Any pumpkin can be used for this dish, as long as it has a firm texture. Jamaican or New Zealand varieties both make good alternatives to kabocha pumpkin.

3 In a saucepan, bring the coconut milk, sugar and salt to the boil.

4 Add the pumpkin and simmer for about 10–15 minutes until the pumpkin is tender. Serve warm. Decorate each serving with a mint sprig and a few toasted pumpkin seed kernels.

Celebration Cake

A mouth-watering gâteau made from fragrant Thai rice covered with a tangy cream icing. Top with fresh berry fruits or pipe on a greeting in melted chocolate.

INGREDIENTS

Serves 8–10

225g/8oz/generous 1 cup Thai fragrant or Jasmine rice
1 litre/1¾ pints/4 cups milk
115g/4oz/¾ cup caster sugar
6 cardamom pods, crushed open
2 bay leaves
300ml/½ pint/1¼ cups whipping cream
6 eggs, separated

For the topping

300ml/½ pint/1¼ cups double cream
200g/7oz/scant 1 cup quark
5ml/1 tsp vanilla essence
grated rind of 1 lemon
30g/1½oz/3 tbsp caster sugar
soft berry fruits and sliced star or kiwi fruits, to decorate

1 Grease and line a deep 25cm/10in round cake tin. Boil the rice in unsalted water for 3 minutes, then drain well.

COOK'S TIP

If you prefer something simpler, turn the cake out and top with sliced fruits or a lovely tumble of berries and stoned cherries. Serve the topping separately, thinning it down slightly with a little milk.

2 Return the rice to the pan with the milk, 115g/4oz/generous ½ cup of the sugar, the cardamom and bay leaves. Bring to the boil, then lower the heat and simmer the mixture for 20 minutes, stirring occasionally.

3 Allow the mixture to cool, then remove the bay leaves and any cardamom husks. Turn into a large bowl. Beat in the whipping cream and then the egg yolks.

4 Whisk the egg whites until they form soft peaks and fold into the rice mixture. Spoon into the prepared tin and bake in a preheated oven at 180°C/350°F/Gas 4 for 45–50 minutes, until risen and golden brown. The centre should be slightly wobbly – it will firm up as it cools.

5 Chill overnight in the tin. Turn out on to a large serving plate. For the topping, whip the double cream until stiff, then mix in the quark, vanilla essence, lemon rind and sugar.

6 Cover the top and sides of the cake with the cream, swirling it attractively. Decorate with soft berry fruits and sliced star or kiwi fruits.

Steamed Coconut Custard

Srikaya is a very popular dessert that pops up all over South-east Asia, rather as crème caramel is found all over Europe or, indeed, wherever Europeans have settled.

INGREDIENTS

Serves 8
400ml/14fl oz can coconut milk
75ml/5 tbsp water
25g/1oz sugar
3 eggs, beaten
25g/1oz cellophane noodles, soaked in warm water for 5 minutes
4 ripe bananas or plantains, peeled and cut in small pieces
salt
vanilla ice cream, to serve (optional)

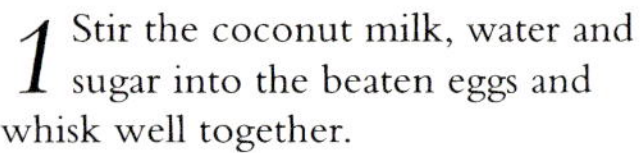

1 Stir the coconut milk, water and sugar into the beaten eggs and whisk well together.

2 Strain into a 1.75 litre/3 pint/ 7½ cup heatproof soufflé dish.

3 Drain the noodles well and cut them into small pieces with scissors. Stir the noodles into the coconut milk mixture, together with the chopped bananas or plantains. Stir in a pinch of salt.

4 Cover the dish with foil and place in a steamer for about 1 hour, or until set. Test by inserting a thin, small knife or skewer into the centre. Serve hot or cold, on its own or topped with vanilla ice cream.

Date and Walnut Crisps

Try this sweet version of fried wontons; they make a truly scrumptious snack or dessert.

INGREDIENTS

Makes 15

25–30 dried dates, stoned
50g/2oz/½ cup walnuts
30ml/2 tbsp light brown sugar
pinch of ground cinnamon
30 wonton wrappers
1 egg, beaten
oil, for deep-frying
fresh mint sprigs, to decorate
icing sugar, for dusting

1 Chop the dates and walnuts roughly. Place them in a bowl and add the sugar and cinnamon. Mix well.

2 Lay a wonton wrapper on a flat surface. Centre a spoonful of the filling on the wrapper, brush the edges with beaten egg and cover with a second wrapper. Lightly press the edges together to seal. Make more filled wontons in the same way.

3 Heat the oil to 180°C/350°F in a wok or deep-fryer. Deep-fry the wontons, a few at a time, until golden. Do not crowd the pan. Remove them with a slotted spoon and drain on kitchen paper. Serve warm, decorated with mint and dusted with icing sugar.

Baked Rice Pudding, Thai-style

Black glutinous rice, also known as black sticky rice, has long black grains and a nutty taste similar to wild rice. This baked pudding has a distinct character and flavour all of its own.

INGREDIENTS

Serves 4–6

175g/6oz white or black glutinous (sticky) rice
30ml/2 tbsp soft light brown sugar
475ml/16fl oz/2 cups coconut milk
250ml/8fl oz/1 cup water
3 eggs
30ml/2 tbsp granulated sugar

1 Combine the glutinous rice, brown sugar, half the coconut milk and all the water in a saucepan.

2 Bring to the boil and simmer for about 15–20 minutes or until the rice has absorbed most of the liquid, stirring from time to time. Preheat the oven to 150°C/300°F/Gas 3.

3 Transfer the rice into one large ovenproof dish or divide it between individual ramekins. Mix together the eggs, remaining coconut milk and sugar in a bowl.

4 Strain and pour the mixture evenly over the par-cooked rice.

5 Place the dish in a baking tin. Pour in enough boiling water to come halfway up the sides of the dish.

6 Cover the dish with a piece of foil and bake in the oven for about 35 minutes to 1 hour or until the custard is set. Serve warm or cold.

Mango with Sticky Rice

Everyone's favourite dessert. Mangoes, with their delicate fragrance, sweet and sour flavour and velvety flesh, blend especially well with coconut sticky rice. You need to start preparing this dish the day before.

INGREDIENTS

Serves 4

115g/4oz sticky (glutinous) white rice
175ml/6fl oz/¾ cup thick coconut milk
45ml/3 tbsp granulated sugar
pinch of salt
2 ripe mangoes
strips of lime rind, to decorate

1 Rinse the glutinous rice thoroughly in several changes of cold water, then leave to soak overnight in a bowl of fresh, cold water.

2 Drain and spread the rice in an even layer in a steamer lined with cheesecloth. Cover and steam for about 20 minutes or until the grains of rice are tender.

3 Meanwhile, reserve 45ml/3 tbsp of the top of the coconut milk and combine the rest with the sugar and salt in a saucepan. Bring to the boil, stirring until the sugar dissolves, then pour into a bowl and leave to cool a little.

4 Turn the rice into a bowl and pour over the coconut mixture. Stir, then leave for about 10–15 minutes.

5 Peel the mangoes and cut the flesh into slices. Place on top of the rice and drizzle over the reserved coconut milk. Decorate with strips of lime rind.

Sugar Bread Rolls

These delicious sweet rolls reveal the influence of Spain on the cooking of the Philippines. They make an unusual end to a meal or a tea-time treat.

INGREDIENTS

Makes 10

350g/12oz/3 cups strong white bread flour
5ml/1 tsp salt
15ml/1 tbsp caster sugar
5ml/1 tsp dried yeast
150ml/¼ pint/⅔ cup hand-hot water
3 egg yolks
50g/2oz/4 tbsp unsalted butter, softened
75g/3oz/¾ cup Cheddar cheese, grated
30ml/2 tbsp melted unsalted butter
50g/2oz/generous ¼ cup sugar

1 Sift the flour, salt and caster sugar into a food processor fitted with a dough blade or the bowl of an electric mixer fitted with a dough hook. Make a well in the centre. Dissolve the yeast in the hand-hot water and pour into the well. Add the egg yolks and leave for a few minutes until bubbles appear on the surface of the liquid.

2 Mix the ingredients for 30–45 seconds to form a firm dough. Add the softened butter and knead for 2–3 minutes in a food processor, or for 4–5 minutes with an electric mixer, until smooth. Turn the dough out into a floured bowl, cover and leave in a warm place to rise until doubled in volume.

3 Turn the dough out on to a lightly floured surface and divide it into 10 pieces. Spread the grated cheese over the surface. Roll each of the dough pieces into 12.5cm/5in lengths, incorporating the cheese as you do so. Coil into snail shapes and place on a lightly greased high-sided tray measuring 30 x 20cm/12 x 8in.

4 Cover the tray with a loose-fitting plastic bag and leave in a warm place for 45 minutes or until the dough has doubled in volume. Bake in a preheated oven at 190°C/375°F/Gas 5 for 20–25 minutes. Brush with the melted butter, sprinkle with the sugar and allow to cool. Separate the rolls before serving.

Exotic Fruit Salad

A variety of fruits can be used for this Vietnamese dessert, depending on what is available. Look out for mandarin oranges, star fruit, pawpaw and passion fruit.

Ingredients

Serves 4–6

75g/3oz/scant ½ cup sugar
300ml/½ pint/1¼ cups water
30ml/2 tbsp stem ginger syrup
2 pieces star anise
2.5cm/1in cinnamon stick
1 clove
juice of ½ lemon
2 fresh mint sprigs
1 mango
2 bananas, sliced
8 fresh or canned lychees
225g/8oz strawberries, hulled and halved
2 pieces stem ginger, cut into sticks
1 medium pineapple

1 Put the sugar, water, ginger syrup, star anise, cinnamon, clove, lemon juice and mint into a saucepan. Bring to the boil and simmer for 3 minutes. Strain into a bowl and set aside to cool.

2 Remove the top and bottom from the mango and remove the outer skin. Stand the mango on one end and remove the flesh in two pieces either side of the flat stone. Slice evenly and add to the syrup. Add the bananas, lychees, strawberries and ginger.

3 Cut the pineapple in half down the centre. Loosen the flesh with a small serrated knife and remove to form two boat shapes. Cut the flesh into chunks and place in the syrup.

4 Spoon some of the fruit salad into the pineapple halves and serve on a large dish. There will be sufficient fruit salad to refill the pineapple halves.

Black Glutinous Rice Pudding

This very unusual rice pudding, *Bubor Pulot Hitam,* which uses bruised fresh root ginger, is quite delicious. When cooked, black rice still retains its husk and has a nutty texture. Serve in small bowls, with a little coconut cream poured over each helping.

INGREDIENTS

Serves 6

115g/4oz black glutinous rice
475ml/16fl oz/2 cups water
1cm/½in fresh root ginger, peeled and bruised
50g/2oz dark brown sugar
50g/2oz caster sugar
300ml/½ pint/1¼ cups coconut milk or cream, to serve

1 Put the rice in a sieve and rinse well under cold running water. Drain and put in a large pan, with the water. Bring to the boil and stir to prevent the rice from settling on the base of the pan. Cover and cook for about 30 minutes.

2 Add the ginger and both the brown and caster sugar. Cook for a further 15 minutes, adding a little more water if necessary, until the rice is cooked and porridge-like. Remove the ginger and serve warm, in bowls, topped with coconut milk or cream.

Deep-fried Bananas

Known as *Pisang Goreng*, these delicious deep-fried bananas should be cooked at the last minute, so that the outer crust of batter is crisp in texture and the banana is soft and warm inside.

INGREDIENTS

Serves 8

115g/4oz self-raising flour
40g/1½oz rice flour
2.5ml/½ tsp salt
200ml/7fl oz /scant 1 cup water
finely grated lime rind (optional)
8 small bananas
oil for deep-frying
sugar and 1 lime, cut in wedges, to serve

1 Sift both the flours and the salt together into a bowl. Add just enough water to make a smooth, coating batter. Mix well, then add the lime rind, if using.

2 Peel the bananas and dip them into the batter two or three times.

3 Heat the oil to 190°C/375°F or when a cube of day-old bread browns in 30 seconds. Deep-fry the battered bananas until crisp and golden. Drain and serve hot, dredged with sugar and with the lime wedges to squeeze over the bananas.

Thai Coconut Cream

This traditional dish can be baked or steamed and is often served with sweet sticky rice and a selection of fruit such as mango and tamarillo.

INGREDIENTS

Serves 4–6

4 eggs
75g/3oz soft light brown sugar
250ml/8fl oz/1 cup coconut milk
5ml/1 tsp vanilla, rose or
  jasmine extract
mint leaves, to decorate
icing sugar, to decorate

1 Preheat the oven to 150°C/300°F/Gas 2. Whisk the eggs and sugar in a bowl until smooth. Add the coconut milk and vanilla or other extract and blend well together.

2 Strain the mixture and pour into individual ramekins or a cake tin.

3 Stand the ramekins or tin in a roasting pan. Carefully fill the pan with hot water to reach halfway up the outsides of the ramekins or tin.

4 Bake for about 35–40 minutes or until the custards are set. Test with a fine skewer or cocktail stick.

5 Remove from the oven and leave to cool. Turn out onto a plate, and serve with sliced fruit. Decorate with mint leaves and icing sugar.

Apples and Raspberries in Rose Pouchong Syrup

This delightfully fragrant and quick-to-prepare Asian dessert couples the subtle flavours of apples and raspberries, both of which belong to the rose family, within an infusion of rose-scented tea.

INGREDIENTS

Serves 4

5ml/1 tsp rose pouchong tea
5ml/1 tsp rose water (optional)
50g/2oz/¼ cup sugar
5ml/1 tsp lemon juice
5 dessert apples
175g/6oz/1½ cups fresh raspberries

1 Warm a large tea pot. Add the rose pouchong tea and 900ml/1½ pints/3¾ cups of boiling water together with the rose water, if using. Allow to stand and infuse for 4 minutes.

2 Measure the sugar and lemon juice into a stainless steel saucepan. Strain in the tea and stir to dissolve the sugar.

3 Peel and core the apples, then cut into quarters.

4 Poach the apples in the syrup for about 5 minutes.

5 Transfer the apples and syrup to a large metal tray and leave to cool to room temperature.

6 Pour the cooled apples and syrup into a bowl, add the raspberries and mix to combine. Spoon into individual dishes or bowls and serve immediately.

SAUCES AND SAMBALS

Dipping sauces are often served with spring rolls, meat, fish, salads and vegetables. Sometimes, they provide a cooling or creamy contrast to hot spiced dishes. More often, they add piquancy and may be very fiery. Sambals, pungent relishes that originated in southern India, are now served throughout South-east Asia, particularly in Indonesia. They may contain chicken or seafood and a mixture of vegetables, sometimes making a quite substantial accompaniment. Whether raw or cooked, they are invariably very hot.

Hot Chilli and Garlic Dipping Sauce

Sambals are placed on the table as a condiment and are used mainly for dipping meat and fish in Indonesia. They are quite strong and should be used sparingly.

Ingredients

Makes 120ml/4fl oz/½ cup

1 garlic clove, crushed
2 small fresh red chillies, seeded and finely chopped
10ml/2 tsp sugar
5ml/1 tsp tamarind sauce
60ml/4 tbsp soy sauce
juice of ½ lime

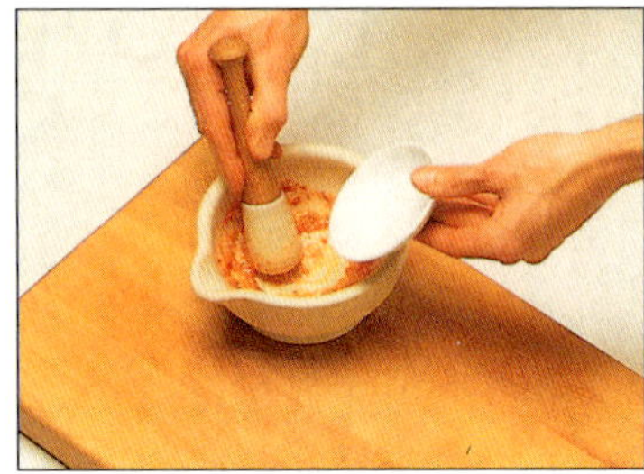

1 Pound the garlic, chillies and sugar until smooth in a mortar with a pestle. Alternatively, grind them together in a food processor.

2 Add the tamarind sauce, soy sauce and lime juice. Stir well.

Hot Tomato Sambal

This is a particularly popular sambal and goes well with most kinds of meat and poultry.

Ingredients

Makes 120ml/4fl oz/½ cup

3 ripe tomatoes
2.5ml/½ tsp salt
5ml/1 tsp chilli sauce
60ml/4 tbsp fish sauce or soy sauce
15ml/1 tbsp chopped fresh coriander

1 Place the tomatoes in a bowl and cover with boiling water for 30 seconds to loosen their skins. Remove the skins, halve and seed the tomatoes, then chop finely.

2 Place the chopped tomatoes in a bowl and mix with the salt, chilli sauce, fish sauce or soy sauce and coriander.

Cook's Tip

If you like really fiery food, you can add 1 or even 2 seeded and finely chopped fresh red chillies.

Sambal Goreng

Traditional flavourings for this dish are fine strips of calves' liver, chicken livers, green beans or hard-boiled eggs. A westernized version is shown here.

INGREDIENTS

Makes 900ml/1½ pints/3¾ cups

2.5cm/1in cube *terasi*
2 onions, quartered
2 garlic cloves, crushed
2.5cm/1in fresh *lengkuas*, peeled and sliced
2 fresh red chillies, seeded and sliced
1.5ml/¼ tsp salt
30ml/2 tbsp oil
45ml/3 tbsp tomato purée
600ml/1 pint/2½ cups stock or water
60ml/4 tbsp tamarind juice
pinch sugar
45ml/3 tbsp coconut milk or cream

1 Grind the *terasi*, with the onions and garlic, to a paste in a food processor or with a pestle and mortar. Add the sliced *lengkuas*, sliced red chillies and salt. Process or pound to a fine paste.

2 Fry the paste in hot oil for 1–2 minutes, without browning, until the mixture gives off a rich aroma.

3 Add the tomato purée and the stock or water and cook for about 10 minutes. Add 350g/12oz cooked chicken pieces and 50g/2oz cooked and sliced French beans, or one of the flavouring variations below, to half the quantity of the sauce. Cook in the sauce for 3–4 minutes, then stir in the tamarind juice, sugar and coconut milk or cream at the last minute, before tasting and serving.

VARIATIONS

Tomato *Sambal Goreng* – Add 450g/1lb of skinned, seeded and coarsely chopped tomatoes, before the stock.

Prawn *Sambal Goreng* – Add 350g/12oz cooked, peeled prawns and 1 green pepper, seeded and chopped.

Egg *Sambal Goreng* – Add 3 or 4 hard-boiled eggs, shelled and chopped, and 2 tomatoes, skinned, seeded and chopped.

Mixed Vegetable Pickle

If you can obtain fresh turmeric, it makes such a difference to the colour and appearance of *Acar Campur*. You can use almost any vegetable, bearing in mind that you need a balance of textures, flavours and colours.

INGREDIENTS

Makes 2–3 x 300g/11oz jars
1 fresh red chilli, seeded and sliced
1 onion, quartered
2 garlic cloves, crushed
1cm/½ in cube *terasi*
4 macadamia nuts or 8 almonds
2.5cm/1in fresh turmeric, peeled and sliced, or 5ml/1 tsp ground turmeric
50ml/2fl oz/¼ cup sunflower oil
475ml/16fl oz/2 cups white vinegar
250ml/8fl oz/1 cup water
25–50g/1–2oz granulated sugar
3 carrots
225g/8oz green beans
1 small cauliflower
1 cucumber
225g/8oz white cabbage
115g/4oz dry-roasted peanuts, roughly crushed
salt

1 Place the chilli, onion, garlic, *terasi*, nuts and turmeric in a food processor and blend to a paste, or pound in a mortar with a pestle.

2 Heat the oil and stir-fry the paste to release the aroma. Add the vinegar, water, sugar and salt. Bring to the boil. Simmer for 10 minutes.

3 Cut the carrots into flower shapes. Cut the green beans into short, neat lengths. Separate the cauliflower into neat, bite-size florets. Peel and seed the cucumber and cut the flesh in neat, bite-size pieces. Cut the cabbage in neat, bite-size pieces.

4 Blanch each vegetable separately, in a large pan of boiling water, for 1 minute. Transfer to a colander and rinse with cold water, to halt the cooking. Drain well.

COOK'S TIP

This pickle is even better if you make it a few days ahead.

5 Add the vegetables to the sauce. Slowly bring to the boil and allow to cook for 5–10 minutes. Do not overcook – the vegetables should still be crunchy.

6 Add the peanuts and cool. Spoon into clean jars with lids.

Sweet-and-sour Ginger Sambal

This sambal is especially delicious with fish, chicken or pork – but beware, it is extremely hot.

INGREDIENTS

Makes 90ml/6 tbsp

4–5 small fresh red chillies, seeded and chopped
2 shallots or 1 small onion, chopped
2 garlic cloves
2cm/¾in fresh root ginger
30ml/2 tbsp sugar
1.5ml/¼ tsp salt
45ml/3 tbsp rice vinegar or white wine vinegar

1 Pound together the chillies and shallots or onion in a mortar with a pestle. Alternatively, grind them in a food processor.

2 Add the garlic, ginger, sugar and salt and continue to pound or grind until smooth. Stir in the vinegar and mix well.

COOK'S TIP

This sambal can be stored in a screw-topped jar in the refrigerator.

Satay Sauce

There are many versions of this tasty peanut sauce. This one is very speedy and it tastes delicious drizzled over grilled or barbecued skewers of chicken. For parties, spear chunks of chicken with cocktail sticks and arrange around a bowl of warm satay sauce.

INGREDIENTS

Serves 4

200ml/7fl oz/scant 1 cup coconut cream
60ml/4 tbsp crunchy peanut butter
5ml/1 tsp Worcestershire sauce
few drops of Tabasco sauce
fresh coconut, to garnish (optional)

1 Pour the coconut cream into a small saucepan and heat it gently over a low heat for about 2 minutes.

2 Add the peanut butter and stir vigorously until the mixture is thoroughly blended. Continue to heat, but do not allow to boil.

3 Add the Worcestershire sauce and Tabasco sauce to taste. Pour into a serving bowl.

4 Use a potato peeler to shave thin strips from a piece of fresh coconut, if using. Scatter the coconut over the sauce and serve immediately.

Vietnamese Dipping Sauce

Serve this dip in a small bowl as an accompaniment to spring rolls or meat dishes.

INGREDIENTS

Makes 150ml/¼ pint/⅔ cup

1–2 small fresh red chillies, seeded and finely chopped
1 garlic clove, crushed
15ml/1 tbsp roasted peanuts
60ml/4 tbsp coconut milk
30ml/2 tbsp fish sauce
juice of 1 lime
10ml/2 tsp sugar
5ml/1 tsp chopped fresh coriander

1 Pound the chilli or chillies with the garlic in a mortar with a pestle.

2 Add the peanuts and pound until crushed. Add the coconut milk, fish sauce, lime juice, sugar and coriander. Mix well.

Thai Dipping Sauce

Nam prik is the most common dipping sauce in Thailand. It has a fiery strength, so use it with caution.

INGREDIENTS

Makes 120ml/4fl oz/½ cup

15ml/1 tbsp vegetable oil
1cm/½in square shrimp paste or 15ml/1 tbsp fish sauce
2 garlic cloves, finely sliced
2cm/¾in fresh root ginger, finely chopped
3 small fresh red chillies, seeded and chopped
15ml/1 tbsp finely chopped coriander root or stem
20ml/4 tsp sugar
45ml/3 tbsp dark soy sauce
juice of ½ lime

1 Heat the vegetable oil in a preheated wok. Add the shrimp paste or fish sauce, garlic, ginger and chillies and stir-fry for 1–2 minutes, until softened, but not coloured.

2 Remove from the heat and add the chopped coriander, sugar, soy sauce and lime juice.

COOK'S TIP

Thai Dipping Sauce will keep for up to 10 days in a screw-topped jar in the refrigerator.

Hoisin Dip

This speedy dip needs no cooking and can be made in just a few minutes – it tastes great with Mini Spring Rolls or prawn crackers.

INGREDIENTS

Serves 4

4 spring onions
4cm/1½in fresh root ginger
2 fresh red chillies
2 garlic cloves
60ml/4 tbsp hoisin sauce
120ml/4fl oz/½ cup passata
5ml/1 tsp sesame oil (optional)

1 Trim off and discard the green ends of the spring onions. Slice the white parts very thinly.

2 Peel and finely chop the ginger.

3 Halve and seed the chillies. Slice finely. Finely chop the garlic.

4 Stir together the hoisin sauce, passata, spring onions, ginger, chillies, garlic and sesame oil, if using. Serve within 1 hour.

Cucumber Sambal

This sauce has a piquant flavour and does not have the heat of chillies found in other sambals.

INGREDIENTS

Makes 150ml/¼ pint/⅔ cup

1 garlic clove, crushed
5ml/1 tsp fennel seeds
10ml/2 tsp sugar
2.5ml/½ tsp salt
2 shallots or 1 small onion, finely sliced
120ml/4fl oz/½ cup rice vinegar or white wine vinegar
¼ cucumber, finely diced

1 Pound together the garlic, fennel seeds, sugar and salt in a mortar with a pestle. Alternatively, grind them together in a food processor.

2 Stir in the shallots or onion, vinegar and cucumber and set aside for at least 6 hours to allow the flavours to combine.

INDEX

Notes

Notes

Notes

NOTES

Notes

Notes

Notes

Notes